Your Windows® 95 Consultant, Pre-Release Edition

Ed Jones
Derek Sutton

201 West 103rd Street
Indianapolis, Indiana 46290

To Nikki and Jarel Jones, the highlights of my life. *Siempre tratar a ser lo maximo que tu puedes!* —Ed Jones

A todas las personas, grande y pequeno. Gracias! —Derek Sutton

International Standard Book Number: 0-672-30611-5

Library of Congress Catalog Card Number: 95-67516

98 97 96 95   4 3 2 1

Interpretation of the printing code: the rightmost double-digit number is the year of the book's printing; the rightmost single-digit, the number of the book's printing. For example, a printing code of 95-1 shows that the first printing of the book occurred in 1995.

Trademarks

All terms mentioned in this book that are known to be trademarks or service marks have been appropriately capitalized. Sams Publishing cannot attest to the accuracy of this information. Use of a term in this book should not be regarded as affecting the validity of any trademark or service mark. Windows is a registered trademark of Microsoft Corporation.

Composed in AGaramond, Futura, and MCPdigital by Macmillan Computer Publishing

Printed in the United States of America

Publisher
Richard K. Swadley

Acquisitions Manager
Greg Wiegand

Managing Editor
Cindy Morrow

Acquisitions Editor
Greg Croy
Grace Buechlein

Development Editor
L. Angelique Brittingham

Production Editor
Kristi Hart

Copy Editors
Fran Blauw, Ryan Rader
Tonya Simpson

Editorial Coordinator
Bill Whitmer

Editorial Assistants
Carol Ackerman, Sharon Cox
Lynette Quinn

Technical Reviewer
Stephen Pedrick, PC PC

Marketing Manager
Gregg Bushyeager

Assistant Marketing Manager
Michelle Milner

Cover Designer
Tim Amrhein

Book Designer
Alyssa Yesh

**Vice President of Production
and Manufacturing**
Jeff Valler

Manufacturing Coordinator
Paul Gilchrist

Imprint Manager
Kelly Dobbs

Team Supervisor
Katy Bodenmiller

Support Services Manager
Juli Cook

Support Services Supervisor
Mary Beth Wakefield

Production Analysts
Angela Bannan, Dennis Clay Hager
Bobbi Satterfield

Graphics Image Specialists
Becky Beheler, Stephen Carlin
Brad Dixon, Teresa Forrester
Jason Hand, Clint Lahnen
Cheri Laughner, Mike Reynolds
Laura Robbins, Dennis Sheehan
Craig Small, Jeff Yesh

Page Layout
Charlotte Clapp, Mary Ann Cosby
Judy Everly, Aleata Howard
Ayanna Lacey, Shawn MacDonald
Jackie Thompson, Mark Walchle
Dennis Wesner, Michelle Worthington
Susan Van Ness

Proofreading
Michael Brumitt, Jama Carter
Donna Harbin, Mike Henry
Donna Martin, Cheryl Moore
Brian-Kent Proffitt, Erich Richter
Suzanne Tully

Indexer
Jeanne Clark

Overview

Introduction   xxxi

Part I Maximizing Windows
1   The Components of Windows 95   3
2   Customizing the Desktop and the Taskbar   13
3   Staying Organized   31
4   Putting It on Paper   45
5   Maximizing Memory   65
6   Exchanging Data Between Applications   71
7   Making the Most of the Bundled Windows
    Applications   83
8   Making the Most of Your Windows Applications   97
9   Running DOS Applications Under Windows   145
10 Windows and Multimedia   165
11 Working with the Registry   181

Part II Maximizing Your Hardware
12 Upgrading Your Memory   189
13 Upgrading Your Hard Drive   205
14 Upgrading Your Video   223
15 Upgrading Your Processor   239
16 Upgrading Your Peripherals   253
17 Choosing and Upgrading Your Windows Printer   261

Part III Windows 95 and the Outside World
18 Installing and Using Windows 95 on a Network   271
19 Windows Communications   301
20 Windows and Laptop Computing   317
21 Troubleshooting Windows   331

Part IV Appendixes
A   Installation   345
B   PC Assembly   353
C   Resources   357

Index   365

Contents

Introduction   xxxi

Part I   Maximizing Windows

1   The Components of Windows 95   3

2   Customizing the Desktop and the Taskbar   13
    Customizing 18

3   Staying Organized   31

4   Putting It on Paper   45

5   Maximizing Memory   65

6   Exchanging Data Between Applications   71

7   Making the Most of the Bundled Windows
    Applications   83
    WordPad 84
        Setting Up WordPad 84
        Creating, Saving, and Editing Documents 84
        Formatting Text 87
        Printing Documents 91
        Making Connections with Other Documents.... 91
    Paint 93

8   Making the Most of Your Windows
    Applications   97
    General Topics 98
    Word Processing 101
        Word for Windows and WordPerfect—
            General Topics.. 101
        Word for Windows Specifics 111
        WordPerfect Specifics 117
    Spreadsheets 119
        All Spreadsheets 119
        Microsoft Excel 120
        Lotus 1-2-3 for Windows 125
        Novell Quattro Pro for Windows 127

Databases 130
Microsoft Access 130
Microsoft FoxPro for Windows 137
Borland dBASE for Windows 141
Borland's Paradox for Windows 143

9   Running DOS Applications Under Windows   145

10   Windows and Multimedia   165

11   Working with the Registry   181

Part II   Maximizing Your Hardware

12   Upgrading Your Memory   189

13   Upgrading Your Hard Drive   205

14   Upgrading Your Video   223
Video Basics 223
Video Standards 226
Purchasing and Installing a Video Card 229
Purchasing and Installing a Monitor 232
Video Troubleshooting 236

15   Upgrading Your Processor   239

16   Upgrading Your Peripherals   253
Keyboards 253
Mice 255
Trackballs 257
Graphics Tablets 257

**17   Choosing and Upgrading Your Windows
Printer   261**

Part III   Windows 95 and the Outside World

**18   Installing and Using Windows 95 on a
Network   271**

19   Windows Communications   301

20   Windows and Laptop Computing   317

21   Troubleshooting Windows   331
Installation Problems 331
Windows Problems 335

Part IV   Appendixes

A   Installation   **345**

Setting Up Windows 345
Upgrading from Windows 3.*x* to Windows 95 347
Uninstalling Windows 95 347
Learning How Setup Works 348
Taking Advantage of Setup's Failure Detection
and Recovery 349
The Event Log... 350
The Detection Crash Recovery Log 350
Deciding Whether to Use Custom Setup 351
Looking At Hardware Requirements 351

B   PC Assembly   **353**

The Basics of a System 353
Common Tools Needed....................................... 355
System Unit Cover Removal 355
Adapter Card Removal 356

C   Resources   **357**

Index   **365**

Question Reference

1   The Components of Windows 95

1.1.   What is Windows 95? 3
1.2.   What's different about Windows 95? 4
1.3.   What's different about the user interface? 4
1.4.   What is the Desktop? 5
1.5.   What is the Taskbar? 6
1.6.   How does task switching work? 7
1.7.   What happened to File Manager? 7
1.8.   What is My Computer? 8
1.9.   What is the Explorer? 8
1.10. Don't My Computer and Explorer accomplish
       the same job? 9
1.11. What is Network Neighborhood? 9
1.12. What are Properties? 9
1.13. All of my Program Manager icons are gone,
       and I liked having them. How can I duplicate
       the Program Manager look? 10
1.14. What happened to Print Manager? 11
1.15. What happened to my CONFIG.SYS and
       AUTOEXEC.BAT files? 11
1.16. What's the Recycle Bin? 12

2   Customizing the Desktop and the Taskbar

2.1.   How much can I accomplish with the Taskbar? 13
2.2.   How and to where can I move the Taskbar? 15
2.3.   How can I hide or unhide the Taskbar? 15
2.4.   How can I customize the Taskbar? 16
2.5.   What are the different ways you can switch
       between programs that are running? 17
2.6.   How can I run a DOS application? 17
2.7.   I just added a program, and it's not on any
       menu. How can I start it? 17
2.8.   How can I customize the Start button? 18
2.9.   How can I edit the names that applications give
       themselves? 18
2.10. How do I change Windows color schemes? 19
2.11. How can I create custom color schemes? 20
2.12. How can I save my custom color scheme? 21
2.13. How can I create custom colors? 21
2.14. How can I change the background pattern? 22

2.15. How can I create my own background? 23
2.16. How can I set up a screen saver? 23
2.17. How can I change mouse settings? 24
2.18. How can I change the repeat speed for my
       keyboard? 26
2.19. How can I change the type of keyboard I am
       using? 26
2.20. How can I change the character layout for my
       keyboard to match a different language? 27
2.21. How can I customize international settings? 27
2.22. How can I assign sounds to system events? 28

3   Staying Organized
3.1. Why think in terms of "objects?" 31
3.2. What advantages does Explorer offer over the File
       Manager of Windows 3.x? 32
3.3. How do I start Explorer? 33
3.4. How do I select different drives? 33
3.5. How can I open and close folders? 33
3.6. How can I open an additional folder window? 34
3.7. How can I copy files or folders? 34
3.8. How can I move files and folders? 34
3.9. How can I move or copy multiple files? 35
3.10. How can I search for files and folders? 35
3.11. How can I duplicate the functionality
       of my Windows 3.x program groups? 36
3.12. How can I get a listing in Explorer comparable
       to what I would see by executing a DIR command
       under DOS? 37
3.13. How can I change Explorer's display? 37
3.14. I prefer to use My Computer for browsing among
       my PC's resources, but I find the clutter of
       numerous windows annoying. Can I force My
       Computer to display all the resources in a single
       window? 38
3.15. How can I change file attributes? 38
3.16. How can I sort files? 38
3.17. How can I print a file? 39
3.18. How can I undelete a file? 39
3.19. How can I create folders? 39
3.20. How can I rename files or folders? 39
3.21. How can I delete files or folders? 40
3.22. How can I format disks? 40

3.23. How can I view disk properties? 40
3.24. If I delete a shortcut from the Desktop,
      do I delete the item? 40
3.25. More than one person uses my computer. Can I
      save and recall the appearance of my Desktop? 41
3.26. How can I associate a particular file with a given
      application? 42
3.27. Is there any simple way of knowing what's in a
      document? 42
3.28. How can I view hidden files? 43
3.29. Why aren't file extensions visible? 43
3.30. Will long filenames be preserved when copying
      files to disks? 43
3.31. Can I use third-party backup programs that I
      used with prior versions of Windows? 44

4 Putting It on Paper

4.1. What's different about the Windows 95 interface
     regarding printing? 45
4.2. Is there a faster way to print documents than
     repeatedly opening them and using File | Print
     from the applications' menus? 46
4.3. How do I install a new printer under Windows? 46
4.4. I tried to install my printer, but it's not listed
     among the list of possible printers. Now what? 47
4.5. How can I change my printer settings? 48
4.6. How does the Printers Folder work? 52
4.7. How can I view the print queue? 53
4.8. How can I change the order of files in the
     print queue? 54
4.9. How can I pause and resume printing? 54
4.10. How can I delete a file from the print queue? 54
4.11. How can I print to a file? 55
4.12. How can I change printer memory usage? 55
4.13. How can I turn off the banner page when
      printing on a network? 56
4.14. How do I assign a printer to a different port than
      the default one? 56
4.15. How do I connect to or disconnect from a
      network printer? 57
4.16. How can I configure a Novell NetWare server
      to support drag-and-drop printing? 57

4.17. I installed a new font cartridge in my printer; why don't the fonts appear in the list of fonts when I try to change fonts from within an application? 58

4.18. How do I manage fonts? 58

4.19. How do I manage soft fonts? 59

4.20. How can I add new soft fonts? 61

4.21. My printer has a number of built-in fonts that appear virtually identical to the TrueType fonts included with Windows. Does it make a performance difference as to which fonts I use? 62

4.22. Where can I obtain more fonts? 62

4.23. How can I change the display fonts used by the Desktop? 63

4.24. When I try to print a page with graphics on it, the page either doesn't print completely or I get an error message displayed on the LCD panel of the printer. 63

5 Maximizing Memory

5.1. Under Windows 95, why bother with memory management? 65

5.2. Can I use my old third-party memory managers by running them through a DOS window? 66

5.3. What are virtual device drivers, and what have they replaced? 66

5.4. What is virtual memory, and how can I use it? 67

5.5. How do I choose between a temporary or permanent swapfile in Windows 95 to support virtual memory? 67

5.6. With Windows' more efficient use of memory, can I get by with 4M of RAM? 69

5.7. How can I conserve memory and/or system resources? 69

6 Exchanging Data Between Applications

6.1. What's the Clipboard, and how does it work? 72

6.2. How can I use the Clipboard with Windows applications? 72

6.3. How can I copy an image of the active window to the Clipboard? 73

6.4. How can I use the Clipboard with DOS applications? 73

6.5.   What is Dynamic Data Exchange, and how does it work? 74

6.6.   What is Object Linking and Embedding, and how does it work? 75

6.7.   How can I establish a link to other data in a document? 76

6.8.   How can I embed an object in a document? 77

6.9.   How can I embed an object that already exists elsewhere? 77

6.10. Having links in my documents noticeably slows down opening and working with those documents. Can I do anything to speed up this process? 78

6.11. Many Windows applications have two choices on the Edit menu: Paste and Paste Link. What's the difference between the two? 79

6.12. After I create linked objects in other documents, can I move the source documents to different folders? 79

6.13. How can I edit a linked object? 79

6.14. Can I create documents with multiple links? 80

6.15. I've created links to other documents, and I don't plan to make any more changes to the data in the source documents. Can I break the links and retain the data? 80

6.16. How can I easily create a logo or decorative title and add it to a document or a spreadsheet? 81

7   Making the Most of the Bundled Windows Applications

7.1.   How can I turn the Toolbar, Format bar, Ruler, and Status bar on and off? 84

7.2.   How can I create a new document? 84

7.3.   How can I save changes to a document? 85

7.4.   How can I open an existing document? 85

7.5.   How can I delete information from a document? 85

7.6.   How can I locate words in a document? 85

7.7.   How can I replace text in a document? 86

7.8.   How can I add the date and time to a document? 86

7.9.   How can I move information between documents? . 87

7.10. How can I copy text between documents? 87

7.11. How can I turn word wrap on and off? 87

7.12. How can I insert a bullet? 87

7.13. How can I select fonts? 88
7.14. How can I change type colors? 89
7.15. How can I change type size? 89
7.16. How can I change the margins? 89
7.17. How can I set tab stops? 90
7.18. How can I delete tabs from a document? 90
7.19. How can I print a document? 91
7.20. How can I preview a document I want to print? 91
7.21. How can I set margins for printing? 91
7.22. How can I change printing options and printers? 91
7.23. How can I insert an embedded or linked object? 92
7.24. When I choose Insert New Object, the list box that appears doesn't show objects from all the Windows programs I have installed. Why is one (or more) object type missing? 93
7.25. How can I draw a straight line? 93
7.26. How can I draw a free-form line? 93
7.27. How can I draw a curved line? 94
7.28. How can I draw different shapes? 94
7.29. How can I draw a square or rectangle? 94
7.30. How can I fill in my shapes? 94
7.31. How can I add text to my pictures? 95
7.32. How can I change the background color? 95
7.33. How can I edit my pictures? 95
7.34. How can I change the appearance of my picture? 95
7.35. How can I copy my picture to use in another application? 96

8 Making the Most of Your Windows Applications
8.1. What are the shortcut keys that work with Windows applications? 98
8.2. Is there a universal print function that works in different applications? 99
8.3. How can I disable call waiting when I use my modem? 99
8.4. Should I keep my Windows installation disks? 99
8.5. The Taskbar overlaps part of my program. Can I move it? 100
8.6. The installation instructions suggest commands that aren't available in Windows 95. What should I do? 100

8.7. How can I access files across the network on another person's computer? 101

8.8. I don't like the default Times New Roman (or whatever) font I'm forced to use each time I start a new document. How can I change this default font? 101

8.9. How can I set the default folder (directory) for saving and opening files so that I don't have to change directories all the time to find the files I use daily? 102

8.10. I lost a document I was working on when the power failed. Is there a way to get my document back? 103

8.11. How can I insert special characters? 104

8.12. How can I select an entire document for formatting? 105

8.13. By default, all my documents are set to print on 8 1/2-by-11-inch paper. For this print job, that's not what I want. How can I change it? 105

8.14. Is there a fast way to select words, sentences, and paragraphs? 106

8.15. I often download files from CompuServe that have hard returns at the end of every line. Is there an easy way to get rid of these? 106

8.16. How can I password-protect a document? 106

8.17. I had the Caps Lock key pressed accidentally, and typed a significant amount of text before noticing. Is there a way to change the case of all the text without retyping it all? 107

8.18. Is there a way to print more than one file at a time from within Word or WordPerfect? 108

8.19. How can I add the date and time to a document? .. 108

8.20. How can I insert a picture into my document? 109

8.21. How can I create a table? 109

8.22. Why do my word processing documents look slightly different when printed than they do on-screen? 110

8.23. When I start Word 6.0, I get the message *Word has caused a General Protection Fault in module WINWORD.EXE*, and the program doesn't load. Do I need to reinstall Word? 111

8.24. How can I line up columns of ASCII text
in Word? 111

8.25. Is there a quick way to move rows or
paragraphs? 112

8.26. How can I speed up printing if all I want is a
draft copy? 112

8.27. Why do I get the error message *Margins outside
printable area of page* when I try to print my
Word document? 112

8.28. How can I print selected pages of a document,
rather than the entire document? 113

8.29. How can I print in reverse order? 113

8.30. Can I delete files from within Word? 113

8.31. How can I print envelopes in Word
for Windows? 113

8.32. How can I remove the field codes from the
screen when I add a bullet to my document? 114

8.33. I've created a macro in Word that I use often.
Can I assign it to a Toolbar button? 114

8.34. How can I simply shell out to DOS while
working on a document in Word 6.0? 114

8.35. How can I make Word for Windows run faster? 115

8.36. How can I use my Word 6.0 files in Word 2.0? 116

8.37. Is there an easy way to insert the commonly used
trademark and copyright symbols? 116

8.38. I installed WordPerfect 6.0 in the same folder
where I had WordPerfect 5.2 installed. Now, I
can't get either program to work! What's wrong? ... 117

8.39. Why is there no Print Preview option in
WordPerfect for Windows? 117

8.40. How can I tell the difference between soft and
hard page breaks in WordPerfect—they both
look alike? 117

8.41. WordPerfect offers a choice of printer drivers:
WordPerfect's own drivers, or the Windows
printer drivers. Which should I use in printing? 118

8.42. How can I make WordPerfect for Windows run
faster? 118

8.43. Is there a way to easily change the format of a
group of cells within a spreadsheet? 119

8.44. Why do my values in a certain cell of my
spreadsheet appear as a string of # characters? 119

8.45. When I enter a formula, I get a beep and an alert box telling me there's an error in the formula, but the alert box doesn't offer any help. 120

8.46. How do I import and export text files in Microsoft Excel? 120

8.47. How can I combine the contents of two cells into one cell? 121

8.48. I want to print a specific area of my Excel worksheet. How can I specify what to print? 121

8.49. Excel adds decimal points to all my numbers, even though I haven't entered them. Why is this happening? 122

8.50. How can I easily print the formulas used in Excel spreadsheets? 122

8.51. When I enter a value with a slash (/) or a hyphen (-), it is formatted as a date. How can I prevent this? 122

8.52. How can I tell Excel to open the same workbook each time I start the program? 123

8.53. How can I designate a default font for all my Excel spreadsheets? 123

8.54. Can I protect most of an Excel worksheet, while leaving some cells editable? 123

8.55. Where can I find a BBS or some other source of ready-to-run programs that I can use with Excel by downloading it or purchasing it? 124

8.56. Why does Excel ignore page breaks I have added? 124

8.57. Is there a way to print more than one file at a time in Excel? 124

8.58. How can I automatically adjust cell widths in Excel? 125

8.59. Is there a way to add currency symbols for foreign currencies in Excel? 125

8.60. How can I load the same 1-2-3 spreadsheet on startup automatically? 126

8.61. How can I convert formulas to values? 126

8.62. Is there an easy way to align labels across columns? 126

8.63. How can I copy formats but not values into another cell? 126

8.64. Is there a simple way to delete files in 1-2-3? 126

8.65. How can I tell 1-2-3 to always use a particular font for all new spreadsheets? 127

8.66. I just installed Quattro Pro, and when I try to load the program, I see the message *Insufficient memory to run this application.* I have plenty of memory and system resources. What's wrong? 127

8.67. When printing multiple copies to my HP DeskJet 500C and 550C, I get only one copy, regardless of the number of I specify. What's wrong? 127

8.68. How do I enter a date or time value into a cell? 128

8.69. I want to enter date values for the 21st century. When I enter a date value like 2/12/05 (for 2/12/2005), Quattro Pro stores February 12, 1905. What's going on? 128

8.70. How can I include page numbers or dates on a printed page in Quattro Pro? 128

8.71. How can I automatically adjust cell widths in Quattro Pro? 129

8.72. How do I export ASCII text files from Quattro Pro? 129

8.73. I have a 386 with 4M of RAM, and Access runs slowly. If I upgrade my processor chip or add a math co-processor, will I see a significant boost in speed? 130

8.74. When I try to start Access, I get a message saying *General Protection Fault.* What's wrong? 130

8.75. How can I get a list of all the objects in my database? 131

8.76. Suddenly all my databases have extra tables with names that begin with "Msys" and "USys." Why are these here, and how can I delete them? 131

8.77. How do I copy all the information from the preceding record on a form to a new record? 131

8.78. Can text stored in a memo field be formatted with different fonts or attributes like boldface or underlining? 132

8.79. How can I quickly create a simple form for use with a table? 132

8.80. Why do I get a *#NAME?* error for a calculated control on a form or a report? 132

8.81. How can I view my data in sorted order? 133

8.82. How can I create calculated fields in a table? 133

8.83. How can I quickly create a simple report? 133

8.84. How do I print reports to a file? 133

8.85. Why do I get extra blank pages between each
page of my report? 134

8.86. My PC has plenty of memory installed, but I
keep getting *Out of memory* errors with my
Access reports. Why is this happening? 134

8.87. I've attached some SQL tables, but they appear
as read-only. Why can't I get write privileges? 135

8.88. How can I prevent an AutoExec macro
from running when I open a database? 135

8.89. How can I dial a modem from Access? 135

8.90. Why does Access place the words *Option
Compare Database* at the top of every module
I create? 136

8.91. We're using Access on a large local area network,
and the more users connected to the database, the
longer it takes to open the database. (During peak
afternoon times, it can take more than a minute
for a user to get into the database!) Is there any
way to reduce these delays we're seeing? 136

8.92. I'm developing an application in Access,
and I've read that I should store my data in one
database and the rest of the objects (forms, reports,
queries, macros, and code) in another database.
Why should I do this, and how do I do it? 136

8.93. I thought FoxPro was a multiuser program right
out of the box, so why am I getting a *File is in use*
message when somebody tries to use the same file
on a network? 137

8.94. I get a *Not enough disk space* error message
when I try to use my application written in
FoxPro on our Novell network. I have more than
200M of disk space available! 137

8.95. I'm using a laptop with no mouse or trackball
attached. How can I design screens with the
Screen Builder without using a pointing device? 138

8.96. How can I quickly create a simple form for use
with a table? 138

8.97. I have designed a screen with a large number
of fields, and I want to change the tab order
with which the insertion pointer moves through
the fields. How can I do this? 138

8.98. Why don't the *@...SAY* program commands
work to display the contents of my general fields
in a screen? 138

8.99. How can I quickly create a simple report? 139

8.100. Must I convert my FoxPro for DOS reports
before I can use them in FoxPro for Windows? 139

8.101. I created a report using the Quick Report option.
Now I want to add another field to the report.
Under FoxPro for DOS, I used the Field option
of the Report menu to add new fields, but there
is no such option in FoxPro for Windows. How
can I add another field? 139

8.102. How can I design multicolumn reports in
FoxPro's Report Writer? 140

8.103. I have a memo field included in my report.
Only the first line prints. What's wrong? 140

8.104. While designing a report, I am trying to move
a text object to a precise location, and it keeps
aligning itself with the grid. How can I prevent
this from happening? 140

8.105. I have a report with a one-to-many relationship
database set up. But only one record for the child
database shows up for one parent record. What is
going on? 140

8.106. I am looking at my report and some of the
numeric fields are appearing with **** instead
of the actual value. What's up? 141

8.107. I am trying to print from FoxPro, but it only
prints after I quit FoxPro. 141

8.108. When I try to start FoxPro, I get a *General
Protection Fault* error message. What's wrong? 141

8.109. I want dBASE for Windows to go to my data files
in my C:\DBASEWIN\PROJECT folder each
time I start the program. How do I do that? 142

8.110. How can I quickly create a simple form for use
with a table? 142

8.111. How can I prevent the Form Expert dialog box
from appearing every time I create a new form? 142

8.112. How can you change a field heading in the
Browse window without modifying the field
name in the table structure? 142

8.113. How can I quickly create a simple report? 143

8.114. How can I put my data in sorted order? 143

8.115. How can I quickly create a simple report? 144

8.116. What is an easy way to move tables in Paradox? 144

8.117. Why do I get a *Locked Record* message when I
have several windows open in Paradox? 144

9   Running DOS Applications Under Windows

9.1. According to what I read, Windows 95 is a
complete operating system, eliminating DOS.
Can I still safely run my DOS applications? 145

9.2. What different ways are there to run a DOS
program under Windows? 146

9.3. Can I easily switch DOS applications between
running in a window and running full-screen? 147

9.4. In Windows 3.*x*, my DOS applications appeared
in a full screen (unless I set them to run in a
window, using the old PIF Editor). In Windows 95,
my DOS applications run in a window by default
(see Figure 9.1). I prefer to see them full-screen. Is
there any way to change this default behavior? 147

9.5. How do I get to a DOS prompt
in Windows 95? 148

9.6. I copied a DOS program from a floppy disk into
a folder using Explorer. I can run it from Explorer
or from My Computer, but I need to run it on a
daily basis. Is there a faster way to launch the
program? 148

9.7. I need to do some low-level hardware maintenance, and I prefer to do it with nothing other than
DOS running. Is there a way to tell Windows not
to load, or must I boot from a floppy disk? 149

9.8. How can I assign a new icon to my DOS
application? 149

9.9. I have a batch file that I run, prior to running a DOS application. (The batch file sets some environmental parameters that should be set before the program runs.) Is there some way to easily run the batch file, and then load the program? 149

9.10. Each of my DOS applications specifies a minimum amount of conventional RAM needed for its operation. Because DOS applications were never designed to run simultaneously, can I safely load more DOS applications than can fit in my PC's conventional memory? 150

9.11. I have a number of games that wouldn't run under Windows 3.x; I always had to exit completely to DOS to run any of these games. Is there a way to use these games under Windows 95? 150

9.12. What is *Single MS-DOS Application Mode*, and how can I use it? 151

9.13. When I run a DOS application in a window, the window has a Toolbar. What's this for, and how can I use it? 152

9.14. How can I force the Toolbar to always appear within a DOS application's window? 153

9.15. Can I cut and paste data using DOS applications? 153

9.16. How can I change the font sizes within a windowed DOS session? 153

9.17. How can I safely terminate a crashed DOS application? 154

9.18. Now that I'm running Windows, the PrtSc key no longer prints data from a screen in my DOS applications to the printer. How can I turn this key back on? 155

9.19. Are there any DOS commands or applications that I shouldn't run from within Windows? 155

9.20. Windows 95 doesn't have a PIF Editor, as did earlier versions of Windows. How can I set specific values in PIF files to optimize how my DOS applications run? 156

9.21. How can I optimize the performance of the DOS applications that I run under Windows? 162

10 Windows and Multimedia

10.1.   What is multimedia? 165

10.2.   What do I need to build a multimedia-ready
        system? 166

10.3.   What is the MPC-2 standard? 166

10.4.   What is a sound card? 169

10.5.   How do I install a CD-ROM drive? 170

10.6.   I've installed a CD-ROM drive and I can't get it
        to work. What do I do now? 171

10.7.   How do I install a sound card? 172

10.8.   How do I add multimedia drivers? 173

10.9.   How can I remove a multimedia driver I'm no
        longer using? 176

10.10. What is Sound Recorder, and how do I use it? 177

10.11. How can I assign sounds to system events? 178

10.12. What is Media Player, and how can I use it? 179

11 Working with the Registry

11.1.   What is the Registry? 181

11.2.   How do I use the Registry Editor? 183

11.3.   Because configuration data is stored in the
        Registry, are the old AUTOEXEC.BAT,
        CONFIG.SYS, and various .INI files still used? 185

12 Upgrading Your Memory

12.1.   I hear a lot about conventional RAM, extended
        RAM, upper RAM, and expanded RAM. Just
        how does my PC's memory work? 190

12.2.   How much memory do I need? 191

12.3.   I see many different types of memory chips
        advertised. Which kind will I need for my
        particular PC's processor? 192

12.4.   I've seen a memory board advertised; I can insert
        memory chips in the board, and just drop the
        board in an expansion slot. Can I go with this
        approach instead of adding SIMMs? 198

12.5.   Does it make sense to buy memory that's much
        faster in speed than the processor? 198

12.6.   How much will more memory cost? 199

12.7.   What are sources for additional memory? 199

12.8.   How do I install SIMMs (or SIPs) in my PC? 199

12.9.   How can I install DRAM chips in my PC? 201

12.10. How do I install a memory expansion card? 202

12.11. I've installed new memory and my PC doesn't
        work. Now what?...203

13 Upgrading Your Hard Drive

13.1. What features can I look for to get good drive
       performance under Windows? 206
13.2. Which drive types should I use? 207
13.3. What's the Enhanced IDE specification? 209
13.4. What's drive caching, and do I need it?.................210
13.5. Does upgrading a hard drive make sense? 211
13.6. Must I upgrade my motherboard and drive
       controller (or entire system) to local-bus
       technology to get really impressive hard drive
       performance under Windows? 212
13.7. I already have one hard drive in my system,
       and I want to add another. Is this feasible?.............213
13.8. How much hard disk space is enough?...................214
13.9. How can I install an IDE hard drive?....................214
13.10. What's a HardCard, and how can I install one? 219
13.11. How do I install an internal SCSI drive? 220
13.12. I've installed a new drive and it doesn't work.
        Now what? 222

14 Upgrading Your Video

14.1. What exactly is monitor resolution, and how do
       the different resolutions affect what I see on the
       screen? 224
14.2. What do I need to consider regarding the amount
       and type of video RAM for my system?..................224
14.3. How does refresh rate affect what I see on the
       screen? 225
14.4. What is the difference between an interlaced
       and a noninterlaced monitor? 226
14.5. What are the different video standards, and
       what do they mean in terms of an upgrade? 226
14.6. What is local bus video? 227
14.7. What is a graphics accelerator card? 229
14.8. What do I need to know before I commit to
       buying a particular video card?..............................229
14.9. Are there any alternatives to installing a new
       video card? 230
14.10. How can I match my card and my monitor?.........230
14.11. How do I install a video card? 231

14.12. What should I consider regarding resolution as I look at different monitors? 232

14.13. What is dot pitch, and how does it affect what I see on the screen? 233

14.14. What types of monitors are there, and what are some key things to consider? 233

14.15. How do I install a monitor? 235

14.16. When it comes to video troubleshooting, what are some common things to check? 236

15 Upgrading Your Processor

15.1. What considerations should I keep in mind when upgrading a processor? 240

15.2. When upgrading motherboards, what is local bus, and is it worth the cost? 244

15.3. I see a number of advertisements for Intel's OverDrive chips. What's OverDrive, and can I take advantage of it? 245

15.4. I've seen advertisements that claim I can upgrade my 80386 system by replacing the processor. Is this possible? 246

15.5. There is a socket for a math coprocessor in my system. How much of a performance gain can I expect if I install one? 247

15.6. How do I install a new motherboard? 247

15.7. How can I install an OverDrive processor? 250

16 Upgrading Your Peripherals

16.1. How do I install a mouse? 258

16.2. I installed a new mouse, but it doesn't work correctly. Now what? 259

17 Choosing and Upgrading Your Windows Printer

17.1. What types of printers should I consider for use with Windows? 261

17.2. What does DPI refer to? 263

17.3. What features should I look for in a printer? 264

17.4. How I increase the performance of my existing laser printer? 265

17.5. What is PostScript, and can I add it to my existing laser printer? 266

17.6. How do I install a printer? 267

17.7. Can you offer some suggestions for trouble-shooting common installation problems with printers? 268

18 Installing and Using Windows 95 on a Network

18.1. What kind of network connectivity does Windows 95 provide? 272

18.2. How does the user interface for Windows 95 support networking? 273

18.3. What are the overall steps involved in setting up peer-to-peer networking for the first time? 274

18.4. How can I browse among the shared resources in my workgroup? 276

18.5. How can I browse among the shared resources in the entire network? 277

18.6. Sharing Windows resources on our peer-to-peer network is slow at times, but we just can't afford a move to a high-performance file server and another network operating system right now. Is there anything else we can do to speed things up? 278

18.7. We're already running Microsoft Windows for Workgroups. Will we keep all the peer-to-peer network capabilities that we currently have if we install Windows 95? 278

18.8. How can I install Windows on a workstation that's already attached to a local area network? 278

18.9. Is there a way to fine-tune the installation options that are used during the install process? 281

18.10. I've added a new type of network adapter to a new computer that I'm adding to the network. How do I install the software needed by this network adapter? 281

18.11. How can I set my network configuration options in Windows? 282

18.12. How can I run the NetWare utilities (such as SYSCON, PCONSOLE, and FCONSOLE)? 285

18.13. How can I change the settings used for a dial-out network cable connection? 285

18.14. What is Chat? 285

18.15. What is Print Server for NetWare, and how can
I use it? 286
18.16. We run a number of NetWare terminate-and-stay-
resident utilities (TSRs) that are compatible with
the Novell NetWare drivers, but are incompatible
with the Microsoft Client for NetWare. How can
we install or change Windows to use the Novell
NetWare drivers? 286
18.17. We don't use NetWare or Microsoft LAN
Manager. Can we install Windows 95 to support
another existing third-party network? 288
18.18. What levels of security are provided by
Windows 95? 290
18.19. How do I access the security options built
into Windows? 291
18.20. How can I set up share-level security
on a network? 294
18.21. How do I establish user-level security? 295
18.22. How do I grant permissions to shared directories
and printers? 296
18.23. How can I monitor resource usage on a peer-
to-peer network? 296
18.24. How can I monitor network activity on a peer-
to-peer network? 299

19 Windows Communications
19.1. How do I install an external modem? 301
19.2. How can I install an internal modem? 302
19.3. I just installed an external modem, but it isn't
functioning. How can I fix it? 302
19.4. I just installed an internal modem, but it isn't
functioning. How can I fix it? 303
19.5. Should I buy an external or an internal modem? 304
19.6. What are surge suppressors, and should
I buy one? 305
19.7. How can I use HyperTerm to connect to another
computer? 305
19.8. How can I dial phone calls from my PC? 306
19.9. Which of the online services should I consider? 306
19.10. How can I select the right online service? 307
19.11. What Is America Online? (AOL) 309
19.12. What Is CompuServe (CIS)? 310

19.13. What Is Dow Jones News/Retrieval with MCI
Mail (DJN/R)? 312

19.14. What Is GEnie? 313

19.15. What Is Prodigy? 314

19.16. What is the Internet? 314

19.17. How can I access the Internet? 315

19.18. Which of the online services offers true Internet
access? 315

19.19. What's the Microsoft Network? 316

20 Windows and Laptop Computing

20.1. Can I install Windows so that it doesn't take up
as much disk space? 318

20.2. I've already installed Windows on my laptop. Is
there any way I can remove parts of it without
running Setup to reinstall the program all over
again? 319

20.3. Are there any files installed by Windows that I
can delete to free up disk space? 319

20.4. How can I make the display on my laptop's
LCD screen easier to read? 324

20.5. How can I make the mouse pointer easier to see? ...325

20.6. What's the Briefcase, and how do I use it? 325

20.7. I don't have a cable I can use to connect my
laptop to my desktop PC. Is there some way I can
keep the files synchronized using a disk? 326

20.8. Can I upgrade my laptop's memory? 327

20.9. Can I upgrade my laptop's processor? 328

20.10. What are some features I need to look for
if I'm buying a laptop to run Windows? 328

21 Troubleshooting Windows

21.1. Windows fails during the installation process,
displaying an error message. What can I do? 331

21.2. The list of installed equipment shown by
Windows doesn't match the actual hardware.
What's wrong? 332

21.3. The mouse pointer appears, but it is frozen
on-screen or jumps wildly around the screen.
Why is this happening? 333

21.4. The installation or setup program for my Windows
application halts abruptly, and I have leftover files
on my hard disk. How do I fix this? 334

21.5. Windows is running very slowly and behaving erratically. How do I fix it? 335

21.6. Windows displays an *Out of memory* error when my application starts, even though my PC has plenty of installed RAM. Why does this happen? ...336

21.7. Windows hangs every time I run a certain Windows application. How can I prevent this from happening? 336

21.8. I get an error message indicating that my hard disk is full in the middle of a Windows operation. What should I do? 337

21.9. I can't save a file to a floppy disk. How can I fix this problem? 337

21.10. When I try to play a particular WAV sound file, I get the error message *Unable to play sound,* or no sound plays. How can I fix this problem? 338

21.11. My printer isn't working. How can I fix it? 338

21.12. My printer works, but some text is missing from the printout. How can I fix this? 339

21.13. My HP laser printer displays an *Error 20* message in its LCD panel in the midst of a document I've sent from within Windows. What does this mean? 339

21.14. My communications software produces a *Cannot Access Serial Port* error message. Why does this mean? 340

21.15. My communications software produces errors when it runs at 9600 bps or more, but it works fine at 2400 bps or less. What should I do? 340

Acknowledgments

We would like to take the opportunity to acknowledge several people who helped in the production of this book, or who just put up with us while we were writing it. Thanks to Greg Croy, who found us an opportunity to write a Windows 95 book in a crowded marketplace. We'd also like to thank the hard-working SysOps on all the CompuServe product forums, whose access to the everyday problems of software have made this a better book. Thanks go to Derek Burton at Wilmer, Cutler, and Pickering for providing insight and experience with Windows 95 on a Novell network. Thanks to our friends and family members for putting up with our ignoring the world and hiding out hunched over computers for long periods of time. And, in a way, we owe some thanks to Carnival Cruise Lines and the people of the Bahamas for providing us with a strong incentive to get the first draft of this book done by November 1994.

About the Authors

Edward Jones is the best-selling author of more than 30 computer books. He provides consulting, planning, software development, and training for federal government agencies, law firms, and corporate clients. He has designed and provided personnel management software to an installed base of approximately 100 companies nationwide through Computer Support Group of Annandale, Virginia. Jones has published articles in *Lotus, Database Advisor,* and *DBMS magazines.*

Derek Sutton is a contributing Sams author who provides consulting services in database management.

Introduction

Welcome to *Your Windows 95 Consultant, Pre-Release Edition*. In this book, you'll find a wide range of hard-to-find answers to your Windows 95 questions in the areas of both software and hardware.

Why This book?

With so many books written for Windows 95, that's a fair question. The majority of the Windows books take you by the hand and guide you step by step through the basics. That approach is fine when you're just learning the Windows environment. However, if you are already basically familiar with Windows 95 (or if you are an accomplished user of Windows 3.*x* and aren't interested in being led by the hand all over again), then what?

This book is designed to meet the needs of your kind of user, the person who wants more than the basics. This book answers questions that go beyond the common "just learning the program" types of questions. And, there is a broad coverage of topics aimed at those who are familiar with earlier versions of Windows, and want to become familiar with Windows 95 while wasting the least possible amount of time.

In particular, this book is designed to help serve as a consultant at your side; it gives you effective answers to the kinds of questions that commonly arise with Windows and with the variety of applications used with Windows today. Those who spend any amount of time supporting computer users in large organizations know about the common questions that don't always have common answers. In effect, these kinds of questions, day in and day out, make up your career as a support person (and, as a side benefit, they pay the rent in the long run). We've spent hundreds of hours making sure that those kinds of questions are covered in this book, so that you'll have a quick and handy access to the answers.

Who Should Read This Book?

This book is for readers who want to get the most out of Windows, out of their Windows applications, and out of their hardware running Windows. It is for readers who want answers to those nagging questions, without having to spend hours on hold on some tech support phone line, or waiting for a return call from the company's overworked PC help-desk person. This book is appropriate for users of all levels, from beginning to advanced. If you're just starting out with Windows, you'll save much time by avoiding the common pitfalls covered by many of the questions that you'll find here. If you're an intermediate to advanced user, you'll add to your existing knowledge base with the tips and techniques that you haven't yet run across. And if, like us, you spend part or all of your work time supporting end users, you'll have a reference for the wide range of hardware and software problems that you must deal with on a daily basis.

How To Use This Book

You can use this book in a number of ways. If you just want to learn as much as you possibly can about Windows 95, you can begin at the front and read straight through. If you're interested in a specific area, you can go to the appropriate section and begin reading there. If you're searching for the answer to a specific question, check the Table of Contents and look in the chapter that covers that specific area. Also, be sure to check Chapter 21, "Troubleshooting Windows," for answers to a range of specific problems.

Conventions Used in This Book

Any commands that you must enter appear in monospaced font, and variables in a command, such as a filename or a disk drive that may differ on different systems, appear in *monospaced italic*.

The first occurrence of a new term appears in italics, and filenames appear in uppercase characters. All figures and tables are numbered sequentially for your convenience. For example, the second figure in Chapter 20 is Figure 20.2.

When we point out a menu option, we designate it like this: Programs | Settings. As an example, a sentence might read "Open the Start menu, and choose Programs | Settings." This indicates that you would select Programs, and then select Settings from the next menu to appear.

A Note About Mouse Buttons

We routinely refer to the mouse buttons as the left mouse button and the right mouse button, following conventional settings for mice. If you use the Windows mouse configuration properties window to reverse the buttons on your mouse, you'll need to use the button that's opposite to the one we refer to.

How This Book Is Organized

In Part I of this book (Chapters 1 through 11), you'll find questions and answers that relate to Windows 95 itself, and to the use of popular Windows applications.

Part II (Chapters 12 through 17) deal with hardware, with a particular emphasis on how you can increase the performance of your hardware, and how you can solve problems that occur when you add equipment or perform an upgrade.

In chapters 18 through 20 of Part III, you'll find questions, answers, and techniques dealing with networks, communications, and the mostly traveling world of portable computers. Finally, there's Chapter 21, which provides common answers in the area of troubleshooting Windows.

Part IV (Appendixes A through C) covers installation and some basics of working with hardware, and provides a resource listing for vendors of hardware and software.

NOTE

The end-user information in this book is based on information on Windows 95 made public by Microsoft as of March 1995. Because this information was made public before the release of the product, we encourage you to visit your local bookstore at that time for updated books on Windows 95.

If you have a modem or access to the Internet, you can always get up-to-the-minute information on Windows 95 direct from Microsoft on WinNews:

On CompuServe: GO WINNEWS

On the Internet:
ftp://ftp.microsoft.com/PerOpSys/Win_News/Chicago
http://www.microsoft.com

On AOL: keyword WINNEWS

On Prodigy: jumpword WINNEWS

On Genie: WINNEWS file area on Windows RTC

You can also subscribe to Microsoft's WinNews electronic newsletter by sending Internet e-mail to news@microsoft.nwnet.com and putting the words SUBSCRIBE WINNEWS in the text of the e-mail.

Maximizing Windows

1	The Components of Windows 95	3
2	Customizing the Desktop and the Taskbar	13
3	Staying Organized	31
4	Putting It on Paper	45
5	Maximizing Memory	65
6	Exchanging Data Between Applications	71
7	Making the Most of the Bundled Windows Applications	83
8	Making the Most of Your Windows Applications	97
9	Running DOS Applications Under Windows	145
10	Windows and Multimedia	165
11	Working with the Registry	181

1

The Components of Windows 95

This chapter provides a general overview of the components behind Windows 95, and what aspects of it differ from the previous versions of Windows that you are likely to be familiar with.

1.1. What is Windows 95?

Windows 95 is a complete 32-bit operating system, as opposed to previous versions of Windows, which were GUI (graphical user interface) environments sitting atop various versions of DOS. It is designed to be easier to use by novices and to eliminate the need to work with the complexities of DOS, while still providing power users with the flexibility they want in order to handle sophisticated operations. Prior versions of Windows, while obviously layered atop versions of DOS, have always meant running a graphical user interface above a character-based operating system. Windows 95 combines the GUI and the operating system into one package, and takes full advantage of 32-bit microprocessors (80386 and higher).

In addition to being a true 32-bit operating system, Windows 95 provides *preemptive multitasking* (meaning that you no longer need to wait for the system to finish certain operations such as copying files), complete support for the 32-bit version of the Windows API, a consistent user interface that is easier for novices to work with, built-in networking support, improved communications, and (finally!) an end to the curse of eight-dot-three filename limitations. Windows 95 also supports Plug-and-Play, a hardware standard that allows Windows to automatically configure itself when plug-and-play compatible hardware is connected to a system.

1.2. What's different about Windows 95?

Windows 95 is not the kind of upgrade that we experienced in moving from Windows 3.0 to Windows 3.1. With the earlier upgrade, major performance improvements took place. But, with the exception of the replacement of the old MS-DOS Executive with the File Manager, the user interface was basically the same between the versions. With Windows 95, on the other hand, the entire user interface (and with it, the ways of using Windows) has changed significantly. Program Manager is gone, as is File Manager. The interface centers around a Desktop that serves as a working surface, and a Taskbar that can be thought of as an efficient program launcher.

1.3. What's different about the user interface?

Figure 1.1 shows the user interface in a nutshell. The Taskbar contains a Start menu that provides quick access to programs, documents, and Help screens; the Start menu can be customized by adding shortcuts to commonly used programs or documents. On the Desktop, icons appear for My Computer, Network Neighborhood (if the computer is connected to a network), and Info Center (if a modem, FAX board, or other e-mail capabilities have been added to the hardware). My Computer provides a visual representation of drives, folders (subdirectories), printers, and other peripherals on the system.

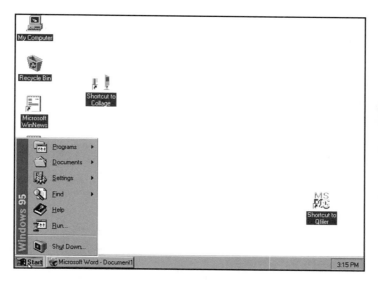

Figure 1.1 *The user interface presented by Windows 95.*

I

1.4. What is the Desktop?

The Windows 95 Desktop is at the core of what you do in Windows. It's the first thing you see after Windows starts. On the Desktop, you see My Computer, the Taskbar, the Recycle Bin, and (optionally) icons for Network Neighborhood and the Inbox.

The new Desktop is much more document-oriented than application-oriented, as the previous version of Windows was. One main idea behind the Desktop and Taskbar combination was to make Windows less visually confusing, and give you an easy way to launch desired programs or open commonly used documents. When Windows boots up, the Taskbar lists all active programs. Clicking on the name of the program activates that program. The Taskbar remains on the screen at all times, making it easy to get to—unless it has been configured otherwise.

With a default installation of Windows 95, only a few graphic items appear on the Desktop, although you can clutter it just as thoroughly as was possible under earlier versions of Windows. The new Desktop contains these items: My Computer, the Recycle Bin, the

Inbox, and the Taskbar at the bottom of the Desktop. (The items you have may vary depending on the options you chose during installation.) In a nutshell, My Computer is used to browse the resources of your PC. The Taskbar is used to start programs and switch tasks with a single mouse-click, which is a lot easier than the awkward task-switching methods of Alt+Tab or Ctrl+Esc. Network Neighborhood (which appears if you're using a Network) is used to browse the resources of a network, which was not an easy task previously. The Inbox is optionally installed and allows access to the Microsoft Exchange.

Q 1.5. What is the Taskbar?

Of all the changes in Windows 95, the Taskbar exemplifies the improvement in the user interface the most. The majority of the most-used applications are easily accessible from the Taskbar. The two most important features of the Taskbar are the Start menu and pushbutton task switching.

The Start menu can be viewed as an efficient program launcher. All programs can be launched from the Start menu. What makes the Start menu so efficient is that during Setup, you can select your frequently used programs, and these are placed in the Programs menu of the Start menu. Later, if you decide to change the programs, you can do so easily by choosing Settings from the Start menu.

The last 15 documents opened are listed in the Documents menu of the Start menu. This makes for quick access to the most recently used documents, and increases efficiency because you don't waste time browsing for particular documents used recently.

The Settings menu gives quick access to the Control Panel and the Printer folder. Also, the Taskbar can be customized from the settings menu by choosing the setup desired.

The Find feature is a big improvement over the File Manager's file Search feature in Windows 3.1. It is no longer necessary to conform to the *.* search syntax because full text can be used as the basis for a search.

Help topics are now more usable and easily accessible from the Start menu. The Help topics are completely different for Windows 95.

Instead of Contents, Search, and Glossary, there are only three Tabs: Contents, Index, and Find.

The Contents tab has gone to a table of contents form of organization. First, the chapters are displayed, and then each can be broken down into subsections by clicking on the Book icon used for the Chapters of Help. The other new feature is that all the help topics fit onto one screen, which prevents having to scroll through complicated and large sections of help screens.

There are also Shortcut buttons to help within all Control Panel tools. This facilitates the use of Help, especially because of the addition of the new question mark icon that appears on the upper-right corner of the title bar. Clicking here causes the cursor to become a question mark that can be dropped anywhere in the dialog box for a brief explanation of whatever was selected.

The Run option gives command-line type functionality via the Start menu, whereas Shutdown safely shuts down Windows. Because there is no separate running of a GUI atop DOS, shutting down Windows takes you to a message screen with the assumption that the computer will be turned off.

1.6. How does task switching work?

Task switching has been made a great deal simpler in Windows 95. As each application is opened, it is given a button on the Taskbar. Therefore, instead of having to switch to a task list, you simply press the application desired on the Taskbar. The Taskbar also can be repositioned to any of the sides of the screen by clicking and dragging with the mouse. To resize the Taskbar, drag the inside edge with the mouse to the desired size. The Auto Hide setting is used to make the Taskbar appear only when the mouse hits the edge of the screen.

1.7. What happened to File Manager?

File Manager has been replaced for the most part with Explorer, a powerful two-pane browsing application with which experienced users can explore drives and directories. Explorer is more than just a file management tool; you can use it to view all system resources under Windows 95, including drives and directories, Control Panel settings, and the configuration of a network.

1.8. What is My Computer?

My Computer is the default method of browsing among the resources of a PC, whether these are files, programs, printers, or system settings. My Computer lets you view the contents of drives and their folders (subdirectories), and it can be used for file management tasks (moving and copying files) as well as for modification of printer and system settings. Additional details on the use of My Computer can be found in Chapter 3, "Staying Organized."

1.9. What is the Explorer?

The Explorer can be thought of as a supercharged File Manager for Windows 95. This file manager is different in many ways, including its power, flexibility, and extensiveness. Unlike the previous File Manager, the Explorer has a different window for each drive, which makes for less confusion.

The Explorer enables you to look at all of Windows 95's resources, local or connected. The zoom option lets you look at all of this at one time, or just a section. My Computer and Network Neighborhood also can be browsed.

The Explorer is also flexible and customizable. A folder's contents can be viewed in several ways via the toolbar and View menu. There is a choice between small or large icons, and list view or detailed view. Network drives can also be mapped from the Explorer toolbar.

Detailed view provides a wealth of information about the folder contents. All of the files have their identifying icons listed, along with drive sizes and space free, which are reported in My Computer. The Control Panel tools are also described in detail view after choosing Control Panel from the toolbar. Printer jobs in queue can also be examined. If operating in a network environment, information on other computers in the Network Neighborhood is provided.

1.10. Don't My Computer and Explorer accomplish the same job?

Basically, yes. In Windows 95, Microsoft provided two tools to meet the same end in order to appeal to novices and experts separately. The old File Manager was found to be difficult to use and understand by novices, but expert users wanted to keep the power designed into File Manager. Microsoft's solution was to provide My Computer to let novices browse among files, perform simple file operations, and change system settings, and to provide Explorer to let the experts do the same kinds of tasks.

1.11. What is Network Neighborhood?

Network Neighborhood allows for the easy browsing of the network. To insulate a user from large networks, the Network Neighborhood is configured by the administrator to display only the PCs, printers, and servers in the user's immediate work group. Network Neighborhood provides an easy-to-use object-oriented interface, which means that network users need not be certified NetWare engineers to figure out what's on a network. If you have multiple servers that you're interested in connecting to, Network Neighborhood lets you browse among those. If you click on a server, you see what shared resources exist on that server, and whether there are printers attached.

To view the entire network, the Entire Network option can be selected from inside the Network Neighborhood.

1.12. What are Properties?

Properties are characteristics of a given object in Windows (such as a hard drive or a printer). Windows 95 makes extensive use of properties to set different characteristics for various parts of the program; think of this as Microsoft's way of bringing object-orientation to the overall Windows environment. As an example, try this:

1. Open My Computer.

2. Right-click on one of your hard drives, and choose Properties from the menu. When you do so, a Properties window opens (see Figure 1.2).

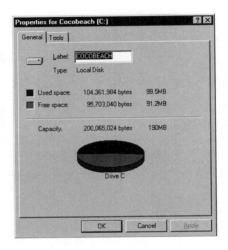

Figure 1.2. *Properties window for a hard drive.*

Properties windows enable you to examine and modify properties for the selected object (in this case, you can examine the free space remaining on the drive, and change the drive's volume label).

1.13. All of my Program Manager icons are gone, and I liked having them. How can I duplicate the Program Manager look?

If you prefer to have favorite icons for all your applications on the Desktop, you can easily do so by adding directly to the Desktop a *shortcut* for the desired application. By default, Windows 95 adds your Windows applications to the Programs section of the Start menu, but you may prefer the icon-on-the-desk approach. Use these steps to add a shortcut to the Desktop:

1. Open My Computer (if you're familiar with Explorer, you can use it for the same task).

2. Open the drive containing the desired program, and navigate into the folder that contains the desired program.

3. Click and drag the program onto the Desktop. An icon
   representing a shortcut to the program will appear.

1.14. What happened to Print Manager?

Both the old Print Manager and the Printer icon in the Control
Panel under earlier versions of Windows are gone from Windows
95. All printer functions are combined into one location, the
Printers Folder.

> **NOTE** You can get to the Printers Folder either from My
> Computer or from the Explorer.
>
> In My Computer, double-click the Printers Folder
> to open it.
>
> In Explorer, scroll to the bottom of the All Folders
> list, and double-click the Printers folder.

From the Printers Folder, you can double-click the Add Printer icon
to install a new printer, or you can double-click any existing printer
to open a window displaying characteristics for that printer. (For
more on working with printers and changing printer settings, see
Chapter 4, "Putting It on Paper.")

1.15. What happened to my CONFIG.SYS and AUTOEXEC.BAT files?

Windows 95 doesn't need individual CONFIG.SYS and
AUTOEXEC.BAT files, as did prior versions of Windows. Windows 95 maintains its own built-in intelligence regarding drivers
and environmental settings, and it loads appropriate driver files and
configuration settings during the process of startup. Because your
existing software (prior to upgrading to Windows 95) may have
required the use of CONFIG.SYS and/or AUTOEXEC.BAT,
Windows 95 reads any existing AUTOEXEC.BAT and
CONFIG.SYS files on startup and uses the information contained
within them to set the global environment.

Q 1.16. What's the Recycle Bin?

The Recycle Bin is a container that stores files you've deleted. (You can delete files by highlighting them in My Computer or in Explorer, and then pressing the Del key.) When you delete a file, Windows 95 doesn't remove it permanently; instead, it stores it in the Recycle Bin. This provides a built-in safeguard. If you later find that you need the file you deleted, you can retrieve it from the Recycle Bin. To see what's in the Recycle Bin, double-click the Recycle Bin icon. The Recycle Bin opens, as shown in Figure 1.3.

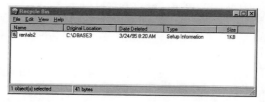

Figure 1.3. *The Recycle Bin containing a deleted document.*

To recover the document, click it to select it, open the File menu of the Recycle Bin, and then choose Restore. You can empty the Recycle Bin by choosing Empty Recycle Bin from the same File menu. Be warned that once you empty the Recycle Bin, the files are gone forever—there is no way to recover them using conventional methods. Also note that, as you run short of disk space, fewer items are kept as recoverable in the Recycle Bin.

Customizing the Desktop and the Taskbar

In this chapter, you will learn how to customize the Windows Desktop and Taskbar, and how to start programs and utilities under Windows. In particular, you will learn how you can customize the Taskbar and its associated properties to best fit how you use Windows.

2.1. How much can I accomplish with the Taskbar?

Microsoft designed the Taskbar to make 95 percent of what a typical Windows user wants to do readily accessible; it serves as more than just a program launcher. One of Microsoft's goals was to make pushbutton task switching easy, even for novice users—it's simple to click on any task and get immediate access to that task. Figure 2.1 shows the Taskbar and its Start menu.

Figure 2.1. *The Taskbar and its Start menu.*

The following paragraphs provide an overview of the Start menu's choices:

Programs
The submenu that opens when you click here contains any Windows 3.1 applications that existed on your hard drive when you installed Windows 95. Also, any new Windows software that you install later is added to this menu (assuming the software's installation routines conform to Windows standards).

Documents
This submenu of the Start menu keeps a running list of the last 10 documents you worked with. By choosing any document from the list, you can launch the corresponding application and load the document simultaneously.

Settings
This option offers fast access to the Control Panel (which is used to control the overall settings in Windows), the Printers folder (which is used to manage printing and to change printer settings), and the Taskbar settings. Choose any of the options shown to customize the items in question.

Find
This option brings up a Find dialog box, which replaces the old search feature of File Manager in prior versions of Windows. Searches can now be done based on partial text, as well as by file size or by last modification date.

Help Topics   This option displays context-sensitive help, which operates differently than in prior versions of Windows. Help screens in many cases can now take you directly to the option you want to perform, and they can "remain on top" so you can view them while working with whatever task it is you asked for help about.

Run   This is the equivalent of File | Run in prior versions of Windows. It enables you to run programs from the command line.

Shutdown   Prepares the PC to be turned off by closing and saving all files and current environmental settings to disk. (If you've modified files that you haven't saved, Windows warns you of that fact.)

2.2. How and to where can I move the Taskbar?

You can move the Taskbar to any position on the perimeter of the screen. You do this by clicking on any of the sections of the Taskbar that do not have any buttons and dragging the Taskbar to the desired position.

2.3. How can I hide or unhide the Taskbar?

You can hide the Taskbar so that it appears only when you want it to, or you can cause it to remain on-screen at all times,

To hide the Taskbar completely, follow these steps:

1. Click the Start button, choose Settings, and then choose Taskbar. The Properties of Taskbar window will appear.
2. Choose Taskbar Options. This switches to the options for the Taskbar.
3. Click the box beside Auto hide. This causes the Taskbar to appear only when you move the mouse pointer to the left corner of the screen. When done, click OK.

4. To unhide the Taskbar, simply return to the Taskbar Options
    window and click the Auto Hide box to force the Taskbar to
    remain on-screen at all times.

2.4. How can I customize the Taskbar?

By right-clicking any blank area of the Taskbar, you can access a
Properties window, where you can customize the Taskbar's charac-
teristics. Click the right mouse button on the Taskbar to open the
Properties menu, and choose Properties to open the Properties for
Taskbar window, shown in Figure 2.2.

Figure 2.2. *The Properties for Taskbar window.*

This window enables you to customize the various Taskbar options
and to change the selected applications that appear on the Start
menu. The first tab on the Properties for Taskbar window is the
Taskbar Options tab. This enables you to customize the Taskbar—
you can select options such as Auto hide and Always on top. As
described earlier, choose Auto hide to hide the Taskbar, or leave the
Always on top choice selected if you want the Taskbar to remain
visible. The second tab, Start Menu Programs, enables you to add
or remove items from the Start menu. To add an item to the Start
menu, click the Add button in the window and specify the name of

the item in the resulting Create Shortcut dialog box. To remove an item from the Start menu, click the Remove button in the window, then choose the item you want to remove from the list in the resulting Remove Shortcuts/Folders dialog box.

2.5. What are the different ways you can switch between programs that are running?

Besides the obvious (clicking on the Taskbar), most of the Windows 3.*x* methods still work. Pressing Alt+Tab cycles you through applications; you can hold Alt and press Tab repeatedly to display all running tasks in sequence, letting up on the Alt key when your desired task appears. Ctrl+Esc no longer brings up a task list, but it will open the Start menu; from there you can keyboard your way to other menu options using the cursor keys.

2.6. How can I run a DOS application?

To run a DOS application, choose Programs from the Start menu, then choose the MS DOS prompt icon. In a moment, the DOS prompt appears, and you can enter the DOS command normally used to start the program.

> **NOTE** You also can run DOS programs from My Computer or from Explorer. Using My Computer or Explorer, find the DOS program's executable (.EXE or .COM) file within its appropriate folder; then, double-click the program file within the folder to run the program.

2.7. I just added a program, and it's not on any menu. How can I start it?

Software that is installed in an unconventional manner may not appear on the Programs menu with your other applications; this is definitely true if your method of "installation" is to drag a program file from a floppy disk onto your hard disk using My Computer or Explorer (or if you copied it with a DOS COPY command). You can run any program by double-clicking it from within its folder in My Computer or Explorer. If you plan on using the program often, it makes sense to add it to the Start menu as an option (see Question 2.8).

Customizing

This section provides techniques you can use to customize various appearance-related aspects of Windows.

2.8. How can I customize the Start button?

Open the Start menu and choose Settings | Taskbar. Next, select the Start Menu Programs tab, and then choose the Add button. You'll be prompted to enter the name and location of the item you wish to add. The Browse button can be used to list the folders. From there you can choose the folder that contains the program or document you wish to use. Click the desired program or document you wish to add, click OK, and then click Next. You still need to select the folder you want to place the shortcut in and enter a name for it. After entering the folder name, click Finished to make the changes. Remember that if you wish to add a document, you'll need to change the File of Type box to All files instead of Programs.

2.9. How can I edit the names that applications give themselves?

It makes sense in many cases to do this; the long names that Windows applications assign themselves can consume more space on your desktop than you're comfortable with. You easily can change a name such as Microsoft Power Point 3.0 to Pwr Point. To do this, click the object to select it, then click inside the box containing the name of the application. This will highlight the name of the application. Next, type the name that you wish to assign the application and press Enter when you're done.

2.10. How do I change Windows color schemes?

To change the Windows color schemes, follow these steps:

1. Open the Start menu, and choose Settings|Control Panel.
2. When the Control Panel opens, double-click the Display icon.
3. When the Properties for Display icon opens, click the Appearance tab to open a Properties window for the Appearance settings (see Figure 2.3).

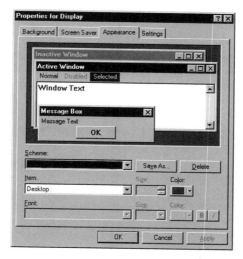

Figure 2.3. *The Appearance tab in the Properties for Display window.*

The Appearance window contains all the items you need for changing the color schemes. Click the Scheme box, and you see a drop-down menu that contains the colors and default fonts for a given color scheme. (Under Windows, a *color scheme* is a collection of colors for various Windows items, such as dialog boxes, active windows, and inactive windows.) The combinations you choose are shown at the top of the screen. This enables you to preview a color scheme before applying it. Click the Item box, and another menu appears that contains all the items to which the different colors can be applied, such as the Desktop, the border captions, menu bar, buttons, and other elements of Windows.

If you wish to customize a specific color scheme, click in the Item list box and choose the desired item, then select a size and color for that item using the Size and Color settings, respectively, in the window. Where appropriate, you also can select a font, along with a size and color for the font. For example, if you select Menu under Item, you can then choose a font, size, and color for the letters used by the menus when your color scheme takes effect. When you finish making changes to the color scheme, click OK.

2.11. How can I create custom color schemes?

You can create custom colors from the Properties for Display window. To open that window, follow the three steps presented in Question 2.10. Click the Appearance tab. On this tab, click the Color box to the right of the Item list box to open the smaller colors box. Click the Other box at the bottom of this box to open the larger colors box. This box contains the Define Custom Colors button. When you click this button, you see the window shown in Figure 2.4.

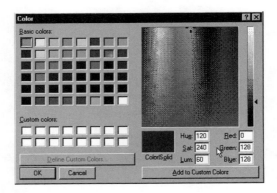

Figure 2.4. *Custom colors window.*

From this window, you can choose a basic color, or you can create a custom color (see Question 2.12 for details on creating a custom color). Once you have chosen a color, click OK, and the item you selected previously takes on the new color. You can repeat these steps to mix and match the colors you want for your custom color scheme.

2.12. How can I save my custom color scheme?

To save the custom color schemes you've created, click the Save As button in the Properties for Display window to open the Save Scheme box. When you do so, you are prompted to enter a filename under which to save your color scheme. Click OK to save the color scheme.

If you no longer want to keep your color scheme, you can remove it. To do this, under the Appearance tab of the Properties for Display window choose the name of the scheme, then click the Delete button.

2.13. How can I create custom colors?

1. Open the Start menu, and choose Settings|Control Panel.
2. When the Control Panel opens, double-click the Display icon.
3. When the Properties for Display icon opens, click the Appearance tab to open a properties window for the Appearance settings, as shown earlier in Figure 2.3.
4. Click the Other box and the Color window opens as shown in Figure 2.4.
5. Click the Define Custom Colors button; when you do so, the color spectrum appears to the right of the window.

To create your own color, click the Add Custom Colors button to activate the cross on the color spectrum. You also can create custom colors by entering values in the text boxes for Hue, Sat, Lum, Red, Green, and Blue. These settings control the shading and the color intensity. You also can drag the cross display to a point on the color spectrum (the larger color box that occupies most of the right side of the dialog box). This causes the color and the shading closest to the new color to appear in the small box below the spectrum. If you wish to use the shading as a basis for the color you create, double-click the desired color and shading, then use the cross display to make changes by clicking and dragging it to the desired location. After you've chosen a general color, you can move the left-pointing arrow on the right of the screen up or down to adjust the intensity of the color until you reach the color you want.

When you finish, click the Add to Custom Colors button, and the color appears on the Custom Colors rows of the color choice box. By default, when both rows are filled, the colors entered first are replaced by any new colors created.

2.14. How can I change the background pattern?

To change the background, right-click at any blank space on the current background to open the Properties for Display window. When the Background tab of this window is selected (see Figure 2.5), you have access to all the settings needed to change the background pattern and to change any wallpaper used for Windows.

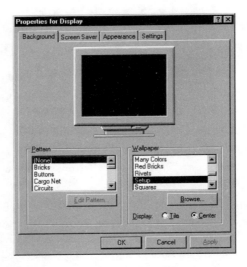

Figure 2.5. *The Background tab in the Properties for Display window.*

The Background tab of the Properties for Display window enables you to see what a particular background will look like when it is applied to the screen. You can change the pattern for this space by changing the settings in the Pattern box on the left of the window. Once you select it, the chosen pattern also is displayed at the top of the window. To change the wallpaper, use the Wallpaper list box at the right of the window. (This list box contains a listing of all the available wallpapers.) To preview what a particular background will look like, click the name and it will appear at the top of the screen as it would on the screen. You also can make the background appear covering the entire screen (Tile), or just in the center of the screen (Center). If you choose Center, Windows leaves a blank space around the chosen background.

2.15. How can I create my own background?

You may want to create your own background with your company name or a logo of your own. To do so, you need to create a bitmap file. (You can do this by using a graphics program such as WinPaint.) After you've created or loaded the desired wallpaper using WinPaint, choose Set as Wallpaper (Tiled) or Set as Wallpaper (Centered), from the File menu in WinPaint. Next, you are asked if you want to save the picture before you set it as wallpaper. After choosing yes, the picture appears as the wallpaper.

2.16. How can I set up a screen saver?

You can set up screen savers by using the Properties for Display window. Open the window the same way you would if you wanted to change the background (right-click on any blank part of the background, and choose Properties from the menu that appears). Click the Screen Saver tab to display the settings for the screen savers (see Figure 2.6).

The upper portion of the window displays the current screen saver, if one is active. Click the arrow to the right of the Screen Saver list box to see all the available screen savers. Select the desired screen saver from the list box—you can preview them at the top of the window. All the screen savers that use lines, such as Bézier and Mystify, enable you to change the characteristics of the lines by using the Settings button; you can change their speed, the colors used for the lines, and the line density. You also can choose Marquee, which enables you to enter a message to display across the screen. Once Marquee has been chosen, clicking the Settings button displays an additional dialog box that enables you to position a marquee, adjust its speed, and set its text and background color.

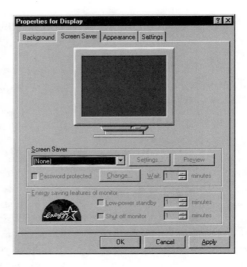

Figure 2.6. *The Screen Saver tab in the Properties for Display window.*

Under the Screen Saver tab in the Energy Saving Features portion of the window, there are two additional options: Low-power standby and Shut off monitor. The Low-power standby option saves power by switching your monitor into a standby mode when the PC is inoperative for the number of minutes indicated in the minutes box. The Shut off monitor option turns the monitor off after the period of inactivity indicated in the minutes box. For either of these options to work, your monitor must support the use of these options.

2.17. How can I change mouse settings?

To change the mouse settings, click the Start button on the Taskbar and choose Settings|Control Panel. Once at the Control Panel, double-click the mouse icon to open the Properties for Mouse window (see Figure 2.7). This window controls all the modifications that can be made to the mouse.

You can change the basic mouse configuration (meaning whether the mouse is "right-handed" or "left-handed") and the double-click speed under the Buttons tab. When the mouse is set for right-handed configuration, the left mouse button selects and drags objects, and the right mouse button opens properties windows.

When the mouse is set for left-handed configuration, the right mouse button selects and drags objects, and the left mouse button opens properties windows.

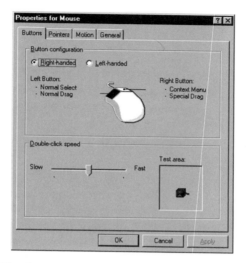

Figure 2.7. *The Properties for Mouse window.*

Under the Pointers tab, you can replace the standard Windows pointers with custom mouse pointers (if you've obtained custom cursor files with *.ANI or *.CUR extensions from some source). To replace a standard Windows pointer, click the Pointers tab, then double-click the desired pointer in the list box of mouse pointers. This causes a Browse dialog box to appear with an entry for File Name. Enter the name of the .ANI or .CUR file that you want to use as a replacement mouse pointer, then click OK.

Under the Motion tab, you can adjust both the pointer speed and the pointer trail for the mouse. The Pointer Speed setting adjusts the speed at which the pointer moves on-screen in response to mouse movement. If you want a pointer with a trail, click the Show Pointer Trails box, and adjust the Pointer Trail setting between short and long, as desired. (Pointer trails can be useful on laptops with LCD screens, where the standard mouse pointers are often hard to see.)

The General tab contains the window that controls the type of mouse being used. To change the type of mouse being used, click the Change button to open the Select Device window. This window displays the current mouse in use and enables you to change the mouse. Show Compatible Devices displays all the mice that are compatible with the one being used. If you wish to see all the available mice, choose Show All Devices. If you are installing a new mouse that is not listed, click the Have Disk button. Doing so displays an Install From Disk dialog box, which asks you to insert the installation disk supplied with the mouse.

2.18. How can I change the repeat speed for my keyboard?

You can change the repeat speeds used by the keyboard by going to the Control Panel (choose Start|Settings|Control Panel). Double-click the Keyboard icon to open the Properties for Keyboard window. The Speed tab displays the properties for the keyboard speed: Repeat Delay and Repeat Speed. To adjust the amount of time that elapses before a character starts to repeat, move the slider under Repeat Delay. To adjust the speed at which the character repeats, move the slider under Repeat Rate. (The setting for Cursor Blink happens also to be in this window, although technically it has nothing to do with your keyboard. Changing this setting changes the speed at which the cursor blinks.)

2.19. How can I change the type of keyboard I am using?

To change the type of keyboard you are using, go to the control Panel. Double-click the keyboard icon, and choose Properties. This opens the Properties window for the keyboard. Next, choose the General tab, then click the Change button to open a Select Device dialog box. In this dialog box, you choose the type of keyboard you wish to use by clicking the Show All Devices button, or if you prefer, you can display only the keyboards that are compatible with your current hardware by leaving the Show Compatible Devices button turned on. If you have an installation disk for the type of keyboard you are installing, click the Have Disk button, insert the disk, and click OK in the resulting dialog box.

2.20. How can I change the character layout for my keyboard to match a different language?

To change the character layout for your keyboard to another language, access the Control Panel, click the Keyboard icon, and then click the Language tab. Next, click the Add button to open the Add Language dialog box. In the Language list box shown within this dialog box, choose the language you want and click OK.

2.21. How can I customize international settings?

You can customize international settings by double-clicking the Regional Settings icon within the Control Panel. This opens the Properties for Regional Settings window, as shown in Figure 2.8. This window has five tabs: Regional Settings, Number, Currency, Time, and Date. Under the Regional Settings tab, you can choose the country or region of the world to use for default Windows settings. The remaining tabs enable you to further customize the symbols used under Windows to display numeric amounts, currency amounts, times, and dates.

Figure 2.8. *The Regional Settings tab of the Properties for Regional Settings window.*

The first tab, Regional Settings, contains a list box of different countries and regions of the world. Select a country or region from the list, and the remaining settings for numbers, currencies, dates, and times will default to the commonly-used conventions for that country or region of the world.

The Number tab changes items such as the symbols used for grouping, the way negative numbers are displayed, where the decimals are placed, and so on.

The Currency tab controls all functions dealing with currency. Here, you can change the symbols used in the currency, the decimal position, the number of digits after the decimal, digit grouping, and the number of digits in each number.

The Time tab enables you to change the time according to the way you want it displayed. Here you can change the time separators and AM/PM designations.

The Date tab enables you to change the date according the format you want: *mm/dd/yy*, *dd/mm/yy*, or *yy/mm/dd*. You also can change the date separator character (a slash by default), and the calendar style used.

2.22. How can I assign sounds to system events?

To assign sounds to system events from the Control Panel, click the Sounds icon. This opens the Properties for Sounds window, as shown in Figure 2.9. In the list box, choose the event to which you want to assign a sound by clicking the event. To choose the sound, select a default sound from the Name list box, or click the Browse button to open the Browse window. From here you have to open the directory with the sound files for your computer. After opening the directory, choose the file you want to use by double-clicking the filename, and the name of the selected file appears in the File box. To test the sound, click the right arrow button in the Preview portion of the dialog box. When done assigning system sounds, click the OK button to activate the sounds.

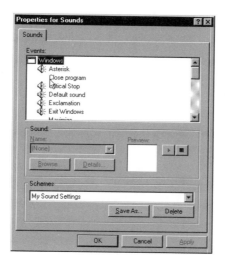

Figure 2.9. *The Sounds tab of the Properties for Sounds window.*

Staying Organized

This chapter presents the common methods used to maintain organization among the files, programs, and resources that you make use of while working with Windows.

Q 3.1. Why think in terms of "objects?"

To understand why Windows object-oriented nature makes sense, it helps to consider the operating system that Windows replaced, which was DOS. DOS and Windows both deal with the same objects—documents (called *data files*), folders (called *directories*), program files, and all the hardware resources (such as disks and printers) attached to a system. The difference between DOS and a GUI environment such as Windows is that with DOS, everything has to be done using commands. The user must figure out how to start programs, open files, and traverse between directories. Learning to use DOS effectively is a challenging task because the system is *procedure-oriented*, which means it relies on a precise series of commands.

With Windows 95, Microsoft has made a noticeable push toward getting Windows to become more object-oriented. This version of Windows is not truly what you would call object-oriented—that will have to wait for a later version of Windows—but it possesses definite object-oriented tendencies. Windows simplifies the process of working with common operations (formerly done using commands under DOS) by grouping them in terms of objects. You can consider most of what you work with in Windows to be one of four types of objects:

- *documents*, or files containing data, such as letters created with a word processor, or spreadsheet files

- *programs*, which are executable files that launch a program when chosen

- *devices*, such as disk drives, CD-ROM drives, printers, and modems, whether connected locally or on a network

- *folders* (known as subdirectories under DOS), which are objects that can be used to store documents, programs, or other folders

As an operating system, Windows follows the "select, then act" methodology in which you first select an object, then perform some action on that object. For example, a common way to print a file under Windows is to select the file from a window where it is visible, then drag it and drop it onto an icon of a printer. Windows provides an object-oriented interface, or *shell*, over the operating system, which lets you control the operating system in a graphical, intuitive manner. It makes sense to understand what Microsoft is trying to accomplish with Windows, and to think more in terms of objects, when getting familiar with the resource management tools, such as Explorer and My Computer, provided under Windows.

3.2. What advantages does Explorer offer over the File Manager of Windows 3.x?

Like File Manager, Explorer provides a two-dimensional hierarchical view of files, but it goes further than this. During the beta-testing phase, one reviewer called Explorer, "File Manager on steroids," and the analogy is an accurate one. Besides providing a way to view your folders and their contents, Explorer also lets you examine and work with other resources as well as system settings. With Explorer, you can delete, move, and copy files; print documents and manage the print queue; browse among the network resources; and change display settings, all from a single location.

3.3. How do I start Explorer?

To start Explorer, open the Start menu and click Programs, then choose Windows Explorer. Explorer opens in a window (see Figure 3.1).

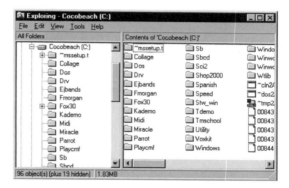

Figure 3.1. *The Explorer window.*

To view the contents of any folder in the right panel of the window, click the desired folder on the left panel of the window. Plus signs, which are visible to the left of the folder names, indicate that the folder contains additional folders within; you can click the plus sign to display the folders within a folder.

3.4. How do I select different drives?

To select different drives in Explorer, click on the drive you wish to view, and the files will appear on the right pane of the window. Alternatively, you can use the keyboard to scroll through the folders. As you move the highlight to each folder, the folder opens and its contents are displayed in the right pane of Explorer.

3.5. How can I open and close folders?

To open and close folders in Explorer, simply click on the folder and the contents will appear in the right pane. You can do the same task in My Computer by double-clicking any desired folder.

3.6. How can I open an additional folder window?

Technically you can't, but in a way, you can. One of the notable differences between Explorer and File Manager of Windows 3.*x* fame is that Explorer has no obvious way to split its display into two windows showing two separate drives. Because you can expand and collapse drives and folders in the left pane, Microsoft's reasoning seems to be that you shouldn't need to open two windows—you can just drag objects between the left and right halves of Explorer. Still, for those who have grown accustomed to working in two separate drive windows, there is a solution: launch Explorer twice, and open the different drives or folders in each session of Explorer. You can drag objects between the two separate Explorer windows just as you would between two sides of the same Explorer window. It's a less messy approach than opening all the windows that clutter the screen if you try using My Computer for the same kinds of tasks.

3.7. How can I copy files or folders?

To copy a file or folder, highlight the icon for the file or folder, and choose Copy from the Edit menu. Doing so copies the file or folder to the Windows Clipboard. Next, click (or use the keyboard to move the highlight to) the area where you want the file or folder copied, and choose Paste from the Edit menu.

3.8. How can I move files and folders?

Windows 95 implements drag-and-drop throughout its interface, which makes it less of a hassle to move objects. To move a file or folder, simply click and drag the icon to the area you want. To maintain compatibility with older habits you learned from earlier Windows versions, you also can choose Cut from the Edit menu, then Paste after choosing where you want the file or folder to be placed.

3.9. How can I move or copy multiple files?

In Explorer and in most other Windows applications, you can hold the Ctrl key while mouse-clicking to select non-contiguous objects (objects that aren't necessarily beside each other). Use the following steps to move or copy multiple files:

1. Click the first file you want to select. With the Ctrl key held down, click on all remaining files you wish to move or copy.

2. If you wish to copy the files, choose Copy from the Edit menu. Then click the folder in which you want to place the files, and choose Paste from the Edit menu.

3. If you wish to move the files, choose Cut from the Edit menu. Then, click the folder where you want to place the files, and choose Paste from the Edit menu. Alternatively, once the files have been selected, you can click and drag the files as a group to the desired folder (click on any of the selected files and hold down the mouse button as you drag).

> **NOTE** Before you copy multiple files to another directory or to a disk, make sure the destination disk contains sufficient space for all the files. (If you run short of space during a copying operation, Windows 95 will display an error message.) You can check on the available space of any disk by right-clicking the disk in question (within Explorer or in My Computer) and choosing Properties from the menu that appears. The properties window that you see as a result will show the disk space used and the space remaining in the form of a pie chart.

3.10. How can I search for files and folders?

Explorer provides a powerful search capability in the Find: All Files dialog box that appears when you choose Find from the Tools menu (see Figure 3.2). In the Named text box, enter some or all of the characters in the name of the file you're looking for. Unlike the Search dialog box in earlier versions of Windows, the Find dialog box enables you to enter partial text without having to use DOS wildcards. Using the Look in Text list box, you can choose a drive or a folder (or you can click on the Browse button to find a particular drive or folder). When you're done, click Find Now to begin the search. Windows displays everything it finds in a columnar display directly below the dialog box.

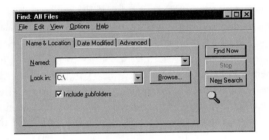

Figure 3.2. *Find: All Files dialog box.*

3.11. How can I duplicate the functionality of my Windows 3.x program groups?

Windows 95 has replaced the old Windows 3.x concept of program groups with a more object-oriented file and folder organization. When you install Windows 95 over an existing Windows 3.x installation, all your old program groups are added as program folders under the Programs section of the Start menu. However, if you installed Windows 95 into a different subdirectory than that of your existing Windows 3.x installation, none of your program groups will appear on the Windows 95 menus. You'll have to add your existing Windows programs to the menu, or add them as shortcuts to the Desktop.

3.12. How can I get a listing in Explorer comparable to what I would see by executing a *DIR* command under DOS?

It won't have that bare-bones look of the character-mode interface that DOS gives you, but you can get a similar display with the following steps:

1. Open Explorer. From the menus, choose View|Options.
2. Click the View tab.
3. Turn off the option, Hide MS-DOS File Extensions for file types that are registered, option, and click OK.
4. From the menus, choose View|Details.

The resulting display is as close as Explorer gets to the kind of listing that a DIR command at a DOS prompt would give you. If you exit Explorer while in this display mode, Explorer will display files in the same way the next time it is next started.

3.13. How can I change Explorer's display?

All the changes to Explorer's appearance can be made from the View menu. The following shows the available choices and what they do:

Toolbar	Turns the toolbar on and off.
Status Bar	Turns the status bar on and off.
Large Icons	Enlarges the icons so they are more visible.
Small Icons	Enables you to have the icons small, making more of them visible.
Lists	Lists all the icons in small form.
Details	Lists the icons, with information on each to the right in the labeled columns.
Arrange Icons	Enables the icons to be arranged by name, type, size, date, or auto arranged.
Refresh	Updates the screen display when running on a network, so that the display reflects the latest

	status of the file structure of the network drives.
Options	Opens the Options window. This window has two tabs: View and File Types. View is used to display or hide certain files and file types. It also enables you to turn the description bar on and off. File Types is used to add or delete file types according to their file extensions.

3.14. I prefer to use My Computer for browsing among my PC's resources, but I find the clutter of numerous windows annoying. Can I force My Computer to display all the resources in a single window?

Through the Properties window for My Computer, you can restrict its display to a single window. Open My Computer, and open the hard drive by double-clicking it. When the window into the drive opens, choose View|Options. In the dialog box that appears, turn on the option, Browse folders using a separate window for each folder, and then click OK.

3.15. How can I change file attributes?

To change the attributes of a file, right-click on the file icon, then choose Properties from the resulting menu. Now the Properties for *filename* window is open (where *filename* represents the name for the file). This window enables you to make a file hidden or read-only by clicking on the corresponding choice (clicking the Hidden box or the Read-Only box, respectively) in the Attributes box.

3.16. How can I sort files?

Sorting the display of files in an Explorer window is deceptively easy. If you're looking for a Sort option on a menu, you won't find it. Once in Details view (from the Explorer menu, choose View|Details), just click on the column you want to be used as the sort. For example, if you click the Size column, the files are sorted by size in ascending order.

3.17. How can I print a file?

To print a file, highlight the file you want to print and then choose Print from the file menu. Windows will then launch the appropriate application to print the file. You also can use drag-and-drop techniques to print: drag the icon of the file above a printer icon, and drop it onto the printer icon to begin printing. (Drag-and-drop printing assumes that the application used to create the file exists on your PC; if it does not, Windows displays an error message.)

3.18. How can I undelete a file?

Double-click the Recycle Bin to open it, and click the name of the desired file. Open the File menu of the Recycle Bin, and choose Restore. In order to restore files, they must still be in the Recycle Bin. If you've used the Empty Recycle Bin option of the Recycle Bin's File menu, an attempted recovery will not be possible.

3.19. How can I create folders?

To create a new folder, launch Explorer or My Computer and choose New from the File menu. Next, choose Folder, and you'll be prompted to enter a folder name. After entering the name, the new folder is added. Windows adds folders to the location where you create them, so if a particular folder is selected when you choose the command, the new folder is created inside the selected folder.

3.20. How can I rename files or folders?

To rename a file or folder, click the name of the file or folder (don't double-click because this will open the file). Click again within the name, and the highlighted name will appear with the cursor flashing. Finally, enter the name with which you wish to replace the old file or folder name.

3.21. How can I delete files or folders?

To delete a file or folder, highlight the file or folder you want to delete, then choose Delete from the Edit menu. As an alternative method, you can right-click on the folder or file and choose Delete from the menu that is opened. After using either method of deleting files or folders, you are asked if this is what you really want to do, which helps prevent accidental deletions.

3.22. How can I format disks?

To format disks in My Computer or in Explorer, right-click the disk drive containing the disk that you want to format. Then, from the popup menu that appears, choose Format. In the dialog box that appears, choose the desired disk capacity, then click Start to format the disk.

3.23. How can I view disk properties?

To view disk properties (including how much free disk space you have remaining), right-click the drive icon of the disk whose properties you want to view, and choose Properties from the menu that appears. The General tab in the resulting dialog box (see Figure 3.3) shows space used versus free space. You also can change the volume label directly from this dialog box by typing a new name in the Label text box. (The Tools tab of this dialog box displays the following information: when you last checked the drive for errors, when you last defragmented the drive, and when you last backed up files on the drive.)

3.24. If I delete a shortcut from the Desktop, do I delete the item?

No. Shortcuts are links to an item (program, folder, or hardware resource such as a printer). If you delete a shortcut, the item still exists where it is stored on disk. On the other hand, if you drag an item from the actual application or document directly onto the Desktop from My Computer or from Explorer and later delete it, you're deleting the actual item. This is why it's important to recognize the difference between a shortcut on your Desktop (which represents a link to the actual item) and having the actual item shown on your Desktop.

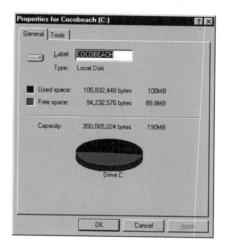

Figure 3.3. *Disk properties.*

3.25. More than one person uses my computer. Can I save and recall the appearance of my Desktop?

You can store the Desktop's layout under a scheme name of your choosing by performing the following steps:

1. Arrange your Desktop the way you like it.
2. Right-click on any blank space in the Desktop, and choose Properties from the resulting popup menu.
3. When the Properties for Display window opens, click the Appearance tab.
4. Click Save As, then give your settings a name in the Save Scheme dialog box that appears.

The name will be included in the Scheme drop-down list on the Appearance tab of the window. Whenever you want to apply your scheme to a Windows session, right-click on the Desktop to bring up the Properties for Display window, and choose your own scheme from the Appearance tab.

3.26. How can I associate a particular file with a given application?

Windows does an admirable job of associating most files with the proper application, but occasionally (usually with applications that aren't written to standard Windows conventions) you'll need to tell Windows which application certain files may be associated with if you want to perform operations such as drag-and-drop or double-clicking a file to launch its application. Perform the following steps to establish an association between data files having a particular extension and a desired application:

1. In My Computer or in the Explorer, open the View menu, and choose Options.

2. Click the File Types tab.

3. In the list of file types that appears, choose the file type that you want to change.

4. Click the Edit button.

5. Specify the program you want to use to open all files that have this extension.

3.27. Is there any simple way of knowing what's in a document?

Windows provides a file viewer that enables you to examine files that are stored in most common file formats, including Word for Windows and WordPerfect documents, Excel and Lotus spreadsheets, and many database files. Use the following steps to open the file in the viewer:

1. Open Explorer, find the file you want to examine, and click it to select it.

2. Open the File menu.

3. Choose Quick View.

Assuming that Windows has a file viewer that is compatible with
the type of file you're viewing, the file appears in a Quick View
window. If the Quick View option is dimmed on the File menu,
Windows may not have a file viewer compatible with the type of file
you are trying to open.

3.28. How can I view hidden files?

Files that have been flagged as hidden can be made visible using the
following steps:

1. Launch Explorer, and open the desired folder.
2. Open the View menu, and choose Options.
3. Click the View tab, then click Show All Files.

3.29. Why aren't file extensions visible?

In its default mode, Windows 95 hides all file extensions.
Microsoft's idea here was to make things less complex for novice
users. The extensions are still there, but they are not visible by
default. You can turn on the display of extensions with the following steps:

1. Launch Explorer, and open the desired folder.
2. Open the View menu, and choose Options.
3. Click the View tab, then turn off the Hide MS-DOS File
   Extensions check box.

3.30. Will long filenames be preserved when copying files to disks?

Yes. If the disk has been formatted using Windows 95, Windows
files—unlike OS/2 files—that make use of long filenames retain
their filename characteristics when copied to disks. If you examine
the files under earlier versions of DOS, the eight-dot-three naming
conventions will still apply; only the first eight characters of your
long filename will appear in the directory structure of the disk.

3.31. Can I use third-party backup programs that I used with prior versions of Windows?

Maybe. If you try it, the results can be unpredictable because backup programs written for earlier versions of Windows don't know how to deal with long filenames. If you stick with the eight-dot-three naming convention for all your files, you may be able to get by with your old software. However, contacting the vendor for a Windows 95-compatible upgrade would be a better idea.

CHAPTER

4

Putting It on Paper

This chapter presents topics related to printing, such as how
Windows prints, how to set up printers, how to print outside
applications, using shared printers and printing to a network,
changing printer settings, and handling printer problems.

Of all Windows' features, the one you're likely to use most often is
printing. Printing is also the Windows operation with more room
for problems to arise than any other. With hundreds of printer types
to support and the complexity of local-area networks entering the
picture, printing under Windows has not always been an easy task.
To reduce the number of user problems that can arise, Windows 95
made major changes in the printing subsystem and in the user
interface related to printing.

4.1. What's different about the Windows 95 interface regarding printing?

Microsoft's efforts to make things less confusing for the end user
have resulted in some major changes in how printer-related
activities are done in Windows 95 compared to earlier versions of
Windows. Previously, printer configuration was done using the

Control Panel, printer characteristics were changed using the File|Print Setup option of most applications, and print spooling was controlled using the Windows Print Manager. In effect, you had to go to three different places to accomplish various printer tasks. In Windows 95, all printer control functions are in one place: the Printers Folder. Underneath the Windows 95 user interface, there also are significant additions to the code, enabling Windows to support drag-and-drop printing, which means you can print documents by dragging them onto the icon of a printer.

4.2. Is there a faster way to print documents than repeatedly opening them and using File | Print from the applications' menus?

You can create a folder that contains your most-often used documents, along with a shortcut to the printer you commonly use. Use the following steps:

1. Create a folder by launching Explorer, selecting the drive or folder where you want to place the new folder, and choosing File|New|Folder from the Explorer menus.

2. Give the new folder a name, and open it.

3. Click and drag the documents that you print often into the new folder.

4. From the Start menu, choose Settings|Printers to open the Printers Folder.

5. Right-click the desired printer, and choose Create Shortcut from the menu that appears. Click Yes in the dialog box that asks if you want to place the shortcut on the Desktop.

6. Drag the printer icon from the Desktop into the new folder.

Now, to print any of your documents, drag them onto the printer icon within the folder. Windows will launch the corresponding application and print the document.

4.3. How do I install a new printer under Windows?

If the printer conforms to the Plug-and-Play standard, simply connect the printer to the PC and restart Windows. Windows will

sense the added hardware and make the configuration automati-
cally. If the printer does not support Plug-and-Play, use the Printers
Folder to install new printers. Double-click My Computer or
Explorer to open it, and open the Printers Folder. When the
Printers Folder opens, double-click Add Printer. An Add Printer
dialog box appears; click Next, and an Add Printer Wizard dialog
box appears, which you can use to select the printer model (see
Figure 4.1).

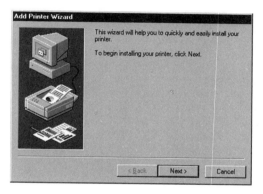

Figure 4.1. *Add Printer Wizard dialog box.*

In the left portion of the window, you choose the manufacturer of
the printer you have. When you do so, the printers made by that
company appear in the right portion of the window. If you have an
installation disk, you can click the Have Disk button and then
insert the disk. If you have no disk, choose the printer you want by
double-clicking it, and Windows will use its own driver for that
printer. Next, the Ports window appears, asking you to choose the
port you want to use with your printer. After choosing the desired
port, one more window appears that enables you to name your
printer with a name you choose, or leave the one supplied by
windows.

4.4. I tried to install my printer, but it's not listed among the list of possible printers. Now what?

Windows 95 does an admirable job of supporting most printers
made for a PC, but there are some lesser-known or older printers

that don't have Windows printer drivers available. Some suggestions if you are faced with making a printer work with Windows:

■ Check your printer's documentation to see if the printer has the capability to emulate some other printer. Many printers can be programmed to emulate popular printers such as Hewlett-Packard laser printers, or Epson or IBM dot-matrix printers. Often, a printer will require settings of DIP switches or some series of menu commands to turn on its emulation mode.

■ Contact a dealer for that particular brand of printer to see if a disk containing a Windows driver is available for the printer.

■ If the printer is a newly introduced model, contact the technical support department of the printer manufacturer to see if you can obtain a driver disk. If none is available, contact Microsoft tech support and ask how you can obtain the latest printer driver disk.

■ If all else fails, install the printer driver labeled Generic/Text Only. This should be considered a less-than-ideal workaround because you won't be able to take advantage of any graphics capabilities.

Q 4.5. How can I change my printer settings?

1. From the Start menu choose Settings, then Printers to open the Printers folder.

2. Right-click the icon for the printer that has the settings you wish to change, and choose Properties to open the properties window for the chosen printer (as shown in the example in Figure 4.2).

This window has six tabs for printer settings: General, Details, Paper, Graphics, Fonts, and Device Options. (If you are using Windows 95 on a network, you may also see a tab entitled "Sharing.")

The General tab (shown in Figure 4.2) contains general information about the printer, such as the type of printer, any comments added, and a Where box that you can use to add a note regarding where the printer is physically located (helpful on a network; rather obvious on a stand-alone system).

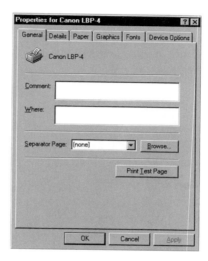

Figure 4.2. *The General tab of the Printer Properties window.*

The Details tab (see Figure 4.3) contains detailed information regarding the printer setup. Use the Print to list box to select the desired printer port, or to tell Windows to print to a file. The Driver list box lets you change your selected printer driver, enabling you to switch printers without leaving the Properties window. The Not Selected entry in the Timeout settings portion of the dialog box lets you specify how much time (in seconds) Windows should wait for the printer to be online before an error is reported. The Transmission retry entry lets you specify how much time Windows should wait for the printer to be ready before reporting an error.

The Capture Printer Port button is used to map the port to a network drive. The Release Printer Port button is the oppsite of the Capture Printer Port button—it removes the mapping of a port from a network drive. You also will see the Add Port, Delete Port, and New Driver buttons. The Add Port button is used to add a port to a network or add a local printer port. The Delete Port button deletes an existing port. The New Driver button updates or changes your printer drivers.

In the case of serial printers, clicking on the Port Settings button brings forth another dialog box that you can use to match serial settings (baud rates and parity) to the printer. The Spool Settings button displays a Spool Settings dialog box, which lets you choose whether to spool print jobs to disk (resulting in faster printing) or to print directly to the printer (no disk space is used, but processing the print job under Windows won't be done until the printer has completed printing).

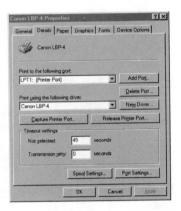

Figure 4.3. *The Details tab of the Printer Properties window.*

The Paper tab contains settings relating to paper sizes and the paper feeding operation. Use the Paper Size box to change the size of the paper being used. (Clicking the arrow opens a window containing different sizes of papers.) The Paper Source option changes the paper source; your options here vary, depending on the model of printer. Most laser printers offer options like upper tray, lower tray, auto, manual, and envelope feed. Use the Number of Copies option to set the number of copies to be printed; and use the orientation check boxes to change the orientation from Portrait, printing in a normal format, to Landscape, printing sideways across the page.

The Graphics tab (see Figure 4.4) is used to set resolution, dithering, and intensity. To set resolution, click on the Resolution box and choose the number of dots per inch. The Dithering box enables you to set the dithering. In dithering, each shade of gray is represented by different numbers of dots in a square grid. The darker the shade is, the more dots there are. The Dithering box enables you to control whether it is set to None, Coarse, Fine, or Line Art. The Intensity bar is used to control the intensity of the shading used in a printer document.

The Fonts tab is used to control which font cartridge is used, and the settings for TrueType fonts. Appearing at the top of the window is a Cartridge list box that lets you change the font cartridges used. (If the font cartridge that you want does not appear in the list, it can be added using the method described in the manual that came with the font package.) The tab also contains two options for printing with TrueType fonts: Download TrueType as Bitmap Soft Fonts and Print TrueType as Graphics. The default (Download TrueType as Bitmap Soft Fonts) enables faster printing with most documents; documents that are graphics-intensive can make better use of the Print TrueType as Graphics option.

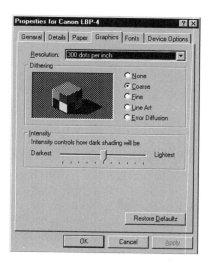

Figure 4.4. *The Graphics tab of the Printer Properties window.*

The Device Options tab contains the settings for the memory of the printer. Clicking the Printer Memory list box enables you to change the memory that Windows thinks is installed in the printer. (The default memory is set for the amount of memory in the standard configuration for the printer.) If sufficient memory is in the printer (and the Printer Memory list box reflects that memory), a Page Protection option may also be available. Turning on Page Protection reserves some of your printer's memory as an output buffer. Some complex documents require page protection to print, but turning on the option consumes more of your printer's memory.

4.6. How does the Printers Folder work?

In Windows 95, the Printers Folder is the single source for most printing operations, including setup of new printers and managing the print queue. To open the Printers Folder, open the Start menu, and choose Control Panel|Settings|Printers. The Printers Folder, shown in Figure 4.5, opens.

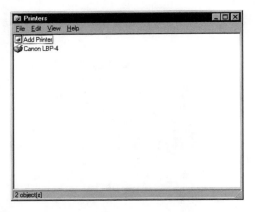

Figure 4.5. *The Printers Folder.*

From the Printers Folder, the File menu contains choices that refer to printing operations. The available choices from the File menu include Open, Pause Printing, Purge Print Jobs, Create Shortcut, Delete, Rename, Properties, and Close.

The Open option opens the window with all the statistics for that specific printer. Pause Printing pauses the printing for the current print job. Purge Printer removes all current print jobs from the print queue. Create Shortcut enables you to create an icon for the printer to be placed on the Desktop. Then, if you want to print a document, click and drag the document to the printer icon and drop it there to print.

Delete Printer deletes the selected printer from the Printers Folder, and Rename Printer enables you to assign a name to your printer (you can enter a name of your choosing or you can leave the default name assigned to the printer by Windows). Properties opens the Properties window for the selected printer, and Close closes the Printers Folder.

The Edit menu of the Printers Folder contains choices for selecting an object within the folder, inverting any selections (deselecting all selected objects and selecting all unselected objects), and selecting all objects, along with the usual Cut, Copy, and Paste options. (These menu choices allow the selection of objects within the folder using the keyboard as an alternative to the mouse.)

The options on the View menu control how the contents of the Printers Folder are displayed. The Toolbar and Status Bar options turn on and off the Printers Folder toolbar and status bar, respectively. The Large Icons and Small Icons options change the size of the icons displayed in the folder; and List View arranges the icons in list form. Detail View places the icons in a fashion that shows the information on each printer, including the number of documents being printed, the status of the documents, the port location for each printer, and any comments on them.

The Arrange Icons option enables the icons to be arranged by name or automatically arranged in rows as printers are added. The Snap Grid option turns on or off a grid to which icons align themselves when they are moved. The Refresh option updates the screen with the latest printer information when Windows is running on a network, and the Options choice opens the Explorer window, which contains the Folder and View tabs.

The Folder tab is used to set the browsing options. A separate window can be used for each folder, or you can use a single window that changes as each folder is opened. The View tab contains two options, Show all files and Hide files of these types. It also lists the hidden files in the list box within this tab. Also on the View tab, there is the option to display the full MS-DOS Path in the title bar—for files not properly registered, you can choose not to show the file extension—and a choice to include a description bar for the left and right panes.

4.7. How can I view the print queue?

To view the print queue, double-click the printer you wish to view and a window titled with the name of that particular printer opens, containing all of the print jobs listed.

4.8. How can I change the order of files in the print queue?

To change the order of the files in the print queue with the mouse, use the following steps:

1. Point at the file whose order you wish to change.
2. Press and hold the left mouse button.
3. Drag the file to the desired place in the queue.
4. Release the mouse button.

To change the order using the keyboard, use the following steps:

1. In the queue, highlight the file whose order you wish to change.
2. Press and hold the Ctrl key.
3. Use the up or down arrow keys to move the file to the desired position in the queue, and release the Ctrl key.

4.9. How can I pause and resume printing?

To pause the printing of a document, first open the Start menu and choose Settings|Control Panel. In the Control Panel, double-click Printers, then double-click the printer being used. Next, open the Printer menu and click Pause Printing.

To resume printing, open the Printer menu, click Pause Printing again, and printing will resume.

4.10. How can I delete a file from the print queue?

To delete a file from the print queue, double-click the desired printer in the Printers folder. Next, open the Document menu and choose Cancel Printing, and the file will be deleted from the print queue.

4.11. How can I print to a file?

You can redirect the printing output to a disk file using the following steps:

1. Open the Start menu, and choose Settings|Printers.
2. Right-click a desired printer.
3. Click the Details tab.
4. In the Port Settings list box, choose File.

Note that the file will contain the codes appropriate to the printer driver you selected in step 2. If you want a file with no printer codes, install the Generic/Text Only printer driver, and use that printer during step 2.

> **TIP** If you need to print (to a file) a document formatted for a specific printer that is not available on your system, you can set up Windows for that printer and print to a file. You can then take the file to a system that has that printer, send the file to the printer, and print.

4.12. How can I change printer memory usage?

To change printer priorities, click Printer Properties from the Printer menu on the Print Queue. The Printer Properties window now opens. Choose the Device Options tab. In the middle of the tab is the Printer Memory Tracking bar, as shown in Figure 4.6. Moving this bar enables you to adjust the usage of the printer's memory.

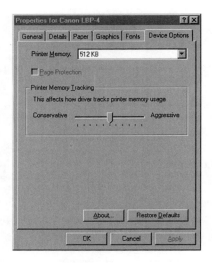

Figure 4.6. *The Printer Memory Tracking bar in the Printer Properties window.*

4.13. How can I turn off the banner page when printing on a network?

To disable the banner page when printing on a network, follow these steps:

1. Open the Printers Folder (from the Start menu, choose Settings|Printers).

2. Right-click the printer you're using, and choose Properties.

3. Click the General tab.

4. Set the Separator Page setting to None.

4.14. How do I assign a printer to a different port than the default one?

Windows assumes that any local printer you install is connected to the default (LPT1) printer port. Sometimes, that is not the case; you may have more than one printer connected to the same PC, with each printer wired to a different printer port to avoid the hassle of a switch box. Use the following steps to change the port assignments for a printer:

1. Open the Start menu, and choose Settings|Printers.
2. Right-click the printer you want to change the port assignment for.
3. Click the Details tab.
4. Choose the desired port from the list box (LPT1, LPT2, LPT3 or COM1, COM2, COM3, or COM4), then click OK.
5. If you selected COM1, COM2, or COM3, click Port Settings and set the proper baud rates and parity for your printer.

4.15. How do I connect to or disconnect from a network printer?

Connecting to a network printer in Windows 95 differs radically from the same operation in earlier versions of Windows. If you're having trouble finding the Network Connections dialog box, that's because it doesn't exist. Physical redirections aren't needed to print on a network. Instead, just double-click the installed network printer in Explorer or in My Computer, or drop a document onto the printer to print it. As soon as you perform any of these actions, Windows establishes the network connection.

If your network operating system software doesn't support Universal Naming Convention (UNC) paths, you can make a connection to a network printer by using the appropriate network commands for your network (such as `net use lpt1:\\server\printer`).

4.16. How can I configure a Novell NetWare server to support drag-and-drop printing?

Assuming that you have administrator privileges for the network, you can configure the NetWare server to save the information needed to support drag-and-drop in the NetWare Bindery. Use the following steps:

1. Open the Control Panel and double-click the Network icon.
2. Click Configuration, and then click Add.
3. Click Service, and then click Add.
4. In the Manufacturers column, click Microsoft.
5. In the Models column, choose the File and Printer Sharing for Novell Networks option.
6. Click OK.

4.17. I installed a new font cartridge in my printer; why don't the fonts appear in the list of fonts when I try to change fonts from within an application?

Unless your printer supports Plug and Play and is capable of sending available font data back to Windows, you must tell Windows when you've installed fonts before they'll register within your applications. See Question 4.18 for directions on installing fonts.

4.18. How do I manage fonts?

Because built-in printer fonts are specific to printers, you can get to them from the properties window for the specific printer. Perform the following steps:

1. Open the Start menu and choose Settings|Printer. The Printers Folder opens.
2. Right-click the desired printer, and choose Properties. A Properties window for the specific printer appears.
3. Click the Fonts tab to display the fonts. Figure 4.7 shows the settings that appear for a Canon LBP-4 laser printer.

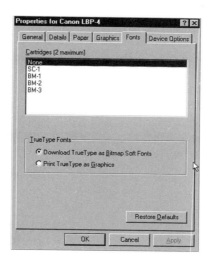

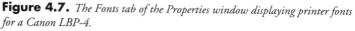

Figure 4.7. *The Fonts tab of the Properties window displaying printer fonts for a Canon LBP-4.*

In the Cartridges list box, you can select your installed cartridges. The TrueType Fonts portion of the dialog box contains two choices: Download TrueType as Bitmap Soft Fonts and Print TrueType as Graphics. Choose your desired option, and click OK.

In general, if you want faster printing, go with the Download TrueType as Soft Fonts option. If your documents are heavy on graphic images, the Print TrueType as Graphics option will likely provide better performance.

4.19. How do I manage soft fonts?

Open the Start menu, and click Settings|Control Panel. When the Control Panel opens, double-click the Fonts icon. The Fonts window appears, as shown in Figure 4.8.

All your installed soft fonts appear in the Fonts window listed in alphabetical order of the font name by default. (If the Toolbar is not visible, choose View|Toolbar from the menu bar to display it.)

Using the Toolbar buttons, you can change how the fonts are displayed—you can list all fonts, or fonts by family name, similarity, or filename. You can also display the actual font as part of the listing. Each of the Toolbar buttons offers ToolTips; if you hold the mouse pointer over the button for a moment, its meaning appears in a ToolTip. Select any font in the list, then open the File menu.

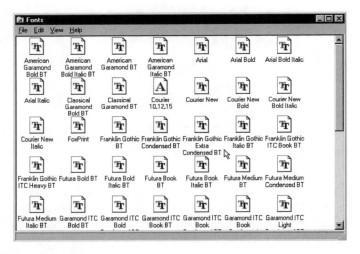

Figure 4.8. *The Fonts window.*

From the File menu, you can show or print a sample of the soft font (choose Open to show the font, or choose Print to print a sample of it), delete a font, install a new font, or show properties for the font. (The same options can also be obtained by right-clicking any font in the list and choosing the desired option from the popup menu.) The Open option, which displays a sample of the font, is useful for getting a representative idea of how a soft font will look in various sizes. Figure 4.9 shows an example of the font sample window that appears when you choose Open for a given font.

Use the View menu to change how the fonts are displayed within the Fonts window (shown previously in Figure 4.8). The Toolbar and Status Bar choices of the menu turn off the Toolbar and Status Bar, respectively, and the remaining options in the View menu perform the same functions as the Toolbar buttons mentioned previously.

Figure 4.9. *Font sample window for Arial Bold.*

4.20. How can I add new soft fonts?

To add new soft fonts, open the Start menu and select Settings|Control Panel|Fonts to bring up the Fonts window. From the window, open the File menu, and choose Install New Font. The Add Fonts dialog box appears (see Figure 4.10).

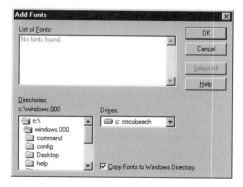

Figure 4.10. *The Add Fonts dialog box.*

Browse among the drives and/or directories until you locate the desired font files, then click OK to display the contained fonts in the List of Fonts list box. Click the desired font or fonts to select them. You can select multiple fonts by clicking the first desired font, holding Ctrl, and clicking any additional fonts. With the desired fonts selected, click OK. Remember that soft fonts consume disk space; many popular TrueType fonts routinely occupy between 50K and 100K of disk space *per font*.

4.21. My printer has a number of built-in fonts that appear virtually identical to the TrueType fonts included with Windows. Does it make a performance difference as to which fonts I use?

If the fonts appear identical, go with the ones that are built-in to your printer. When Windows uses a TrueType font, it must scale the font's outline in memory to create the image of the character—a process that is not necessary with built-in fonts. Hence, actual printing might be slightly slower when the document is composed of TrueType fonts as opposed to built-in fonts.

4.22. Where can I obtain more fonts?

The popularity of TrueType fonts has resulted in an abundant supply of available fonts—in some ways, too much of a good thing exists. Literally thousands of fonts are available inexpensively or as shareware, depending on your sources. But much of what's available is junk, and it may take some looking to find font collections that are worth the disk space.

TrueType fonts are routinely available in collections, sold along with other printer utilities at computer and software stores, or packaged on disks available at hardware flea markets and swap meets. Most bulletin boards also maintain collections of fonts online, as do the commercial online services like CompuServe and America Online. Microsoft offers its own package of assorted TrueType fonts on the retail market for under $50 (and no, we're not paid to say this).

4.23. How can I change the display fonts used by the Desktop?

Right-click in any blank area of the Desktop, and choose Properties from the popup menu to open the Properties for Display window. Click the Settings tab, then choose the desired font size in the Font Size list box. In addition, you can click the Custom button in the dialog box to display another dialog box, which enables you to click and drag a visible ruler to establish a custom size for your screen fonts.

4.24. When I try to print a page with graphics on it, the page either doesn't print completely or I get an error message displayed on the LCD panel of the printer.

When this happens, it doesn't indicate a Windows problem; it indicates that there is insufficient memory in the printer to handle the graphics that you are trying to send. You can either install more RAM in the printer or cut down on the amount of graphics information in the document you are sending. One important point is that if the printer doesn't support Plug and Play, make sure Windows knows how much memory really is installed in the printer by opening the Printers Folder, right-clicking the desired printer, and choosing Properties from the menu that appears. When the Properties window opens, click the Device Options tab to check the amount of RAM setting for the printer.

Maximizing Memory

This chapter covers memory-oriented topics. Although memory management is simplified greatly over earlier versions of Windows, there still are various tips and techniques you can take advantage of to make the most of your PC's memory, and improve performance as a result.

5.1. Under Windows 95, why bother with memory management?

Although the replacement of DOS and the capability of Windows to dynamically alter its environment to maximize memory may appear to eliminate the need for memory management, you still can take some steps to better customize how Windows handles your system's available memory. By using Windows' System Properties settings, you can change settings for the use of virtual memory.

5.2. Can I use my old third-party memory managers by running them through a DOS window?

Attempting to do so is not a wise idea. Windows 95 uses a *flat memory model* to reference a virtual address space (meaning, Windows looks at all of your PC's installed memory as a single area), rather than the old 16-bit segmented memory model that memory managers dealt with. Although you could exit directly to the operating system (by choosing Start | Programs | MS-DOS Prompt) and run a DOS memory manager from the DOS prompt, this would accomplish little because Windows works to dynamically manage memory and resources, regardless of what your memory manager does. Many of the changes made by memory managers to the old CONFIG.SYS and AUTOEXEC.BAT files are read by Windows 95 only to help it set the overall environment. The effects of device drives used by memory managers are in effect replaced by Windows' use of virtual device drivers (see Question 5.3). Third-party memory managers are designed to work under Windows 3.*x* from one portion of your hard drive, and Windows 95 is designed to work from another portion.

5.3. What are virtual device drivers, and what have they replaced?

Virtual device drivers are 32-bit drivers that Windows provides to manage system resources, such as hardware devices or installed software, enabling more than one application to use the system resource at the same time. Microsoft uses the term *VxD* to refer to virtual device drivers, where *x* represents the device driver type. VPD, for example, represents device drivers for a printer. Windows 95 uses virtual devices to enable DOS-based applications to multitask; each hardware part of the system is virtualized so that it appears (to the software) that each DOS application is running on its own computer. Windows uses these virtual devices to perform I/O operations for a specific application, without interfering with other applications. Windows 95 uses virtual device drivers to replace a number of the old device drivers (SYS files) used by Windows 3.*x* (including SmartDrive), drivers for CD-ROM file systems, mouse drivers, SHARE.EXE, disk controller drivers (including those that support SCSI controllers), and Network drivers for Novell Netware.

5.4. What is virtual memory, and how can I use it?

Windows uses virtual memory to make disk space look like added RAM to your PC. *Virtual memory* is space on your hard disk that is used as a replacement for available RAM. Windows moves temporary data to and from the disk, saving the data as needed in a *swapfile*. The use of virtual memory helps your PC's performance significantly if it is short on memory. Virtual memory is needed greatly in 4M machines and often is a wise idea in machines with 8M. If you have 16M or more of memory, the use of virtual memory probably offers minimal benefit, unless your idea of multitasking is at least two dozen applications running at the same time. By default, Windows makes use of virtual memory; you can fine-tune how it does this by using the virtual memory settings (see the next question).

5.5. How do I choose between a temporary or permanent swapfile in Windows 95 to support virtual memory?

In a way, you do, and in a way, you don't. The old swapfile design that was implemented in Windows 3.*x* had it drawbacks—not the least of which was the difficulty in deciding whether to use a temporary or a permanent swapfile, how much disk space to allocate to the swapfile, and whether to enable 32-bit disk access to the swapfile. The swapfile in Windows 95 still exists, but it now is dynamic, expanding and contracting in size as needed depending on the available space and the demands on your system. You still can adjust the virtual memory settings, but it's a much less complex task. To change the settings, follow these steps:

1. Open the Start menu, choose Settings, and then choose the Control Panel option.
2. When the window opens, double-click the System icon.
3. Click the Performance Tab.

4. Click the Virtual Memory button to reveal the virtual
    memory settings (see Figure 5.1).

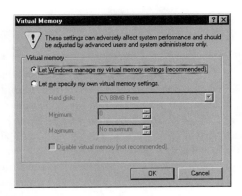

Figure 5.1. *Virtual Memory dialog box.*

There are two options for handling virtual memory settings in this
dialog box. You can let Windows manage the settings for you, or
you can specify your own settings.

The first option, titled "Let Windows manage my virtual memory
settings," is the setting that Windows selects at installation. It causes
Windows to dynamically allocate disk space to serve as virtual
memory on an as-needed basis. This option is Microsoft's recom-
mendation.

If you prefer to do things the way you did them under an earlier
version of Windows, however, you can check the second option,
titled "Let me specify my own virtual memory settings." Choose a
disk drive under Hard disk, and then enter a Minimum and
Maximum size for the virtual memory in the Property window.

TIP	Because a swapfile takes contiguous (or nonstop) chunks of disk space, you should defragment your hard disk from time to time. Performing a defragmenting operation relocates disk space into a contiguous chunk, maximizing performance of Windows' use of virtual memory.

> **NOTE** Windows does not enable you to use a Network drive for storage of the virtual memory's swapfile. You also cannot use a drive that has been compressed with a third-party compression utility.

5.6. With Windows' more efficient use of memory, can I get by with 4M of RAM?

As with Windows 3.*x*, having 4M of RAM on a machine is a judgment call; as Microsoft says, a Windows PC will run with 4M of RAM. More RAM (a minimum of 8M), however, is highly recommended; overall performance increases noticeably if you have 8M or more of RAM installed. Because Windows 95 greatly improves on the handling of system resources, users of 4M machines now can run a number of applications simultaneously without encountering the dreaded Low Memory dialog box; however, performance under such circumstances is considerably less than stellar.

One notable difference exists for users of Windows attached to a Novell network. Under Windows 3.*x*, many 4M machines would not successfully run any Windows applications after loading the NetWare shells, because the memory remaining after the shells were loaded was insufficient to handle Windows. With Windows 95, you can run a machine under Novell with 4M of RAM, because Windows loads its own Novell drivers as virtual drivers, avoiding the use of precious base RAM.

5.7. How can I conserve memory and/or system resources?

You can use some small but helpful techniques to cut down on low-memory errors. These techniques follow:

- Avoid running DOS applications in a window; where possible, run the applications full screen (use Alt+Enter to switch between applications).
- Avoid the multitasking of DOS applications.

- Be judicious in the use of wallpaper. Wallpaper consumes memory and system resources. Change the wallpaper setting to None and consider using tiled bitmaps instead if you must have some sort of background decor.

- Check the Clipboard viewer by choosing the Start menu, Programs, Accessories, and Clip Book Viewer to see what is on the Clipboard. Then save the contents or trash them.

Be aware that some ill-behaved Windows applications have a bad habit of not freeing all the resources they have used. If you open and close such an application repeatedly, you gradually reduce available resources to the point where Windows does not run your application at all. In such cases, the only solution is to shut down all running applications and restart Windows.

6

Exchanging Data Between Applications

One of the benefits Windows has offered from early on in its development process is the capability to exchange data between applications. For many users, this is a significant reason behind moving to Windows in the first place. Even if nearly all your daily work is in a single application—WordPerfect for Windows, for example—you probably are accustomed to the ease with which Windows enables you to move and copy data between portions of the same document, or from one document to another. Of course, the data-sharing capabilities of Windows go far beyond that, making it possible to copy and move data between different applications of different types, and between Windows and non-Windows applications. And as Windows has progressed through its various versions, advanced data-sharing features such as Dynamic Data Exchange (DDE) and Object Linking and Embedding (OLE) were added to the picture. This chapter tells you how to put these significant features of Windows to work in your everyday tasks.

6.1. What's the Clipboard, and how does it work?

The Clipboard is nothing more than an area of memory in which Windows stores data that is cut or copied from an application. Think of it as a kind of scratch pad—a temporary holding area. As data gets copied into the Clipboard, it replaces any data that previously was there; the Clipboard can hold only a single object at a time, whether that object is a paragraph of text, an entire file, a photograph, or a selected range of cells in a spreadsheet.

6.2. How can I use the Clipboard with Windows applications?

The basic steps for using the Clipboard as a means of data transfer are virtually identical, regardless of what Windows application you are using. Follow these steps:

1. In the Windows application that is serving as the source of the information, select the data you want to move or copy.

2. If you want to move the data to another application, open the Edit menu and choose Cut. To copy the data to another application, open the Edit menu and choose Copy.

3. Switch to the application that is to receive the data, and move the insertion pointer to the place where you want to insert the data.

4. Open the Edit menu and choose Paste.

As an example of this process, suppose that you want to copy a block of cells from an Excel spreadsheet into a letter you are composing in WordPerfect for Windows. Start by opening the Excel spreadsheet, clicking at one corner of the desired block of cells and dragging to the other corner, and choosing Edit | Copy. Then switch to WordPerfect for Windows, open the letter, place the insertion pointer where you want to insert the data, and choose Edit | Paste from the menus.

6.3. How can I copy an image of the active window to the Clipboard?

Windows has a hot-key combination that you can use to copy the current window to the Clipboard. Press Alt+PtrSc to copy the active window's contents into the Clipboard as a graphic. This can be a useful technique if you have to produce user documentation and you want to include graphics of how different windows in certain programs appear. Capture the window by pressing Alt+PrtSc, switch to your word processor where you are writing the documentation, and choose Edit | Paste to insert the image where you want it.

6.4. How can I use the Clipboard with DOS applications?

Although DOS never was designed initially to support the kind of data exchange that Windows is capable of, you can use the Windows Clipboard along with DOS applications, with a few limitations. You can copy data from a DOS application to the Clipboard, but you cannot cut data from a DOS application to the Clipboard. If you are running a DOS application that is a graphics application as a full screen, you cannot copy data from that application to the Clipboard; you must switch to running the application in a window (by pressing Alt+Enter) before you can copy data from it to the Clipboard.

To copy data to the Clipboard from a windowed DOS application, follow these steps:

1. Open the DOS application in an active window.

2. Press Alt+space bar to open the Control menu.

3. Choose Edit.

4. From the next menu that opens, choose Mark.

5. Use the arrow keys to move the cursor to the upper left corner of the area that you want to copy.

6. Press and hold the Shift key, move the cursor to the lower right corner of the area you want to copy, and release Shift.

7. Press Alt+space bar to open the Control menu.

8. Choose Edit | Copy from the menu.

9. Switch back to the Windows application and press Edit | Paste.

To copy data to the Clipboard from a DOS application that is running full screen, just press the PrtSc key. Windows pulls the data from the entire screen and inserts it into the Clipboard. (If you don't need the entire screen, just delete what you don't need after you paste the data into the destination application.)

To paste data from the Clipboard into a DOS application, use these steps:

1. Open the DOS application in an active window. If the application is running full screen, press Alt+Enter to switch to a windowed display.

2. Using the mouse or the arrow keys, place the cursor at the location in the DOS application where you want the data to appear.

3. Press Alt+space bar to open the Control menu.

4. Choose Edit | Paste from the menu.

6.5. What is Dynamic Data Exchange, and how does it work?

Dynamic Data Exchange (DDE) is a system of sharing data, first implemented in Windows 3.0, that enables you to exchange data between applications by means of dynamic links. The basic concept is similar to that demonstrated earlier, by means of the Clipboard. With DDE, however, the data that you paste is *dynamic*—it changes as the data changes at the source. When you paste information from a source document into a destination document using DDE, you establish a *link* between the data that is in the source document and the copy of the data existing in the destination document. The advantage of this approach is that if you update the data in the source document, the copy of the data in the destination document gets updated as well. DDE can be used through commands in many programming languages such as the variants of BASIC that are built into many Microsoft applications, but that is a topic beyond the scope of this book. From an interactive standpoint, you can make use of DDE by using the Edit I Copy and Edit I Paste Link commands within many Windows applications (particularly those that do not support OLE).

6.6. What is Object Linking and Embedding, and how does it work?

Object Linking and Embedding (OLE) is actually a superset, or enhanced implementation, of DDE. Object Linking and Embedding was introduced to the Windows environment with version 3.1 of Windows, and enables you to use various menu options from your Windows applications to establish links with data stored using other applications, or to embed portions of a document created in one application inside a document created in another application. With OLE, you can insert a copy of data from a source document created by another application and have that data linked to the source document, or you can embed a copy of data from a source document created in another application.

When you *link* to an OLE object, the object is stored elsewhere, and your document maintains a link to the source document. If pictures in CorelDRAW! are linked to an OLE object you insert in a Word for Windows document you are creating, for example, the drawings exist only in the CorelDRAW! documents in which they originally were stored. Linking is the preferred method to use when you want the data in your destination document to be updated whenever the data in the original document changes.

> **WARNING** When you use linking, it may be important to remember that you used linking, rather than embedding. If you delete an object in a source document that is linked, you will lose the object in the destination document as well.

When you *embed* an object in a document, the object becomes part of that document. (It still exists in the original source document, but the object is a virtual copy of the original source object.) After the object is embedded, there is no longer a connection between it and the original object; hence, any further changes made to the original object are not reflected in the embedded object. Suppose that you embed a series of CorelDRAW! images in a Word for Windows document. You can change the images by double-clicking them (which launches CorelDRAW!, where you can make your changes). The images are stored as a part of the Word for Windows document, however, and the original application (CorelDRAW!) is used only to make changes to the object. The original CorelDRAW! image files remain unchanged when changes are made to the images in Word for Windows.

6.7. How can I establish a link to other data in a document?

Whenever you have data in another Windows application, you can link that data to your current document by using the following steps:

1. Place the insertion pointer in the document where you want to insert the linked data.
2. Switch to the server application (use the taskbar).
3. Select the data that you want to link.
4. Open the Edit menu and choose Copy.
5. Switch back to the destination application.
6. Open the Edit menu and choose Paste Link or Paste Special to create the link and paste the data into your destination

application. If a dialog box opens, choose the Link or Paste Link option within that dialog box, and then click OK. (Whether you see this dialog box depends on the design of your application.)

6.8. How can I embed an object in a document?

I

The steps you use to embed an object in a document follow. (Precisely which steps you carry out varies, depending on the design of your particular software package.)

1. Place the insertion pointer in the document where you want to embed the data.
2. Open the Insert menu and choose Object (or, if this command doesn't exist in your software, open the Edit menu and choose Insert Object). An Object Type dialog box appears, showing the different types of objects that can be created by the Windows applications on your system.
3. Choose the object type you want from the list (this starts the corresponding application).
4. Create the data that you want to embed.
5. Open the File menu and choose Exit and Return to leave the server application and embed the object in your document.

6.9. How can I embed an object that already exists elsewhere?

If the data that you want to embed in your document already exists elsewhere on disk, you can use the Edit I Copy and Edit I Paste Special commands to embed a copy of the object in your document. Use these steps:

1. Place the insertion pointer in the document where you want to embed the data.
2. Switch to the server application (use the taskbar).
3. Select the data that you want to embed in the document.
4. Open the Edit menu and choose Copy.
5. Switch back to the document in the destination application.

6. Open the Edit menu and choose Paste Special. A dialog box appears, asking which data type should be pasted into the document.

7. Choose the data type's appropriate format to complete the embedding operation.

6.10. Having links in my documents noticeably slows down opening and working with those documents. Can I do anything to speed up this process?

Two possibilities exist: one is software-related and the other is hardware-related. On the software side, OLE by default creates *automatic links* between your source and your destination documents. Assuming that you don't update the source documents very often, you can speed up things from a performance standpoint by using manual updating of your OLE links. You can use these steps to turn off automatic updating of links:

1. Open the destination document.

2. Open the Edit menu and choose the appropriate option that enables you to edit the document links. Usually, this command is Edit | Links or Edit | Edit Links. A dialog box opens, displaying the source of the link and whether updating is set to Automatic or Manual.

3. In the dialog box, select the link you want to change. (If you need to change only one link in your document, you can avoid this step by selecting the linked object within the document before performing step 2.)

4. In the Update portion of the dialog box, choose Manual. Then click OK.

After you switch to manual updating, remember that your linked objects do not reflect changes made to the source documents unless you open the document in the destination application and choose Edit | Update Links.

Another way to speed up opening and editing documents containing linked (or embedded) objects involves improving your hardware. Although Windows' minimum configuration is a 386SX with

4M of RAM, this combination does not effectively support extensive work with OLE. If you are going to work with compound documents on a regular basis, you should consider a 486DX with 8M of RAM to be a minimum system, and take the memory to 16M if your company can manage the expense.

6.11. Many Windows applications have two choices on the Edit menu: Paste and Paste Link. What's the difference between the two?

Edit | Paste uses the Windows Clipboard to paste a copy of the data from the source application to the destination application. The copy's data is *static*—it is in no way linked to the original document. When you use Edit | Paste Link, you are using DDE (in older Windows applications) or OLE (in newer applications that support it) to create a dynamic link to the source document that changes automatically when the source data changes.

6.12. After I create linked objects in other documents, can I move the source documents to different folders?

Not without causing major problems. Moving a *compound document* (any document containing OLE objects) to a different folder changes its actual location in a directory of the hard disk that is managed by Windows. When you link objects, Windows stores the object's folder location along with the object as part of the compound document. If you move the source document out of its original folder, the destination document is not able to find the source document, and you see an error message when you try to open the destination document. You get the same problem if you delete the source document.

6.13. How can I edit a linked object?

To edit a linked object, first open the destination document containing the object. Then, double-click the object to launch the source application, and make the desired changes. Save the changes and exit the application (or use the taskbar to switch back to the destination document). Assuming that you have automatic links turned on within the document, you see the updated data in the destination document.

6.14. Can I create documents with multiple links?

Yes. You can have as many links as needed to accomplish a task. In a proposal written in Microsoft Word, for example, you might have a portion of an Excel spreadsheet, a graph stored in PowerPoint, and a report from an Access database. In theory, there is no practical limit to the number of fields or embedded objects that you can have in a compound document. In practice, a large number of objects in a document may cause a slower response time when working in the document.

6.15. I've created links to other documents, and I don't plan to make any more changes to the data in the source documents. Can I break the links and retain the data?

Yes. When you no longer need the capability of Windows to automatically update linked data, you can break the link and keep the information as *static data* (not linked to any other source) in your document. Use these steps:

1. Open the destination document.
2. Click the linked object to select it.
3. Choose Links from the Edit menu.
4. In the dialog box that appears, choose the appropriate option to terminate the link (this option may be called Break Link, Cancel Link, or Delete).
5. Click OK.

After you break the link, the data stays in your document. Windows no longer updates the information if the data in the source document changes, however.

6.16. How can I easily create a logo or decorative title and add it to a document or a spreadsheet?

You can use Paint and the cut-and-paste techniques described in the first part of this chapter, but creating a company logo in Paint isn't necessarily easy. If you have Word for Windows (version 2.0 or 6.0) installed, you can use *WordArt* (a design miniapplication provided with Word) to create fancy titles or logos that you can embed in a word processing document or a spreadsheet. Use these steps:

1. Open the document where you want to add the title or logo, and place the insertion pointer in the desired location.

2. From the menu bar, choose the Insert | Object command.

3. In the Object dialog box that appears, choose MS Word Art, and then click OK.

4. Create the logo or title by typing the text in the Enter Your Text Here box.

5. Use the toolbar and/or menu options of WordArt to format the text; then click Update Display.

6. When you have finished designing the logo or decorative text, click anywhere outside the logo to exit WordArt and return to your document.

Making the Most of the Bundled Windows Applications

This chapter details user tips and tricks for the bundled Windows 95 applications, with an emphasis on WordPad and Paint. If you are familiar with prior versions of Windows, and you've always dismissed the bundled applications such as Write, Cardfile, Calendar, and Paintbrush as lightweights, consider taking another look at the applications bundled with Windows 95. Write, Cardfile, Calendar, and Paintbrush are all gone, as is Notepad. Paintbrush has been replaced with an improved drawing tool called Paint. Write and Notepad both get a sorely needed replacement with WordPad. In terms of power, WordPad can be thought of as a slimmed-down version of Microsoft's Word for Windows; it uses the same style of interface, offers most of the basic features provided by Word, and saves files in Word format (though you can force WordPad to save its files as ASCII text).

WordPad

WordPad is a richly featured, although somewhat limited, word processor. It is limited only in that it doesn't have the full feature set of a full-scale word processor such as Word for Windows or WordPerfect for Windows. WordPad has replaced Write, which came with previous releases of Microsoft Windows.

Setting Up WordPad

You can customize WordPad to fit the way you might like to work.

7.1. How can I turn the Toolbar, Format bar, Ruler, and Status bar on and off?

If you want to show or hide any of these, open the View menu as shown in Figure 7.1. If a check appears beside one of the entries, the item is shown on the screen. If you choose to hide an item, click the item and the check is removed. The item is now hidden on the screen.

Figure 7.1. *The View menu.*

Creating, Saving, and Editing Documents

After you set up WordPad to work the way you want it to, you're ready to create, save, and edit documents.

7.2. How can I create a new document?

To create a new document, click File on the menu bar. Then choose New from the File menu and a new file is created as "Untitled." To name the file, choose Save As from the File menu and give the file a name. As an alternative, you can also use the Toolbar and click the New icon at the far left (or use Ctrl+N).

7.3. How can I save changes to a document?

To save changes to a document, open the File menu and choose Save. Alternatively, you can click the Save icon on the Toolbar, which is the third of the first three menu options. (You can also press Ctrl+S.)

7.4. How can I open an existing document?

To open an existing document, choose Open from the File menu. Next, either type the name of the file in the Filename box or scroll through the list of files to find the file you want to open. On the Toolbar is a File open icon that also brings up the Filename dialog box. (You can also use Ctrl+O.)

7.5. How can I delete information from a document?

There are two options you can use to delete information or blocks of text. You can choose Clear from the Edit menu after highlighting the information that you want to delete, or you can click and drag to highlight the information, then press Delete on the keyboard.

7.6. How can I locate words in a document?

To find words or phrases in a document, choose Find from the Edit menu to activate the Find window (or press Ctrl+F). When the Find dialog box opens, as shown in Figure 7.2, you are prompted to enter the string of characters for which you are looking. In the Find window, you also have the option to either match the word only, or do a match case to find the exact occurrence of the character string entered. Activate these by clicking the box beside them.

Figure 7.2. *The Find dialog box.*

7.7. How can I replace text in a document?

To replace text, perform the following steps:

1. Choose Replace from the Edit menu (or press Ctrl+H). When you do so, the Replace window is opened and you are prompted to enter the string of characters to be found and replaced.

2. Enter the character string to be replaced in the Find what: box, use the Tab key or click in the Replace with box.

3. Enter the word or phrase you want to replace existing text or characters with (the information in the box above it). Here too, you have the option to search for just the word or a match case to find the exact occurrence. The Replace window also has an option that lets you search for each occurrence of an item: simply click Replace. You may also replace every occurrence of an item in the document at once by clicking the Replace all button.

7.8. How can I add the date and time to a document?

To add the date and time to a document, choose Date and Time from the Insert menu or click the Date and Time icon on the Toolbar. This opens the Insert Date and Time dialog box, as shown in Figure 7.3. The Date and Time window enables you to choose the format you want for the date—long or short form—or if you want the day and or time included, or even just the time.

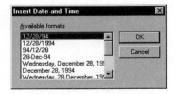

Figure 7.3. *The Insert Date and Time dialog box.*

7.9. How can I move information between documents?

To move information between documents, click and drag to highlight the text to be moved, then choose Cut from the Edit menu. (You can also use the Cut icon on the Toolbar.) This moves the text to the Clipboard. Next, open the document to which you want to move the information and choose Paste from the Edit menu to insert the information to your document.

7.10. How can I copy text between documents?

To copy text between documents, highlight the desired text, and either choose Copy from the Edit menu (or press Ctrl+C) or click the Copy icon on the Toolbar. This places a copy of the highlighted information onto the Clipboard. Then open the document in which you want to place the information and either click the Paste icon or choose Paste from the Edit menu (or press Ctrl+V).

Formatting Text

Formatting text in WordPad is similar to formatting in Microsoft Word for Windows and is easy to do.

7.11. How can I turn word wrap on and off?

Word wrap can be turned on and off by choosing Options from the View menu. This opens the View Options dialog box, as shown in Figure 7.4. This box enables you to turn Word wrap on and off or turn the Ruler on or off. In the Measurement unit box, you can change the measurement units to centimeters, inches, pints, or picas. You also can change the default file type by canceling the Prompt for file type.

7.12. How can I insert a bullet?

To insert bullets, simply choose Bullet from the Insert menu before typing the sentence that begins with the bullet. This automatically places a bullet each time you press Enter. To end bullet placements, return to the Bullet choice on the Insert menu and click it to turn it off. You may also use the Bullet icon in the same way: click it on and off to place bullets in your document.

Figure 7.4. *The View Options dialog box.*

7.13. How can I select fonts?

You can select fonts by choosing Font from the Format menu. This opens the Font dialog box, which contains a list of all the fonts available in WordPad, as shown in Figure 7.5. If the Format bar is active, clicking the arrow beside the font box opens a drop menu with a list of the available fonts. Use the arrow keys or click the font you want to choose.

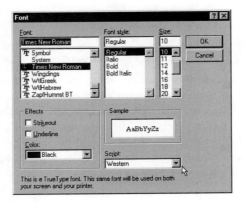

Figure 7.5. *The Font dialog box.*

7.14. How can I change type colors?

To change the color of the type that appears on your screen, choose
Font from the format window to open the Font dialog box. Click
the color arrow at the bottom-left corner of the dialog box, as
shown in Figure 7.6. You also can click on the color change icon
located on the Format bar.

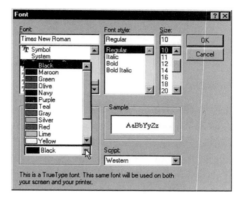

Figure 7.6. *The Font dialog box with colors displayed.*

7.15. How can I change type size?

To change type size, with the Format bar active, click the type size
arrow and choose the size you want using the arrow keys or by
clicking it. You can also open the fonts window by choosing Font
from the Format menu, then choosing the type size from the Size
box.

7.16. How can I change the margins?

To change the margins of a document, choose Paragraph from the
Format menu. This opens the Format Paragraph dialog box, as
shown in Figure 7.7. Here you can change the left and right

margins of your document to the desired size. You also may set a first line indent for paragraphs in a document by choosing the number of centimeters you wish to indent the first line in the First line box.

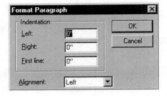

Figure 7.7. *The Format Paragraph dialog box.*

7.17. How can I set tab stops?

To set tab stops, click the section of the ruler where you wish to place the tab stop, and a tab stop will be placed there. You may also choose Tabs from the Format window to open the Format Tabs dialog box, as shown in Figure 7.8. This enables you to set a tab in a specific place on your document.

Figure 7.8. *The Format Tabs dialog box.*

7.18. How can I delete tabs from a document?

With the ruler showing, click the tab stops and drag them to the left of the ruler. If you wish to delete all the tab stops, choose Tabs from the Format menu, open the Format Tabs window, and click the Clear All button.

Printing Documents

Creating and editing documents almost always ends in printing. This is now much smoother than in previous versions of Windows.

7.19. How can I print a document?

To print a document, either choose Print from the File menu (or press Ctrl+P), or click the Print icon on the Toolbar.

7.20. How can I preview a document I want to print?

To preview a document, simply click the Preview icon on the Toolbar or choose Preview from the File menu.

7.21. How can I set margins for printing?

Choose Page setup from the File menu to open the page setup window. Here you can set the margins for the top, bottom, right, and left of a document to be printed.

7.22. How can I change printing options and printers?

To change print options, choose Print from the File menu to open the Print dialog box, shown in Figure 7.9. You can change the printer options from this dialog box by clicking the Properties button.

Making Connections with Other Documents

Embedding and linking objects in WordPad is easier than ever before.

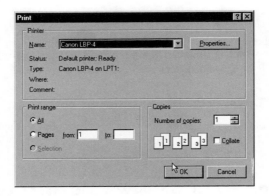

Figure 7.9. *The Print dialog box.*

7.23. How can I insert an embedded or linked object?

To insert an object into a document, choose Insert New Object from the Insert menu. This opens the Insert Object dialog box, as shown in Figure 7.10. From here, choose the object type you wish to insert and click OK. This opens a window for the type of file you want; from there, you can choose the file you want and insert it into your document.

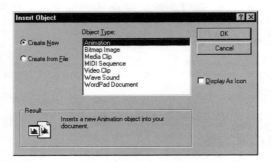

Figure 7.10. *The Insert Object dialog box.*

7.24. When I choose Insert New Object, the list box that appears doesn't show objects from all the Windows programs I have installed. Why is one (or more) object type missing?

The available object types list is taken directly from the Windows Registry, which keeps track of all installed Windows software. If a type of object doesn't appear in the list, you must reinstall the software package so that the Windows Registry is updated with the list of objects that package is capable of creating.

Paint

You can easily illustrate documents with the easy-to-use, but rich, set of drawing tools that comes in Paint.

7.25. How can I draw a straight line?

To draw a straight line, choose the Line icon; then at the bottom of the toolbox, select the width of the line you want. Also at the bottom of the toolbox, you can choose the color of the line you want. If you want to make a horizontal line, press Shift while you are drawing the line.

7.26. How can I draw a free-form line?

To draw a free-form line, click the Pen icon in the tool bar. Then you can drag the mouse pointer in the direction in which you want to make a line, as you desire. Again, if you want to make a horizontal line, simply press Shift while you are drawing the line.

| TIP | If you are switching between freeform and straight lines, you can use the pen and simply press Shift when you want to make straight lines. |

7.27. How can I draw a curved line?

Choose the Curve Line icon from the toolbox. Next, choose the width you want for the line. First, draw a straight line with the mouse. To add the curve, you simply have to click where you want the line to curve, then drag. As you click and drag, the line will curve. After you have curved the line to your liking, move to the toolbox and choose any other button to make the curve in the line permanent.

7.28. How can I draw different shapes?

To draw an oval, circle, rectangle, square, or any shape, you will first need to specify whether you want it opaque or transparent. Do this by choosing the appropriate icon from the toolbox. Again, before drawing the shape, you will need to choose the color of the line by clicking the color palette, and the width of the line by clicking the line width while one of the line drawing icons is pressed.

To make a circle, simply click the circle icon and press Shift while you click and drag. The same icon is used for making ovals. The process is the same, but you don't press the Shift key.

7.29. How can I draw a square or rectangle?

To draw a square or rectangle choose the square/rectangle icon. After choosing the width of the line and the color of the line, click and drag to make a rectangle. If you want to make a square, use the same process, but press Shift and you will create a square.

7.30. How can I fill in my shapes?

To make your shapes transparent or opaque, open the Options menu and choose Transparent or Opaque as desired. This will fill in your shape. You may also choose the Fill icon, which is used to fill in areas; this too will fill in your shapes.

Q.31. How can I add text to my pictures?

If you wish to add text to your pictures, click the Add Text icon in the toolbox. Next, click the area in which you want the text to appear. This causes a frame to appear, which defines the typing area. To make the frame larger, click and drag diagonally. Finally, click in the frame and begin typing. You also can change the color of the text by clicking the color you want the text to be before you type.

I

Q.32. How can I change the background color?

After choosing a color, click on the area and it becomes filled with your chosen color. This method can also be used to fill in shapes or other objects with closed borders.

Q.33. How can I edit my pictures?

If you want to, you can erase small areas of your picture by clicking the Eraser icon. Then choose the eraser size you wish to have. This enables you to edit in a large or small area of your picture.

The background color shows the color that will be left behind after the erasing. If you want to change the color, use the right mouse button and click the color you want. The Color Pick-up icon can be used to erase one pixel at a time.

To erase a large area of a picture, click either of the top buttons on the toolbox and define the area you want to erase. After defining the area you want to erase, the selected background color shows what will appear after the area is erased.

Q.34. How can I change the appearance of my picture?

To look at your picture in different ways, go to the View menu. Here you have a choice for Normal Size, Large Size, and Custom. Choosing Zoom; Large enables you to get a large view of your picture. Choosing Zoom; Custom enables you to look at your picture at a zoom of 100, 200, 400, 600, or 800 percent. This is useful in looking at sections of the picture for editing purposes. Use the magnifying glass from the toolbox to take you through the magnification strengths.

7.35. How can I copy my picture to use in another application?

If you want to copy your picture to another application, you must first highlight the picture by choosing the icon in the top-right corner of the toolbar. This icon is used to select information for editing. After you have done this, choose either Cut (if you wish to move the picture to another application), or Copy (if you wish to leave an active copy in Paint) from the Edit menu. After you have switched to the other application and chosen where you want to place the object, choose Paste from the Edit menu.

Making the Most of Your Windows Applications

This chapter focuses on common applications used with Windows, with a view toward detailing the tips and techniques that you can use to make your work with these applications less complicated and more effective on a daily basis. You look at the overall areas of word processing, spreadsheets, and databases. Some questions apply to a category of products (such as spreadsheets), but most are directed toward a specific product (such as Quattro Pro for Windows or Excel for Windows). Although many of the tips have been written to apply to as many versions of the different products as possible, note that they have been tested specifically with the most recent versions at the time of this writing. These versions include Word 6.0 for Windows, WordPerfect 6.0 for Windows, Excel 5.0, and Quattro Pro 5.0.

Because this chapter covers common questions for a variety of products, there are references throughout that assume a familiarity with the specific product. If a reference isn't familiar, the Search option of the Help screens in that product (or the product's documentation) should provide some assistance.

General Topics

If you're new to Windows, you're probably anxious to avoid problems with the applications you run. Even experienced users are bound to have questions arise from time to time regarding basic Windows operations. Although many techniques are discussed throughout this book, this section addresses some of the more general topics applicable to most programs that run under the Windows operating system.

8.1. What are the shortcut keys that work with Windows applications?

Every Windows user should know a number of Ctrl+key and Alt+key combinations, because these combinations perform the same functions in nearly all Windows applications. Table 8.1 shows these common keys and their functions.

Table 8.1. Common key combinations in Windows.

Key Combination	Action
Home	Moves to start of line
End	Moves to end of line
Ctrl+Home	Moves insertion point to start of document
Ctrl+End	Moves insertion point to end of document
Shift+Ctrl+Home	Selects text from insertion point to start of document
Shift+Ctrl+End	Selects text from insertion point to end of document
Alt+F4	Closes the application window
Alt+Tab	Switches between current and prior Windows application
Alt+Esc	Switches to next application
Ctrl+F4	Closes child window
Ctrl+Esc	Opens Start menu

Key Combination	Action
Alt+Backspace	Undoes typing over selected text or erases prior word
Tab	Moves to next field or moves forward in dialog box
Shift+Tab	Moves to previous field or moves backward in dialog box

I

8.2. Is there a universal print function that works in different applications?

You can press Ctrl+P to bring up the Print dialog box in most Windows applications. You then can click OK to print one copy of the active document to the default printer. (The Alt+F+P combination also performs the same task in most Windows applications.)

8.3. How can I disable call waiting when I use my modem?

Fax-modem users who have call waiting know that all too often sessions are disrupted or even terminated because of call waiting. Most phone systems have a way to disable call waiting before placing a call—often by dialing *70 followed by a comma for a two-second pause before dialing the number. (Call your local phone company for the correct code that is used in your area.) You can add the code to your modem's dialing string in your communications software's modem setup screen; in most cases, the string begins with ATDT*70, as in ATDT*70,555-1234, for example. If you dial from a rotary system (pulse dial), try using 1170 instead of *70.

8.4. Should I keep my Windows installation disks?

It is a good idea to keep your Windows installation disks handy even after you install Windows. Often, Windows needs other files from the installation disks when different options are changed (particularly with regard to hardware reconfigurations). If you purchased Windows 95 on CD-ROM, this is as simple as leaving the CD in your drive. However, swapping floppy disks can become a nuisance as you install any program. A simpler approach is to copy the installation disks to your hard disk if you have a spare 20M or so. You can place the disks in a folder called C:\WINDISKS, if you like. Then, the next time Windows asks you for Windows disk #*n*, just type the path C:\WINDISKS (assuming that your hard disk is drive C).

8.5. The Taskbar overlaps part of my program. Can I move it?

The Taskbar is designed to always be visible as you use Windows. Sometimes, this Taskbar gets in the way of applications designed for Windows 3.*x* by covering up their status bar, scroll bar, or other important part of the program. You can quickly hide it (minimize to a thin line) by clicking the top edge of the Taskbar and dragging it to the bottom of the screen. To view the Taskbar again, simply reverse the process. If you want the Taskbar to hide automatically as you move the pointer away and to reappear as the pointer passes over its thin minimized line, you can right-click on the Taskbar, choose Properties from the context menu, and enable Auto hide.

8.6. The installation instructions suggest commands that aren't available in Windows 95. What should I do?

Windows 95 was designed to run all Windows 3.*x*-version applications. However, the installation instructions that come with those applications do not explain steps for installing under Windows 95. Essentially, there are three items to consider. First, to install a program, choose Start | Run, and enter the drive and filename (Windows 3.*x* used File | Run). Second, if you absolutely need the old Windows 3.*x* File Manager, you can invoke it by running the Winfile program. Choose Start | Run, type `Winfile`, and click OK. Last, once a program is installed, shortcuts are placed in the Programs folder. Instead of opening a Program group as was done in Windows 3.*x*, simply choose Start | Programs, and select the Program group.

8.7. How can I access files across the network on another person's computer?

In order to access the files on another person's computer, you must map, or assign, a drive letter to it. This creates a bridge between the other person's computer and yours. To do this, open Explorer and choose Map Network Drive from the Tools menu. Enter the path of the person's computer and shared folder (directory) in the Map Network Drive dialog box. Of course, this must follow the UNC (Universal Naming Convention) format, such as `\\Marty's 486\c\database`.

Word Processing

Of all Windows applications, perhaps the most commonly used is the word processor. The graphical WYSIWYG appearance gives you the ability to create professional-looking documents, and other features make it the best way to create a document. Also, because the Windows interface has helped integrate disparate word-processing applications, many of these topics apply just as well to other word processors.

Word for Windows and WordPerfect—General Topics

This section covers common issues of the two most popular word processors—Microsoft Word and Novell WordPerfect for Windows.

8.8. I don't like the default Times New Roman (or whatever) font I'm forced to use each time I start a new document. How can I change this default font?

In Word for Windows, you can change the font used for all documents by using these steps:

1. From the menu bar, choose Format | Font.

> **TIP** You also can press Ctrl+D to access the Font dialog box.

2. Select a font name in the Font box, and then type or select a font size in the Size box.

3. Click the Default button. When Word asks if you want to change the default font, click Yes.

> **NOTE** You quickly can change the default formatting in Word by selecting text that has the formatting you want. Then choose Format | Font, click the Default button, and click OK.

In WordPerfect for Windows, you can change the font used for all documents by following these steps:

1. From the menus, choose File | Printer.

2. Click the File icon to select it.

3. From the menu bar, choose the printer driver you want, and then choose Initial Font.

4. Select the font and styles you want and click OK.

8.9. How can I set the default folder (directory) for saving and opening files so that I don't have to change directories all the time to find the files I use daily?

In Word for Windows, use these steps to change the default folder (directory):

1. From the menu bar, choose Tools | Options.

2. Click the File Locations tab.

3. In the File Types list, choose Documents; then click the Modify button.

4. Type or select the drive and directory you want to use as the default; then click OK.

5. Click Close.

In WordPerfect for Windows, use these steps to change the default directory:

1. From the menu bar, choose File | Preferences.
2. Double-click the File icon to select it.
3. Click the Documents/Backup radio button.
4. Enter the folder (directory) name you want in the Default Directory text box.
5. Click OK and then click Close.

8.10. I lost a document I was working on when the power failed. Is there a way to get my document back?

In both Word and WordPerfect, you can turn on an Autosave option that automatically backs up your work at timed intervals. If the power goes out, restart Windows. Then, once you launch your word processor, the document will be resurrected. Of course, this only works if the Autosave feature is enabled *before* the power goes out.

In Word for Windows, perform these steps:

1. From the menu bar, choose Tools | Options.
2. Click the Save tab.
3. In the Save Options area, place an x in the Automatic Save Every check box.
4. Enter an interval (in minutes) in the Minutes box; then click OK.

In WordPerfect, follow these steps:

1. From the menu bar, choose File | Preferences.
2. Double-click the File icon.
3. Click the Documents/Backup radio button.
4. Select Timed Document Backup in the dialog box that appears.
5. Specify the interval (in minutes) in the Timed Backup spin box.
6. Click OK and then click Close.

> **NOTE** If power fluctuations and outages are a problem in your area, you may want to consider getting an uninterruptible power supply for your computer.

8.11. How can I insert special characters?

Sometimes, you need characters that aren't on the normal US/English keyboard, such as the trademark or registry symbol, or accented characters used in the alphabets of other languages. To insert special characters in Word for Windows, use these steps:

1. Place the insertion pointer where you want to insert the character.
2. From the menu bar, choose Insert | Symbol.
3. In the Font list box, select the font that contains the character you want to insert.
4. Double-click the character. (If you can't find the character you want, try selecting another font in the Font list box.) You can insert additional symbols by moving the insertion pointer to the next location and repeating steps 3 and 4.
5. When you finish inserting the characters, click Close.

To insert special characters in WordPerfect, use these steps:

1. Place the insertion pointer where you want to insert the character.
2. From the menu bar, choose Insert | Character.
3. In the Character Set popup, choose the set of characters that contains the character you want.
4. In the Characters list box, select the character you want.
5. Click Insert. (You can move the insertion pointer and repeat steps 3 through 5 for any other characters you want to insert.)
6. Click Close.

8.12. How can I select an entire document for formatting?

Selecting an entire document is a useful technique when you want to apply a common formatting to the whole document, such as when you want to apply a single font or font size throughout, or to change line spacing universally. In Word for Windows, press Ctrl+A to select the entire document. In WordPerfect, choose Edit | Select | All to select the entire document.

8.13. By default, all my documents are set to print on 8 1/2-by-11-inch paper. For this print job, that's not what I want. How can I change it?

In Word for Windows, use these steps to change the paper size:

1. Place the insertion pointer anywhere in the section of the document where you want the paper size change to take effect.

2. From the menu bar, choose File | Page Setup.

3. Click the Paper Size tab.

4. In the Paper Size list box, choose the paper size you want. (You can use a custom paper size by entering the paper's measurements in the Height and Width boxes.)

5. In the Orientation area, choose Portrait or Landscape.

6. In the Apply To box, choose how much of the document you want the paper size change to apply to; then click OK.

In WordPerfect, use these steps to change the paper size:

1. Place the insertion pointer at the point in the document where you want the change to take effect. (If you want the change to be in effect for the entire document, place the insertion pointer at the beginning of the document.)

2. From the menu bar, choose Layout | Page | Paper Size.

3. In the Paper Size dialog box that appears, highlight a paper size from the Paper Definitions list and click Select to confirm the choice.

8.14. Is there a fast way to select words, sentences, and paragraphs?

Yes. In Word for Windows, double-click a word to select it. Ctrl-click anywhere in a sentence to select the sentence. Double-click to the left of any paragraph to select that paragraph. In WordPerfect, double-click a word to choose it. Triple-click a word to select the sentence it is in. Click four times on a word to select a paragraph.

8.15. I often download files from CompuServe that have hard returns at the end of every line. Is there an easy way to get rid of these?

When e-mail is downloaded or cut and pasted into your document, hard returns appear at the end of every line. This occurrence is frustrating when you want to edit the text. A caret (^) and a lowercase *p* represent the hard return at the end of each line in the document. To fix this problem, use the Find and Replace feature of your word processor to turn the hard returns (paragraph marks) into single spaces. In Word for Windows, search for ^p and replace it with a space. In WordPerfect, search for [HRt] and replace it with a space.

8.16. How can I password-protect a document?

Password-protection enables you to hide your document from unauthorized eyes. One point to keep in mind is that if you protect a document, you must not lose the password; the tech support line at your software vendor will not be able to help you open the document or retrieve the password.

In Word for Windows, you can password-protect a document with these steps:

1. Open the document that you want to password protect.
2. From the menu bar, choose Tools | Options.
3. Click on the Save tab.
4. In the Protection Password box (or in the Write Reservation Password box), enter a password and click OK.

5. Enter the password again in the Confirm Password dialog box and click OK.

In WordPerfect, you can password protect a document by using these steps:

1. Open the document that you want to password protect.

2. From the menu bar, choose File | Save As. If the document is unnamed, enter a name in the File Name box.

3. In the dialog box that appears, click the Password Protect check box.

4. Click OK, enter a password, and click OK again.

5. Retype the password and click OK.

8.17. I had the Caps Lock key pressed accidentally, and typed a significant amount of text before noticing. Is there a way to change the case of all the text without retyping it all?

In Word for Windows, you can reverse the case of what you typed by using these steps:

1. Select the text containing the case you want to change.

2. From the menu bar, choose Format | Change Case.

3. In the Change Case dialog box that appears, choose Toggle Case; then click OK.

TIP	You also can press Shift+F3 to toggle the case (after you highlight the text).

In WordPerfect, there is no specific way to reverse all the case (that is, change all uppercase to lowercase while changing all lowercase to uppercase). You can do most of that task, however, by selecting all the affected text and choosing Edit | ConvertCase | Lowercase from the menus. Then you only need to recapitalize those letters that should be in uppercase within the selection.

8.18. Is there a way to print more than one file at a time from within Word or WordPerfect?

You can select multiple files for printing from within Word by performing these steps:

1. From the menu bar, choose File | Find File to open the Search dialog box. (If you've used the Find File feature previously, this will open the Find File dialog box instead. If so, go on to step 3.)

2. In the Search For area, click the File Name list box and specify the document extension. In the Location list box, specify the drive and path. (Click Include Subdirectories if you want to search folders beneath this one.) Click OK to search.

3. From the listed files, select the files that you want to print by holding the Ctrl key and clicking on each file you want.

4. Click Commands and then choose Print.

5. In the Print dialog box click OK.

To print multiple files simultaneously from WordPerfect, perform these steps:

1. Choose Open from the File menu.

2. Highlight the files you want to print by Ctrl-clicking on the desired files.

3. Click the File Options button and choose Print.

4. In the Print File dialog box, click Print. If the file is text (or a format other than WPWin), a Convert File Format dialog box will appear wherein you can click OK to continue.

8.19. How can I add the date and time to a document?

In Word for Windows, follow these steps:

1. Place the insertion pointer where you want to add the date and/or time.

2. From the menu bar, choose Insert | Date and Time.

3. In the dialog box that appears, select the format you want for the date and/or time; then click OK.

In WordPerfect, use these steps:

1. Place the insertion pointer where you want to add the date and/or time.

2. From the menu bar, choose Insert | Date | Date Text.

If you want a different date or time format than what is inserted, choose Tools | Date from the menu bar, and then choose Date Format. In the dialog box that next appears, choose the options to select the date or time format you want and click OK.

8.20. How can I insert a picture into my document?

1. In Word for Windows, choose Insert | Picture from the menu bar. In WordPerfect, choose Graphics | Figure from the menu bar.

2. Select the picture file you want from the dialog box that appears.

3. Click OK.

After you insert the picture, in Word for Windows you can choose Format | Picture from the menu bar to change the size and position of the picture. In WordPerfect, you can use the Graphics menu and the Graphics Box toolbar to change the size, appearance, and placement of the picture.

8.21. How can I create a table?

In Word for Windows, you can create a table by using the following steps:

1. From the menu bar, choose Table | Insert Table.

2. In the Number of Columns text box, enter the number of columns you want.

3. In the Number of Rows text box, enter the number of rows you want.

4. Click OK to place the table in the document.

> **TIP** You can create a table quickly in Word by clicking the Insert Table button on the Toolbar. Drag to the desired dimension. In WordPerfect, click the Table Quick Create button on the Power Bar and drag to the desired dimension.

To create a table in WordPerfect, perform these steps:

1. Choose Tables from the Layout menu.
2. Choose Create.
3. In the Columns text box, enter the number of columns you want.
4. In the Rows text box, enter the number of rows you want.
5. Click OK.

To insert text in the table (using Word or WordPerfect), move the insertion pointer to the cell where you want to type the text, and type the text. You can move between the cells of a table by pressing Tab or Shift+Tab, or by using the mouse.

8.22. Why do my word processing documents look slightly different when printed than they do on-screen?

The difference between what you see and what you get is due to the fact that some Windows printer fonts do not have identical matching screen fonts. With fonts that aren't TrueType, Windows must use one font for the printer, and another font for the screen display. Windows tries to use a screen font that is closest in appearance to the chosen printer font. In some cases, however, differences are apparent; this is particularly true with printer fonts that are of an unusual design (such as with most fonts that simulate script handwriting). You can eliminate the "what you see is not what you get" problem by using TrueType fonts for all of your printing. For more information on fonts and printing in general, see Chapter 4, "Putting It on Paper."

Word for Windows Specifics

As you work more closely with Word for Windows, you'll want to know about commonly encountered issues. This section discusses these topics.

8.23. When I start Word 6.0, I get the message *Word has caused a General Protection Fault in module WINWORD.EXE,* and the program doesn't load. Do I need to reinstall Word?

Perhaps, but perhaps not. First, try the following steps:

1. Find the file called NORMAL.DOT. (Usually, this file is in the TEMPLATE folder that resides in the WINWORD folder.)

2. Use Explorer or My Computer to locate and rename the file NORMAL.DOT to another filename.

3. Try to restart Word. If Word starts normally, the template file NORMAL.DOT was corrupted. Word automatically creates a new template, although you need to reset any default fonts and redo any global macros you had stored in the file. If you still get the error, rename the file back to NORMAL.DOT, and then proceed to the next step.

4. Change your Windows display driver to 16 color, restart Windows, and try to restart Word again. If Word runs OK, contact the vendor of your video hardware for an updated video driver.

If Word doesn't restart, you probably need to reinstall Word to resolve the problem.

8.24. How can I line up columns of ASCII text in Word?

If you're having problems with this, it's because the ASCII files are based on fixed-width characters, whereas most Windows fonts are *proportional,* meaning the characters have different widths. This causes the columns that lined up in an ASCII file to appear out of line when imported into Word. The solution is to use a fixed-width font in Word (Courier New is a good suggestion).

8.25. Is there a quick way to move rows or paragraphs?

You can move rows and paragraphs in Word without using the Cut and Paste options. First, highlight the row or paragraph you want to move. Second, press Shift+Alt+Down arrow (or up arrow, depending on the direction in which you want to move the text). The row or paragraph moves up or down by one row each time you press this key combination. Adjacent rows or paragraphs shift up or down accordingly. You also can use the mouse to click and drag the highlighted row or paragraph to the desired location.

8.26. How can I speed up printing if all I want is a draft copy?

Use these steps to get a draft copy that prints faster but has minimal formatting:

1. From the menu bar, choose File | Print.
2. In the dialog box that appears, click Options.
3. In the Printing Options area, choose Draft Output.
4. Click OK twice to print the document.

8.27. Why do I get the error message *Margins outside printable area of page* when I try to print my Word document?

This message occurs because you have set your page margins to specifications that your particular printer is not physically capable of meeting. Most printers (including virtually all laser printers) can print reasonably close to the paper's edge, but not all the way up to the edge. Windows knows about these dimensions because they are stored with other data in your installed printer drivers; when you try to print, Windows warns Word (which then warns you by means of the dialog box) that the data you're sending to the printer falls outside the printer's physical boundaries. The only solution is to change your page margins so that your printer can handle them; most laser printers need from 1/4 inch to 1/2 inch of space at the top, bottom, left, and right edges of the page.

8.28. How can I print selected pages of a document, rather than the entire document?

Choose File | Print. When the Print dialog box appears, click the Pages button. Then enter the page numbers or a range of pages (separated by commas) in the text box beside the button. Entering 2,4,7-12 in the box, for example, causes Word to print page 2, page 4, and pages 7 through 12 of the document.

8.29. How can I print in reverse order?

Word 6.0 enables you to print in reverse order. Choose Print from the File menu. Next, select Options and then place an x in the Reverse Print Order box in the Printing Options area and click OK. Finally, click OK in the Print dialog box.

8.30. Can I delete files from within Word?

Yes (although it's just as easy to task switch to the Find utility and do it from there). To delete files from within Word, use these steps:

1. From the menu bar, choose File | Find File.
2. In the Search dialog box, enter the desired criteria in the File Name and Location text boxes; then click OK.
3. Select the files that you want to delete in the Listed Files list box.
4. Choose Commands, and then choose Delete.
5. Click Yes to confirm the deletions.
6. Click Close.

8.31. How can I print envelopes in Word for Windows?

You can use Word's envelope-printing feature to make this a simple task. Perform these steps:

1. From the menu bar, choose Tools | Envelopes and Labels.

2. In the dialog box that appears, enter the mailing address and the return address in the appropriate text boxes.

3. Click the Options button and click the Envelope Options tab. Choose the envelope size you want in the Envelope Size list box.

4. Click the Printing Options tab and choose the appropriate feed method for your envelopes. Click OK to return to the Envelopes and Labels dialog box.

5. Click the Print button to start printing.

8.32. How can I remove the field codes from the screen when I add a bullet to my document?

If you want to see the actual bullet instead of the field code, choose Options from the Tools menu. Next, click the View tab and uncheck the Field Codes check box. Click OK.

8.33. I've created a macro in Word that I use often. Can I assign it to a Toolbar button?

Yes. Follow these steps:

1. Choose Tools | Customize.

2. Click the Toolbars tab and, in the Categories list, highlight Macros. This lists the available macros.

3. Click on the macro you want and drag it up to the desired location on a toolbar.

4. From the Custom Button dialog box, choose a button face for this macro or provide text for the button's name, and click Assign.

5. Click on Close.

8.34. How can I simply shell out to DOS while working on a document in Word 6.0?

A simple way to go from Word for Windows to DOS and back again is to write a one-line macro, and even assign it to the toolbar if you want. Follow these steps:

1. Choose Macro from the Tools menu.

2. Type TODOS in the box for the Macro name and click Create.

3. Between the lines Sub Main and End Sub, type Shell "MS-DOSPR.PIF".

4. Choose Save All from the File menu.

5. Click Yes in response to any confirmation requests, and then choose Close from the File menu.

If you want to make your macro easily accessible, you can create a shortcut keystroke or an icon on the standard toolbar. If you prefer the keystroke combination, follow these steps:

1. Open the Tools menu and choose Customize.

2. Select the Keyboard tab. Scroll down the categories list, and when you reach Macros, select it. Then select TODOS from the list of macros.

3. With the mouse, click in the Press New Shortcut Key text box. Then press the key combination you want to use to shell out to DOS. Alt+D is a good example.

4. When you have completed your work, click Assign.

If you want to assign a button to the toolbar to shell out to DOS, refer to Question 8.33.

8.35. How can I make Word for Windows run faster?

You probably will see this enough times in this book to become sick of it, but *more memory* is the most significant addition you can make to increase performance, and this applies equally to Word 6.0 for Windows. In practice, 8M should be considered a minimum amount to run Word acceptably. Some additional techniques you can use to increase performance follow:

- If you still are using an unaccelerated video card, consider replacing it with an accelerated video card.

- Try to keep 4M to 6M of free disk space on the drive where Word stores its temporary files (usually C:\WINWORD).

- From the menu bar, choose View/Normal. The Normal mode of display is Word's fastest display mode.

■ If your document includes graphics, choose Tools | Options from the menu, click the View tab, and turn on the Picture Placeholders option.

■ Wherever possible, don't run other major Windows applications while Word is running.

■ If you commonly work with documents greater than 50 pages in length, break them down into smaller chunks.

8.36. How can I use my Word 6.0 files in Word 2.0?

If you are a user of Word 2.0 and you need to read files from Winword 6.0, the following is a helpful suggestion for reading 6.0 documents in 2.0.

Microsoft created an import/export converter for this very task. The converter kicks in when a document created in 6.0 is opened in 2.0. It then enables you to both save and load documents in the new file format. Although the converter cannot handle document elements created with the new features of Word in 6.0, such as OLE 2.0 links, it's an extremely useful program to have. You can get this converter from the Microsoft forum on CompuServe (GO MSWORD), or from Microsoft's direct download BBS at (206) 936-6735. The filename is MSWRD6.EXE and is 731K.

8.37. Is there an easy way to insert the commonly used trademark and copyright symbols?

You can use shortcut keys to insert special characters in your documents. You can enter a trademark symbol by pressing Ctrl+Alt+T. To insert a registered trademark, press Ctrl+Alt+R; or if you need to enter a copyright symbol, press Ctrl+Alt+C. If you want to use other symbols, choose Symbol from the Insert menu, choose the special character or symbol you want, and click Insert Close.

WordPerfect Specifics

As you work more closely with WordPerfect, you'll want to know about commonly encountered issues. This section discusses these topics.

8.38. I installed WordPerfect 6.0 in the same folder where I had WordPerfect 5.2 installed. Now, I can't get either program to work! What's wrong?

There are some basic design incompatibilities that make it impossible for you to run these two versions of WordPerfect for Windows from the same folder (subdirectory). If you must run both versions, you need to install them in separate folders. Erase all the files from the current folder, and install one version or the other. Then create another folder and install the other version of WordPerfect there.

8.39. Why is there no Print Preview option in WordPerfect for Windows?

Actually, there is, but it isn't called Print Preview. Open the View menu and choose Page. The on-screen representation that you get when you choose View | Page is what WordPerfect considers to be a print preview; it is true WYSIWYG (what-you-see-is-what-you-get), and the way your document appears here is the way it will print.

8.40. How can I tell the difference between soft and hard page breaks in WordPerfect—they both look alike?

You can switch to Draft view, or you can turn on Reveal Codes. In Draft view, the page breaks look different (a soft page break appears as a single line, while a hard page break appears as a double line). With Reveal Codes turned on, soft page breaks appear as [Spg], while hard page breaks appear as [Hpg].

8.41. WordPerfect offers a choice of printer drivers: WordPerfect's own drivers, or the Windows printer drivers. Which should I use in printing?

In general, you can use either without problems. WordPerfect has included its own printer drivers for maximum compatibility with WordPerfect for DOS 6.0, which uses the same printer drivers. If you use WordPerfect for DOS simultaneously (or work in an organization where others who share files are using the DOS version), you should stick with the WordPerfect printer drivers. If you don't need to work with files from the DOS version, and you use other Windows programs extensively, you should stick with the Windows printer drivers.

8.42. How can I make WordPerfect for Windows run faster?

First, if you are using version 6.0, make sure that you have upgraded to version 6.0a. (It's a free upgrade that cures some performance problems that were inherent in the first release of version 6.0 of WordPerfect for Windows. You can get the upgrade by calling the support number listed in your WordPerfect documentation.) Also, consider the following suggestions:

- If you are running on a system with 4M of RAM, consider upgrading to at least 6M.
- Use Draft view instead of Page view whenever possible.
- On machines with minimal memory, don't open more than one document at a time unless absolutely necessary.
- Turn off Reveal Codes if you have them turned on.
- Turn off the display of graphics (you can do this from the Display Preferences dialog box).
- Don't display comments.
- Whenever possible, don't run other CPU-hungry Windows applications while WordPerfect is running.

Spreadsheets

Once used only by accountants and financial gurus, spreadsheets are commonplace among all computer users. What's more, today's Windows-based spreadsheets give you extensive text and number handling capabilities similar to the popular word processors.

All Spreadsheets

A benefit to the Windows interface is that it narrows the differences between applications. This section takes a look at topics common among all spreadsheets.

8.43. Is there a way to easily change the format of a group of cells within a spreadsheet?

In an increasing number of spreadsheets (including recent editions of Microsoft Excel and Novell's Quattro Pro for Windows), you quickly can change cell formatting through properties accessed with a right-click of the mouse. Select the group of cells you want, and then right-click anywhere on the selection. From the menu that appears, choose the Format or Format Cells option, and use the choices in the dialog box that appears to set the cell's formatting.

8.44. Why do my values in a certain cell of my spreadsheet appear as a string of # characters?

Virtually all spreadsheets display numeric data that is too wide to fit in a column as a series of # symbols. To correct the problem, you must widen the column. You can widen the columns in Windows spreadsheets by placing the mouse pointer at the right border of the column and clicking and dragging the border to the width you want.

Q 8.45. When I enter a formula, I get a beep and an alert box telling me there's an error in the formula, but the alert box doesn't offer any help.

Occasionally, the alert box that appears in response to a formula error indicates the source of the error, but often you appear to be on your own. Take advantage of the context-sensitive help built into most Windows spreadsheets. When the error message appears, press F1. The dialog box that opens indicates the most common sources of the formula error.

Microsoft Excel

A heavyweight in the spreadsheet arena, Excel gives you all the power you need for manipulating financial data, solving what-if scenarios, and just plain number-crunching. This section looks at topics specific to Microsoft Excel.

Q 8.46. How do I import and export text files in Microsoft Excel?

In reality, importing a file is handled by Excel's internal import filters, so there is no formal import procedure. However, you do need to indicate how you want the incoming information displayed. In Excel 5.0, the Text Import Wizard handles this. Follow these steps:

1. From the menu bar, choose File | Open.

2. To view all files with TXT, PRN, and CSV filename extensions, select Text Files in the List Files of Type area. As soon as you type or select the filename you want, the Text Import Wizard starts. Note that if you have a file with a CSV (comma-separated variable format) filename extension, the file is opened and the text spreads across columns automatically, bypassing the Text Import Wizard.

3. Follow the steps outlined by the Text Import Wizard. During these steps, you designate whether the file is in a delimited or fixed-width format, set the starting row of the data you want

to import, choose one or more delimiters, create and move column break lines if your data is of fixed width, and set the format for each of the columns.

Just like importing, exporting a document simply saves it in a different format. However, you must indicate how the data should appear in the resulting document. To export a document from Excel, do the following:

1. From the menu bar, choose File | Save As.

2. In the Save File as Type list box, select the desired "export" format. This format can be for another spreadsheet, text, even a database!

3. Enter a name in the File Name text box and click OK.

4. Close the document.

8.47. How can I combine the contents of two cells into one cell?

You can use the CONCATENATE() function. If cell A1 contains "Mary" and cell A2 contains "Smith", for example, you can display the text "Mary Smith" by entering the following formula in cell A3:

```
=CONCATENATE(A1," ",A2)
```

If you want to enter text into the cell, whether to separate words or to form complete sentences, the text must be surrounded by quotes. The example shows cell A1 followed by a space (in quotes) followed by the contents of cell A2. Note that this function is new to Excel 5.0; if you're using an earlier version of Excel, you cannot use this function.

8.48. I want to print a specific area of my Excel worksheet. How can I specify what to print?

To print a certain area of the worksheet, simply highlight with your mouse the cells or area you want to print and then click the Printer button on the Toolbar.

8.49. Excel adds decimal points to all my numbers, even though I haven't entered them. Why is this happening?

You can cure this problem by turning off Excel's Fixed Decimal option. Use these steps:

1. Choose Tools | Options.
2. Click the Edit tab.
3. Click the Fixed Decimal check box to remove the x from it.
4. Click OK.

8.50. How can I easily print the formulas used in Excel spreadsheets?

To use the easiest method of printing formulas, follow these steps:

1. Choose the Tools | Options command.
2. Click the View tab and select the Formulas check box. This action displays the formula text instead of the results. All the columns must be wide enough to display the formulas completely. To do this, click on the box at the intersection of your worksheet's row and column headings and choose Format | Column Auto Fit Selection.
3. Choose File | Page Setup, click the Sheet tab, and select the Row and Column Headings check box.
4. Print as you normally would.

8.51. When I enter a value with a slash (/) or a hyphen (-), it is formatted as a date. How can I prevent this?

Use the Text number format to tell Excel to display the hyphens or slashes that you enter in the cell as text. Follow these steps:

1. Select the cell or range of cells in which you want to enter the data.
2. From the menu bar, choose Format | Cells.

3. Click the Number tab.

4. In the Category area, choose the Text option; then click OK.

When you enter values in the chosen cells, they appear in the cell as you type them.

8.52. How can I tell Excel to open the same workbook each time I start the program?

Use Explorer or My Computer to move the workbook that you want to load on startup into the XLSTART folder inside the EXCEL folder. (If you're comfortable with DOS commands, you can accomplish the same thing by getting into a DOS window and copying the workbook file into the EXCEL\XLSTART subdirectory.)

8.53. How can I designate a default font for all my Excel spreadsheets?

To designate a default font for the Normal Style, follow these steps:

1. From the menu bar, choose Format | Style.

2. Click Modify, and in the Format Cells dialog box click the Font tab.

3. Choose the options you want in the Font, Font Style, and Size list boxes.

4. Click OK twice to return to the worksheet.

8.54. Can I protect most of an Excel worksheet, while leaving some cells editable?

Yes. To protect most of your worksheet, follow these steps:

1. If you already have protected the worksheet, choose Tools | Protection and select Unprotect Workbook or Unprotect Sheet; then click OK.

2. Select the cells you want to be able to edit.

3. Choose Format Cells.

4. Click the Protection tab.

5. Turn off the Locked check box in the dialog box that appears.

6. Click OK.

7. From the menu bar, choose Tools | Protection.

8. Choose Protect | Workbook or Protect | Sheet and click OK.

8.55. Where can I find a BBS or some other source of ready-to-run programs that I can use with Excel by downloading it or purchasing it?

One of the largest software libraries can be found on CompuServe. There you can find a vast amount of free and shareware templates, macros, and utilities in the Lotus and Microsoft Excel forums. You also may find a list of reputable mail-order distributors of shareware and freeware from the Association of Shareware Professionals. You can contact them at (616) 788-5131.

8.56. Why does Excel ignore page breaks I have added?

Turn off Excel's Fit To option (it overrides your manual page breaks). Use these steps:

1. From the menu bar, choose File | Page Setup.

2. Click the Page tab.

3. Click the Adjust To option button. Make sure it's set to 100%.

4. Click OK.

8.57. Is there a way to print more than one file at a time in Excel?

Certainly. You can select multiple files for printing from within Excel by performing these steps:

1. From the menu bar, choose File | Find File to open the Search dialog box. (If you've used the Find File feature previously, this will open the Find File dialog box instead. If so, go on to step 4.)

2. Click Search to open the Search dialog box.

3. Enter `*.XL*` in the File Name box and click Include Subdirectories (which are subfolders in Windows 95); then click OK.

4. When the worksheet files appear in the Find File dialog box, select the files that you want to print by pressing the Ctrl key while clicking on each desired file.

5. Click Commands; then choose Print.

6. Click OK.

8.58. How can I automatically adjust cell widths in Excel?

To automatically adjust cell widths to accommodate the longest entry you have, choose the columns or the entire worksheet. Then double-click the right border of the selected column's heading. If you want to adjust the height of the row automatically, choose the rows or the entire sheet, and double-click on the bottom border of any row's heading.

8.59. Is there a way to add currency symbols for foreign currencies in Excel?

Yes. You can add special characters for pound sterling, cents, or yen. Press and hold the Alt key while using the numeric key pad; type 156 for the British pound or 157 for the Japanese yen symbol. If you work with small numbers, type 155 for the cents sign.

If you want a specific currency setting throughout the entire worksheet, you can modify the regional settings to match your needs. For more information on changing regional settings, refer to Chapter 2, "Customizing the Desktop and the Taskbar."

Lotus 1-2-3 for Windows

Lotus 1-2-3 is another popular and powerful spreadsheet. This section looks at topics specific to Lotus 1-2-3 for Windows.

8.60. How can I load the same 1-2-3 spreadsheet on startup automatically?

You can do this by renaming it AUTO123.WK4. Then every time you start it, 1-2-3 will load that spreadsheet.

8.61. How can I convert formulas to values?

To convert formulas to values in a cell, press F2 to activate Edit mode. Press F9 (Calc) and then press Enter or click on the check mark to the left of the cell value.

8.62. Is there an easy way to align labels across columns?

To align text (a label) evenly over a range of cells, select a cell range and be sure the label to be aligned is in the first cell. Choose Style | Alignment and then click on the Across columns option.

8.63. How can I copy formats but not values into another cell?

Copy style settings such as colors, shading, borders, and fonts to the Clipboard by choosing Edit | Copy. Then click on the destination, choose Edit | PasteSpecial, click on the Styles Only option, and click OK.

8.64. Is there a simple way to delete files in 1-2-3?

Use 1-2-3's alphabetical file list to delete files. This list is familiar to DOS users. Use the list to delete files rather than using File Manager. Use 1-2-3 Classic menu commands File | Erase | Worksheet, highlight a file, and press Enter.

8.65. How can I tell 1-2-3 to always use a particular font for all new spreadsheets?

To use the current default font for more than just the current worksheet, choose Style | Worksheet Defaults, and click Make Default.

Novell Quattro Pro for Windows

Users who require powerful data analysis features and presentation graphics in a single package will be pleased with Novell Quattro Pro for Windows. Similar features are available in Borland Quattro Pro for Windows.

8.66. I just installed Quattro Pro, and when I try to load the program, I see the message *Insufficient memory to run this application.* I have plenty of memory and system resources. What's wrong?

Due to reasons a bit too technical to go into here, you can get this message due to a hard disk that's almost full and heavily fragmented. During the installation process, if files critical to Quattro Pro's operation are installed on fragmented sectors of the hard disk, they can be corrupted, and the message you see results. Delete all the files from the folder where you installed Quattro Pro, and use the disk defragmenter in Windows to defragment your hard disk. Then repeat the installation process.

8.67. When printing multiple copies to my HP DeskJet 500C and 550C, I get only one copy, regardless of the number of copies I specify. What's wrong?

This problem is due to an incompatibility between Quattro Pro for Windows and some Windows drivers for the HP DeskJet printers. No matter how many copies you choose in the Print dialog box, you get only one copy from the printer. You can work around this problem by changing printer drivers and using the driver from the original HP DeskJet. (However, this driver doesn't support color, so you lose the capability to print in color if you switch to this driver.) If you need the color capability, another workaround is to create a macro that repeats the {Print.DoPrint} command to produce more than one copy with a single command in Quattro Pro. The macro would look like this:

```
C1: {GETNUMBER "Number of copies? ",A1}
C2: {FOR A2,1,A1,1,C4}
C4: {Print.DoPrint}
```

(This macro assumes that the Page Setup, Printer Setup, and Print blocks have been defined correctly.)

8.68. How do I enter a date or time value into a cell?

To enter a date in Quattro Pro, hold down the Ctrl and Shift keys and press D. Then enter the date or time.

8.69. I want to enter date values for the 21st century. When I enter a date value like 2/12/05 (for 2/12/2005), Quattro Pro stores February 12, 1905. What's going on?

Quattro Pro bases the century it stores on the system date within your PC's clock. Therefore, if you enter the date 2/12/05 and today's date is 03/24/1995, you get the date 02/12/1905. If your computer's clock is set to a date greater than 01/01/2000, then you get dates with years in the 21st century. If you need to perform data entry for a number of dates in the 21st century, use the Date/Time icon within the Windows Control Panel to change your PC's system date to any date in the 21st century. Then perform the data entry and change your system clock back when you're done.

8.70. How can I include page numbers or dates on a printed page in Quattro Pro?

You can include special codes within the page headers or page footers to produce page numbers or dates. The codes you can include are shown in Table 8.2.

Table 8.2. Page header and footer codes.

Code	Action
#	Enters current page number
@	Enters current date
#d	Enters current date in Short International format (MM/DD)
#D	Enters current date in Long International format (MM/DD/YY)
#ds	Enters current date in Std Short Date format (DD-MM)
#T	Enters current time in Long International format (HH:MM:SS)
#ts	Enters current time in Std Short Time format (HH:MM AM/PM)
#Ts	Enters current time in Std Long Time format (HH:MM:SS AM/PM)
#p	Enters the current page number
#P	Enters the total number of pages in the printout

8.71. How can I automatically adjust cell widths in Quattro Pro?

To set a column width exactly to hold the text or values, click on the AutoFit button in the toolbar. To add extra space at the end of a column, so that text from one column is not flush against text in the next column, select the Auto Width option of the Property Inspector's Column Width property. Specify the amount of extra space to be added to the longest entry in a column.

8.72. How do I export ASCII text files from Quattro Pro?

To export a text file, select the page with the text to be exported. Then choose File | Save As and name the file with a TXT extension. (Alternately, you can use the Notebook | Extract command to export a selected block as ASCII text.)

Databases

Databases in general have become simpler to use and much more powerful. Most companies depend on these databases for their survival and can't afford problems or "quirks" that negatively affect their productivity. This section discusses many of the common issues surrounding Windows databases.

Microsoft Access

A relative newcomer to the database arena, Access has become one of the most widely used applications, particularly among "power users." Here are many of the common topics encountered when running Access under Windows.

8.73. I have a 386 with 4M of RAM, and Access runs slowly. If I upgrade my processor chip or add a math coprocessor, will I see a significant boost in speed?

A math coprocessor will have virtually no effect, except on some numerical report and query calculations, because the operations done by Access in handling your database needs aren't math-intensive. Although a faster CPU contributes to better Access performance, the best thing you can do is increase your PC's memory to a minimum of 8M. Although Microsoft specifies that Access will run with 4M, it doesn't run very well. Access runs significantly better with 8M than with 4M, and if you plan on multitasking with other major Windows applications, 16M is a good idea.

8.74. When I try to start Access, I get a message saying *General Protection Fault.* What's wrong?

Usually, this problem stems from incompatible or incomplete video drivers. Try changing Windows back to the standard VGA video driver. If the problem disappears, contact the vendor of your video card for the latest drivers. Video drivers for Diamond Stealth video cards are known for having these kind of incompatibilities with Access.

I

8.75. How can I get a list of all the objects in my database?

You can use a feature of Access called the Database Documentor to perform this task. Follow these steps:

1. Open the database. Then from the menu bar, choose File | Add-Ins.

2. From the submenu that appears, choose Database Documentor.

3. After the Database Documentor dialog box appears, click the Object Type list box and choose All Object Types from the list.

4. Click Select All; then click OK.

The Database Documentor examines all objects in the database and produces an Object Definition report showing details of all the objects. You can choose File | Print, or click the Print icon on the toolbar, to print this listing. Note that the process may take some time, particularly with databases that contain a large number of objects.

8.76. Suddenly all my databases have extra tables with names that begin with "Msys" and "USys." Why are these here, and how can I delete them?

These are the system tables, and you don't want to delete them, because Access needs these tables to operate. You can hide them by choosing View | Options from the menu bar, choosing the General category, and setting Show System Objects to No.

8.77. How do I copy all the information from the preceding record on a form to a new record?

When you find the record you want to copy, follow these steps:

1. From the menu bar, choose Edit | Select Record.

2. Copy the record to the clipboard by choosing Edit | Copy, or simply clicking the Copy button on the Toolbar.

3. Press Ctrl+*plus* (the + key) to insert a new record.

4. Again, choose Edit | Select Record from the menu bar.

5. Paste the data into the new record by choosing Edit | Paste, or simply clicking the Copy button on the Toolbar.

8.78. Can text stored in a memo field be formatted with different fonts or attributes like boldface or underlining?

You can format text stored in a memo field, but you can use only one style for all the text within the field; you cannot mix different formatting attributes (like bold or underline) in the same field. If you need this kind of formatting, you should consider storing the data as OLE objects, and inserting formatted text written in Microsoft Word (or any word processor that supports OLE) in the text fields of the table.

8.79. How can I quickly create a simple form for use with a table?

Open the Database window and click a table or query to select it. Then click the AutoForm button on the toolbar. Access builds a default form for the chosen table or query.

8.80. Why do I get a #NAME? error for a calculated control on a form or a report?

You may be attempting to use the same name for a calculated text box as a name that already exists within the expression. As an example, consider the following expression:

```
=[City]&", "&[State]&" "&[ZIP]
```

If you attempt to use this expression within a control that is called City, State, or ZIP, you get a #Name? error. This happens because the use of the control name within the control's expression creates a circular reference. You can solve this problem by changing the name of the control that contains the expression to anything other than the name of the control.

8.81. How can I view my data in sorted order?

By default, Access displays data in the order of the primary key (unless there is none, in which case data is displayed according to *natural order*, or the order in which it was entered). To view your data in a different order, click the Sort Ascending or Sort Descending button on the toolbar. Or open the Records menu, choose Quick Sort, and choose either Ascending or Descending.

8.82. How can I create calculated fields in a table?

You can't, but you can add them to a query. Because Access queries are updatable, this technique accomplishes the same result. Design a query that contains all the fields of the desired table, and then add a calculated field to the query. (Open the query in Design mode and enter the expression for the calculation in the Field row of the Query grid.)

8.83. How can I quickly create a simple report?

Open the Database window and click a table or query to select it. Then click the AutoReport button on the toolbar. Access builds a default report for the chosen table or query.

8.84. How do I print reports to a file?

Open the report in Preview mode, and choose File | Output To from the menu bar. In the dialog box that appears, you can choose whether to send the report's output as text, rich-text format (RTF files, compatible with Microsoft Word), or Microsoft Excel (XLS) files. Note that there are limitations to this; any graphics items in the report are not included in the output, and subreports are not included in the output.

8.85. Why do I get extra blank pages between each page of my report?

The common cause of this problem is a report containing a design surface that extends beyond the size of the printed page. To correct this problem, open the report in Design mode and pull in the right margin as far as possible to the left and the bottom margin as far as possible to the top. If the design surface is as small as possible and you still get the extra blank page, check the File | Print Setup menu option and make sure that the margins are correct for the paper size you are using.

8.86. My PC has plenty of memory installed, but I keep getting *Out of memory* errors with my Access reports. Why is this happening?

To understand why this occurs, it helps first to understand how reports are handled internally by Access. Reports use a query, combined with an underlying data source, for each section of the report. Hence, the report header is based on a query, the page header is based on a query, the group header is based on a query, the detail section is based on a query, and so on.

When the report runs, all these queries are combined into a *segmented virtual table.* The way that Access is designed, the final output or SQL string based on this virtual table must compile and run within a 64K limit. If your report runs up against this limit, an Out of memory error occurs.

You can do several things to avoid this error:

- Use table names, column names, and control names that are as short as possible.

- Minimize the use of expressions within the underlying queries that are used by the reports.

- Avoid stacking your queries (don't base a report on a query that is based on another query, that is based on a table, for example). If a particular report that is based on a select query produces an Out of memory error, try turning your select query into a make-table query and basing the report on the resulting table instead.

8.87. I've attached some SQL tables, but they appear as read-only. Why can't I get write privileges?

If the attached tables reside on SQL servers, they are read-only whenever the tables don't have unique indexes. Access allows updates to attached tables only when the tables have unique indexes. For the same reason, Access does not allow updates to Paradox tables when the Paradox tables lack primary keys. (Finally, don't overlook the possibility that the attached table has been marked as read-only by the network operating system software.)

8.88. How can I prevent an AutoExec macro from running when I open a database?

Hold down the Shift key as you open the database.

8.89. How can I dial a modem from Access?

You can go into Form Design mode and use the Button Wizard to add a button with autodialer capability. Use these steps:

1. Open a form in Design mode where you want to add a Dial button, and display the toolbox by choosing View/Toolbox.

2. In the Toolbox, click the Control Wizards icon to turn on the Control Wizards.

3. In the Toolbox, click the Command Button icon, and then click in the form where you want to place the button.

4. When the Command Button Wizard dialog box appears, click Miscellaneous in the Categories list; then click Autodialer. Click Next to continue.

5. Follow the remaining instructions presented by the Wizard to finish adding the button, and save the form in the usual manner.

If you're curious about the program code needed to perform this task, you can examine the code that the Wizard attaches to the button. (Right-click the button and choose Build Event from the context menu to look at the resulting program code added by the Wizard.)

8.90. Why does Access place the words *Option Compare Database* at the top of every module I create?

The words Option Compare Database tell Access to use its standard order when sorting data, which is the same default order that Access uses in queries. Many experienced Access programmers suggest that you add a single line containing the words Option Explicit directly after this line. This forces you to declare all your variables, which can reduce code errors due to typos.

8.91. We're using Access on a large local area network, and the more users connected to the database, the longer it takes to open the database. (During peak afternoon times, it can take more than a minute for a user to get into the database!) Is there any way to reduce these delays we're seeing?

The delay that you are seeing is actually in the time Access takes to make the connection to the SYSTEM.MDA file, and not in connecting to the database itself. The solution to this problem is to place a copy of SYSTEM.MDA on each user's machine, and point Access to that. You will eliminate the locking contentions you are having for the system files, and all users will gain fast access to the database.

8.92. I'm developing an application in Access, and I've read that I should store my data in one database and the rest of the objects (forms, reports, queries, macros, and code) in another database. Why should I do this, and how do I do it?

Access developers routinely split the designs of an application into two databases, with all the data residing in one database and all other objects stored in the other database. The advantage to this scheme is that it becomes much easier to update your application;

simply replace the CODE database while leaving the DATA database intact. To do this, first build and thoroughly test and debug your application as a single database. When the application is debugged completely, create another database, and copy the tables to the new (DATA) database. Then delete the tables within the CODE database, and from within the CODE database, attach to the tables in the DATA database.

Microsoft FoxPro for Windows

Primarily a developer's tool, Microsoft FoxPro for Windows pleases others with its speed of execution and flexibility. The user can extend FoxPro's features by using its programming language.

8.93. I thought FoxPro was a multiuser program right out of the box, so why am I getting a *File is in use* message when somebody tries to use the same file on a network?

FoxPro is multiuser, out-of-the-box program. However, EXCLU-SIVE is ON by default. In the Command window, enter SET EXCLUSIVE OFF to open the files in Shared mode.

8.94. I get a *Not enough disk space* error message when I try to use my application written in FoxPro on our Novell network. I have more than 200M of disk space available!

More than likely, one or more of the files your application uses has been flagged with the N/A parameter. Use the Novell NDIR command to view the ownership rights. (Consult your Novell documentation for details on how you can give these files valid ownerships.)

8.95. I'm using a laptop with no mouse or trackball attached. How can I design screens with the Screen Builder without using a pointing device?

You can't. The way FoxPro is designed, you must have some sort of pointing device attached to successfully use the Screen Builder.

8.96. How can I quickly create a simple form for use with a table?

From the menu bar, choose File | Catalog Manager. When the Catalog Manager appears, click the Screen button, and then click New. In the Create Screen dialog box, choose a table or query, and then click the Screen Wizards button. Follow the directions that appear in the Screen Wizards dialog boxes; in the last dialog box that appears, click the Save and Run Screen option, and then click Finish.

8.97. I have designed a screen with a large number of fields, and I want to change the tab order with which the insertion pointer moves through the fields. How can I do this?

Open the screen in Design mode, and choose Screen/Object Order from the Screen Builder menu to open the Object Order dialog box. To change the tab order for the objects, click the button to the left of each object, and drag the object to its new order. (The object at the top of the list is accessed first, the object below it is accessed next, and so on.) When done, rebuild the application so that the new tab order is included.

8.98. Why don't the @...SAY program commands work to display the contents of my general fields in a screen?

General fields contain OLE objects, which cannot be displayed using @...SAY commands. Use the Picture tool instead to place a picture object in the screen's design.

8.99. How can I quickly create a simple report?

From the menu bar, choose File | Catalog Manager. When the Catalog Manager appears, click a table or query to select it, and then click the AutoReport button on the toolbar. FoxPro builds a default report for the chosen table or query.

8.100. Must I convert my FoxPro for DOS reports before I can use them in FoxPro for Windows?

This isn't necessary. FoxPro for Windows has the FoxPro/DOS Report Engine built into its code, so that it can process and run reports created in the DOS version of FoxPro with no changes. If you want to modify the reports so that you can include graphic elements of Windows or add other features, you must convert the reports to FoxPro for Windows report format.

8.101. I created a report using the Quick Report option. Now I want to add another field to the report. Under FoxPro for DOS, I used the Field option of the Report menu to add new fields, but there is no such option in FoxPro for Windows. How can I add another field?

In FoxPro for Windows, you use the Field tool located in the toolbox (the toolbox is at the left edge of the Design window) to add a field to an existing report. Follow these steps:

1. Open the report in Design mode, and then click the Field tool in the toolbox (the third icon from the top).

2. Click in the report's design where you want to place the field, and in the dialog box that appears, click the Expression button.

3. After the Expression Builder appears, click the field you want in the Fields list box.

4. Click OK twice to add the field, and size the field as desired.

8.102. How can I design multicolumn reports in FoxPro's Report Writer?

Open the Report menu and choose Page Layout. In the dialog box that appears, use the Columns spinner to choose the desired number of columns. FoxPro automatically modifies the size of the Report Layout window to reflect the new widths of the columns.

8.103. I have a memo field included in my report. Only the first line prints. What's wrong?

You must turn on the Stretch Vertically property of the field before it will expand during the reporting process to show the additional data. Open the report in Design mode and double-click the field. Then choose the Top - Field Can Stretch option from the Position Relative To item. This option enables the field to grow in size, proportional to the length of the contents of the memo field.

8.104. While designing a report, I am trying to move a text object to a precise location, and it keeps aligning itself with the grid. How can I prevent this from happening?

FoxPro aligns objects that you place in a report with the grid by default. To prevent this from happening, open the Report menu, and choose Snap to Grid to turn off the option.

8.105. I have a report with a one-to-many relationship database set up. But only one record for the child database shows up for one parent record. What is going on?

Make sure that the one-to-many relationship is set up correctly. You can do this by entering the SET SKIP TO *child database* command while you are in the parent database work area.

8.106. I am looking at my report and some of the numeric fields are appearing with **** instead of the actual value. What's up?

If there is not enough space for the numeric value to appear, FoxPro places **** in the field instead of the actual value. You can avoid this problem by resizing the field so that the numeric value can fit.

8.107. I am trying to print from FoxPro, but it only prints after I quit FoxPro.

After you print something from FoxPro, the information is sent over the printer queue in Windows. To release this job while inside FoxPro, issue the SET PRINTER TO command in the Command window.

8.108. When I try to start FoxPro, I get a *General Protection Fault* error message. What's wrong?

You can experience this problem in FoxPro due to incompatible or incomplete video drivers. Try changing Windows back to the standard VGA video driver. If the problem disappears, contact the vendor of your video card for the latest drivers. Video drivers for the ATI Ultra Graphics, Mach32, Genoa 7900, SpeedStar 24x, and TIGA (in 1024×768 mode) video cards are known for having these kind of incompatibilities with FoxPro. Also, the video driver hardware built into the motherboards of some computers has been known to cause this problem, particularly in modes other than standard VGA.

Borland dBASE for Windows

Perhaps the longest surviving database, dBASE gives you all the traditional tools and power a developer needs. The dBASE programming language has been enhanced with many Windows-oriented commands. Here are many of the common topics encountered when running dBASE for Windows.

8.109. I want dBASE for Windows to go to my data files in my C:\DBASEWIN\PROJECT folder each time I start the program. How do I do that?

Go into the Navigator, and change the current directory to the folder that you want to use. Then exit completely from dBASE. After you exit the program, dBASE writes the current directory setting from the Navigator into the DBASEWIN.INI file that's read on startup of the program.

8.110. How can I quickly create a simple form for use with a table?

Open the desired table in a window. Then, click the Quick Form button on the SpeedBar.

8.111. How can I prevent the Form Expert dialog box from appearing every time I create a new form?

You can disable the Form Expert by performing these steps:

1. Create a new form.
2. Choose Properties | Form Designer from the menu to open the Form Designer Properties dialog box.
3. In the Form Expert box, turn off the Invoke for New Forms option.
4. Click OK to save the changes.

The next time you create a form, dBASE will not bring up the Form Expert dialog box.

8.112. How can you change a field heading in the Browse window without modifying the field name in the table structure?

Access the Browse Window, and perform the following steps:

1. Choose Properties | Table Records Window to display the Table Records Properties dialog box.

2. Highlight the field with the heading you want to change, and then click the Properties push button.

3. In the Options box, type the heading that you prefer in the Heading field.

4. Click OK to save the changes. Then click OK again to close the dialog box.

Your new heading name now appears in the Browse window.

8.113. How can I quickly create a simple report?

Version 5.0 of dBASE for Windows doesn't offer an easy way to create a quick report from any menus or the SpeedBar, due to its reliance on a separate program (Crystal Reports) as a means of report design. You can enter dBASE commands in the Command window to produce a basic listing, however. Use the format

```
LIST name1, name2, name3,...nameX TO PRINT
```

where *name1* through *nameX* represent the names of your fields. Given a table with fields named LASTNAME, FIRSTNAME, and PHONE, you could enter the following command in the Command window to produce a simple listing:

```
LIST LASTNAME, FIRSTNAME, PHONE TO PRINT
```

Borland's Paradox for Windows

Another widely used database, particularly rich with programming tools, Paradox for Windows is a robust database system. Here are many of the common topics encountered when running Paradox under Windows.

8.114. How can I put my data in sorted order?

Open a table, and from the Table menu choose Sort. In the dialog box that appears, click the field that should serve as the primary sort field, and then click the right-pointing arrow to add the selected field to the Sort Order list box. Use the same technique to add any other fields you want included as the basis of the sort, and click OK to reorder the records.

8.115. How can I quickly create a simple report?

Make the window that contains the desired table the active table, and then click the Quick Report icon on the SpeedBar (or press Shift+F7).

8.116. What is an easy way to move tables in Paradox?

Instead of using Tools | Utilities | Copy and
Tools | Utilities | Delete to move a table, you can use
Tools | Utilities | Rename from the menu. Select a table from the Rename dialog box, click in the To text box, and type the full path and name for the new table. The benefit to *moving*, rather than *copying* and then *deleting*, is that it takes less time to rename a table to a different location than performing the copy and delete steps. This process moves the Paradox table to its new folder.

8.117. Why do I get a *Locked Record* message when I have several windows open in Paradox?

You probably have more than one window open for the same table or form. You should check the windows you have open by selecting Window from the toolbar and seeing the list of windows open. If there are any duplicate windows, you can fix the problem simply by closing the duplicate window.

9

Running DOS Applications Under Windows

This chapter covers the use of DOS applications under Windows 95. Included in the chapter are topics to help you customize the behavior of your DOS applications under Windows, modify the appearance of DOS programs within Windows, and fully utilize the features of Windows that are designed to help DOS applications better coexist with Windows applications.

9.1. According to what I read, Windows 95 is a complete operating system, eliminating DOS. Can I still safely run my DOS applications?

Although it's true that Windows 95 replaces the use of DOS and Windows 3.x combined, support for your old DOS favorites (including device drivers and TSRs) doesn't go away. Windows 95 actually offers more robust support for the running of DOS applications than Windows 3.x was ever able to manage. Like its predecessors, Windows 95 lets you launch and run DOS applications inside what are known as *virtual machines*. The functionality that you get with Windows 95 is equivalent to the functionality you get when running DOS applications under MS-DOS 6.*x.* The design of Windows 95 also provides some notable improvements in how your DOS applications behave, including the following:

■ Protected-mode portions of your DOS applications use no conventional memory.

■ Compatibility for running DOS applications is improved.

■ DOS games get better support (including, in many cases, the capability to run in a window).

■ DOS applications that you previously had to run by completely exiting Windows can now be run from Windows.

■ Properties for DOS applications can be customized from a single location, rather than through a collection of .PIF and .BAT files.

■ DOS applications running in a window offer a Toolbar, which can be used for quick access to common tasks.

■ Using TrueType fonts, windows containing DOS applications are now user-scalable.

9.2. What different ways are there to run a DOS program under Windows?

You can use any of the following methods to launch a DOS application:

■ Find the DOS program in Explorer or in My Computer, and double-click its icon (or right-click the icon and choose Open from the popup menu).

■ Open the Start menu and choose Run. In the dialog box that appears, enter the program name (including its folder path), or click the Browse button to locate the program; then, click the program to select it, click Open, and click OK.

■ Open the Start menu, and choose Programs|MS-DOS Prompt. When the DOS prompt appears, run the application as you would from DOS.

9.3. Can I easily switch DOS applications between running in a window and running full-screen?

Pressing Alt+Enter switches a DOS application between running within a window and running full-screen. Keep in mind that some DOS applications, due to their design, will not run in a window. Also note that a DOS application that's running full-screen uses less memory and system resources than one that's running in a window.

9.4. In Windows 3.x, my DOS applications appeared in a full screen (unless I set them to run in a window, using the old PIF Editor). In Windows 95, my DOS applications run in a window by default (see Figure 9.1). I prefer to see them full-screen. Is there any way to change this default behavior?

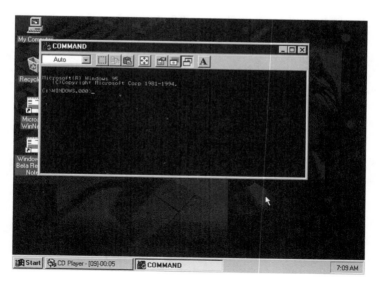

Figure 9.1. *DOS application running within a window.*

Windows 95 does differ from Windows 3.*x* in that the default behavior is to run the application windowed, similar to the example shown in Figure 9.1. You can determine whether an application should start windowed or full-screen. Perform the following steps to set the default window size of a DOS application:

1. In My Computer or Explorer, find the DOS application.
2. Right-click the application's icon, and choose Properties from the popup menu that appears.
3. In the Properties window, click the Screen tab.
4. Under Screen Usage, click Full-screen.
5. Click OK.

9.5. How do I get to a DOS prompt in Windows 95?

Open the Start menu, and click Programs. In the Programs menu, choose MS-DOS Prompt. After the DOS prompt appears, you can use the Alt+Enter key combination to switch between running DOS in a window or as a full-screen. When done with your work in DOS, type EXIT and press Enter to return to Windows.

9.6. I copied a DOS program from a floppy disk into a folder using Explorer. I can run it from Explorer or from My Computer, but I need to run it on a daily basis. Is there a faster way to launch the program?

You can create shortcuts to DOS applications, just as you can create shortcuts to Windows applications. Perform these steps to add a shortcut to the DOS application to your Desktop:

1. In My Computer or in Explorer, locate the icon or filename representing the DOS application.
2. Right-click the icon or filename, and choose Create Shortcut from the popup menu that appears.
3. When the icon for the shortcut appears in My Computer or in Explorer, click it and drag it onto the Desktop.

From this point on, you can double-click the icon on the Desktop to launch the DOS application.

9.7. I need to do some low-level hardware maintenance, and I prefer to do it with nothing other than DOS running. Is there a way to tell Windows not to load, or must I boot from a floppy disk?

You can bypass Windows and load just a core version of MS-DOS in its place. Turn on or reboot the system, and when the message Starting Windows appears on the screen, immediately press the F4 key. MS-DOS will be loaded, leaving you at a DOS prompt.

9.8. How can I assign a new icon to my DOS application?

Use these steps to change the default icon for an application:

1. In My Computer or Explorer, find the DOS application.
2. Right-click the application's icon and choose Properties from the popup menu that appears.
3. In the Properties window, click the Programs tab.
4. Click the Change Icon button.
5. Choose a new icon in the dialog box that appears and then click OK twice.

9.9. I have a batch file that I run prior to running a DOS application. (The batch file sets some environmental parameters that should be set before the program runs.) Is there some way to easily run the batch file, and then load the program?

You can specify that a batch file must be run before a particular DOS application runs; you make this determination through the Environment properties for the application. Use the following steps:

1. In My Computer or Explorer, find the DOS application.
2. Right-click the application's icon, and choose Properties from the popup menu that appears.
3. In the Properties window, click the Program tab.

4. In the Batch File text box, enter the name of the desired batch file and click OK (or, click the Browse button, find the desired file in the list box that appears, and click OK twice).

The capability of Windows to assign batch files to DOS applications is similar to letting you have a separate AUTOEXEC.BAT file for each of your DOS applications. This avoids a significant disadvantage of the old AUTOEXEC.BAT file used with MS-DOS and earlier versions of Windows, which was that the environmental settings established by AUTOEXEC.BAT applied to every DOS application you launched under Windows, whether you wanted it to or not.

9.10. Each of my DOS applications specifies a minimum amount of conventional RAM needed for its operation. Because DOS applications were never designed to run simultaneously, can I safely load more DOS applications than can fit in my PC's conventional memory?

In Windows 95, you can load as many DOS applications as can fit in your machine's extended memory; you're not limited to conventional memory. Windows creates a separate virtual machine in a protected portion of memory for each DOS application that you load. Windows has the capability to swap significant portions of itself out of memory as you work with your DOS applications. This reduces the amount of memory needed for the operating system, freeing more memory for your DOS applications. However, because each DOS application must have its own dedicated virtual machine under Windows, you can run up against memory limits if you try to load a number of memory-intensive DOS applications. At some point, you'll try to load another DOS application, and you'll get an error indicating that there is insufficient memory to load the application.

9.11. I have a number of games that wouldn't run under Windows 3.x; I always had to exit completely to DOS to run any of these games. Is there a way to use these games under Windows 95?

Yes. (Finally! Hot games and Windows getting along.) See the next question.

9.12. What is *Single MS-DOS Application Mode,* and how can I use it?

Single MS-DOS Application Mode is a special mode of operation that exists under Windows 95, and permits the running of DOS applications that previously ran only under DOS and required virtually all system resources to operate. Some DOS applications (typically games) have a well-documented history of not getting along with prior versions of Windows. These applications usually require close to 100 percent of the CPU time, often write directly to video memory, and demonstrate an annoying habit of taking over hardware resources such as your CD-ROM drive or sound card.

To provide support for *intrusive* DOS applications of this nature, Windows 95 has the capability to place itself in a *holding pattern,* store its current state of operation to disk, and remove all but a tiny fraction of itself from memory as it turns over control of the operating system to the DOS application in question. After the DOS application exits, Windows reloads itself into memory and continues running. (Obviously, this design means that other Windows applications cannot remain running in the background while the DOS application runs.)

To run a DOS application in Single MS-DOS Application Mode, you turn on the Single MS-DOS Application Mode property from the Program tab in the properties for the application. When this property has been set, you can run the application at any time, using the usual methods for launching a DOS application. Perform these steps to set the property:

1. In My Computer or Explorer, find the DOS application.
2. Right-click the application's icon, and choose Properties from the popup menu that appears.
3. In the Properties window, click the Programs tab.
4. Turn on the Single MS-DOS Application Mode check box.
5. Click OK.

After you've set this property, whenever you run the DOS application, Windows will display a dialog box asking whether you want to end all tasks that are currently running. Click OK and Windows shuts down any existing applications, loads a real-mode copy of MS-DOS, and launches the chosen DOS application. This whole process is equivalent to exiting earlier versions of Windows, running the application under DOS, and then returning to Windows.

9.13. When I run a DOS application in a window, the window has a Toolbar. What's this for, and how can I use it?

The MS-DOS Application Toolbar (see Figure 9.2) is an addition to this version of Windows that provides you with quick access to commonly used operations when working with DOS programs. (If you don't see a Toolbar when you open a DOS application inside a window, press Alt+Spacebar to open the window's Control menu, and choose Toolbar.)

Figure 9.2. *MS-DOS Application Toolbar.*

You can use the Toolbar buttons to change the fonts and the font sizes used by the DOS application; to select, copy, and paste data into and out of the Windows Clipboard; to change from the windowed display to a full screen; to access the properties for the application; and to indicate whether the application should run exclusively (not yielding available CPU time to other applications) or in the background. The Toolbar has built-in ToolTips to explain the purpose of each button; hold the mouse pointer over any button for more than one second, and a ToolTip appears showing the button's purpose.

If you would rather not have the Toolbar taking up real estate on your screen, open the Control menu (press Alt+Spacebar or click the icon in the upper-left corner of the window) and choose Toolbar to turn the Toolbar off.

9.14. How can I force the Toolbar to always appear within a DOS application's window?

Use these steps to set the default presence (or absence) of the Toolbar:

1. In My Computer or Explorer, find the DOS application.
2. Right-click the application's icon, and choose Properties from the popup menu that appears.
3. In the Properties window, click the Screen tab.
4. Turn on or off the Display Toolbar option, as desired.
5. Click OK.

9.15. Can I cut and paste data using DOS applications?

Yes. An easy way to do this is to display the Toolbar (see the prior question), and use the Toolbar's Mark, Cut, and Paste buttons along with your mouse. For more specifics, see this topic under Chapter 6, "Exchanging Data between Applications."

9.16. How can I change the font sizes within a windowed DOS session?

If the Toolbar isn't visible, press Alt+Spacebar to open the Control menu, and choose Toolbar. Click the arrow at the right of the Font Size list box, to display the available fonts (see Figure 9.3). Choose the desired size from the list. Note that you can also click the font button at the right side of the Toolbar to open the Font tab of the Properties window and change the fonts from the list box contained within the window.

The fonts that are available will vary, depending on your installed video drivers and what TrueType fonts are available. You can use any screen fonts and any TrueType fonts that are on your system for the fonts used within a DOS application.

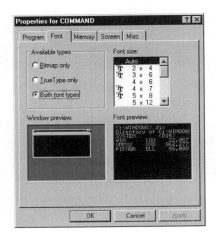

Figure 9.3. *List box of fonts.*

9.17. How can I safely terminate a crashed DOS application?

The famous (or infamous, depending on how you view it) three-finger salute still continues to work in this version of Windows, but it's been further refined to show you precisely which DOS applications are running, and to enable you to choose the one you want to shut down. Press Ctrl+Alt+Del simultaneously, and Windows will display the Close Program dialog box, shown in Figure 9.4.

Figure 9.4. *Close Program dialog box.*

Click the desired application in the list box, and then click End Task to close that specific application. (If you click Shut Down, Windows shuts down completely after asking for confirmation.)

9.18. Now that I'm running Windows, the PrtSc key no longer prints data from a screen in my DOS applications to the printer. How can I turn this key back on?

Actually, the PrtSc key is working, but it works differently under Windows. Pressing PrtSc causes an image of the entire screen to be copied to the Windows Clipboard. (Pressing Alt+PrtSc does the same trick, but just for the contents of the active window, and not for the entire screen.) To get a printout of the screen of a DOS application, paste the contents of the Clipboard into a word processing document within a Windows word processor (you can use WordPad), and print the document. You can do so by performing these steps:

1. When in the DOS application, press Alt+PrtSc.

2. Switch back to Windows and get to a blank document in your favorite word processor (or if you don't have one, open the Start menu and choose Programs|Accessories|WordPad).

3. From the menus, choose Edit|Paste.

4. Print the document, using the usual print commands (in WordPad, click the Print icon, or choose File|Print from the menus and click OK).

9.19. Are there any DOS commands or applications that I shouldn't run from within Windows?

Although this version of Windows is smart enough to recognize and halt most illegal operations attempted by DOS applications, there are still some DOS programs and commands that shouldn't be run from Windows. When you run a DOS application (or go to a DOS window), much of Windows remains in memory, and it keeps a number of files open. Any DOS programs that attempt to modify the basic file structure of the operating system can wreak havoc. Avoid any of the following types of commands or programs:

- DOS commands that attempt to perform any sort of reorganization on the hard disk, such as CHKDSK /F, FORMAT C:, and RECOVER. (Windows will intercept a CHKDSK /F command and refuse to process it, displaying an error message.)

- DOS-based disk optimization programs. These work by rearranging the physical layout of the files on your hard disk, arranging data in contiguous sectors so that overall data access improves. Popular programs that fall into this category include the optimization routines in PC Tools, the Norton Utilities, and SpeedDisk.

- File undelete utilities, which are often included in disk utility software packages.

- DOS-based backup programs. These programs, designed to backup your hard disk, often bypass the disk operating system and read and write files directly, using Direct Memory Access (DMA) channels of the hardware. Avoid this kind of software and use a Windows backup utility instead.

- Disk-cache programs. Attempting to use caching programs written to work with versions of DOS won't accomplish anything under Windows 95, because the operating system that is a part of Windows handles its own disk caching, using virtual drivers.

- Memory-resident programs (also called TSRs). These programs load into memory and are designed to be accessed with a *hot-key* combination. Most of these are actually stable under this version of Windows, but it still makes sense to avoid playing with fire. Some of the more ill-behaved TSRs can interfere with normal memory operation under Windows.

9.20. Windows 95 doesn't have a PIF Editor, as did earlier versions of Windows. How can I set specific values in PIF files to optimize how my DOS applications run?

In Windows 95, PIF files aren't used, so the PIF Editor is no longer necessary. In its place are customizable properties for each specific DOS application. You can change these properties for any DOS application by using these steps:

1. In My Computer or Explorer, find the DOS application.
2. Right-click the application's icon, and choose Properties from the popup menu that appears.

Figure 9.5 shows an example of a Properties window for a DOS application. In the example, the General tab of the Properties window is displayed.

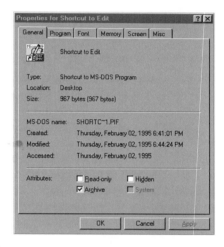

Figure 9.5. *General tab of the Properties window.*

The Properties window is divided into six categories, accessed using the tabs at the top of the window. These six tabs contain the different options that you can use to tightly control the behavior of your DOS applications running under Windows. Click on any of the tabs at the top of the window to display and modify the settings for that particular category. If you want detailed information on any of the options contained within any of the tabs, you can click the desired option to select it, and then press F1. A help screen explaining the purpose of that option then appears. Each tab's contents are explained in the following paragraphs.

General   This tab (shown above in Figure 9.5) shows the size and folder location of the application, along with its creation date. The only changeable attributes here are the Read-only, Archive, and Hidden properties, which you can turn on and off by clicking in the respective check boxes.

Program   This tab contains options for the program's title
           (as it appears in a folder or within Explorer), the
           command line entry used to start the program,
           the working directory (if any), and an optional
           shortcut key that can be used to start the
           program (see Figure 9.6). (To set the shortcut
           key, click in the Hot key text box, then press the
           key combination that you want to use as the
           shortcut.) You also can choose whether the
           window should close when you exit the DOS
           application, whether Windows programs should
           be allowed to be called by the DOS application,
           and whether the DOS application should run in
           a normal window, minimized, or maximized.
           From this tab, you can use the Advanced button
           to display an Advanced Program Settings dialog
           box; you can use the settings within this dialog
           box to choose whether to run the program in
           Single MS-DOS Application Mode (see Ques-
           tion 9.12, earlier in this chapter, for more
           details).

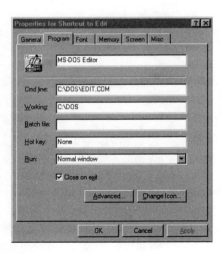

Figure 9.6. *Program tab of the Properties window.*

Font   This tab can be used to change the fonts that are
           used within a DOS application that runs inside a
           window (see Figure 9.7). The options in this tab

let you choose the types of fonts available for use by an application (bitmapped or TrueType), and the font size (selectable in the Font Size list box). As you select different font sizes, representations of both the overall window size and the appearance of the font appear in the Window preview and Font preview sections of the tab.

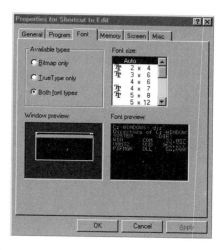

Figure 9.7. *Font tab of the Properties window for a DOS application.*

Memory   This tab contains the settings that relate to the use of memory (see Figure 9.8). The tab is divided into four portions: Conventional memory, Expanded (or EMS) memory, Extended (or XMS) memory, and DOS Protected Mode memory. Within each of the portions, you can choose specific amounts for each memory type. In the case of conventional memory, you can turn on the Protected check box, which tells Windows to protect system memory from inappropriate modifications to the memory by the application. In the case of extended memory, you can specify whether the DOS application should be allowed to use the HMA (high memory area).

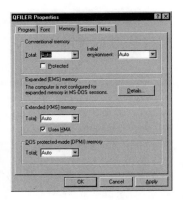

Figure 9.8. *Memory tab of the Properties window for a DOS application.*

Screen   This tab contains settings that affect the screen display of the application (see Figure 9.9). Under Usage, you can specify whether the application should run full-screen, in a window, or convert automatically. (If you click the Convert automatically option, the program runs in a window when in text mode, and automatically switches to full-screen when in graphics mode.) Click the Initial size list box to specify the initial number of screen lines for an application. (Note that DOS applications that reset the screen display to their own setting will override this setting.) Under Window, use the Display toolbar option to specify whether the MS-DOS Toolbar should be displayed when the program is running in a window, and use the Restore settings on startup option to restore all settings for the window (including its size, position, and font) when you start the program in a window. Under Performance, use the Fast ROM emulation option to specify whether the display driver should write to the screen faster by emulating video functions in ROM. Turn on the Dynamic memory allocation option if your DOS program uses several modes and you wish to maximize the amount of memory made available to other programs while this program runs.

Figure 9.9. *Screen tab of the Properties window for a DOS application.*

Misc This tab lets you change various options relating to foreground and background operation of DOS applications, mouse use in a DOS application, how the application terminates, and which hot-keys are allowed (see Figure 9.10). In the Foreground and Background portions of the window, you can turn on or off the options shown, in order to determine whether Windows handles tasks exclusively in the foreground, whether screen savers are allowed, and whether tasks in the background should always be suspended. Under Mouse, the QuickEdit option specifies whether the mouse should work exclusively with the application when it is running. The Exclusive mode option determines whether the mouse can be used to make selections within the application for cutting, copying, and pasting to other Windows applications. You can use the option under Termination to specify whether Windows should warn you before tasks are terminated by the operating system. You can also change the idle sensitivity, which specifies how much of the CPU resources should be made available to other applications while your chosen DOS application is waiting for keyboard input. Under Other, use the Fast pasting option to specify whether Windows can use a faster method of pasting data into the DOS program. (This option works with most DOS programs, but trial-and-error is the only way to find out.) Use the options under Windows hot keys to specify shortcut keys that should be reserved for use with Windows. (If you turn off the check box for any of these key sequences, Windows ignores that key sequence when you are using the DOS program.)

Figure 9.10. *Misc tab of the Properties window.*

9.21. How can I optimize the performance of the DOS applications that I run under Windows?

There are some overall steps you can take to improve the performance of your DOS applications. These steps are summarized in the following paragraphs:

- Shut down any applications you aren't using. This improves performance throughout Windows, especially with DOS applications, in which each application has to consume the equivalent of a virtual machine inside the Windows environment.

- Operate your DOS applications in full-screen mode whenever possible.

- If you use a large number of DOS applications and few Windows applications, change the Idle Sensitivity settings on the Tasking properties tab for the DOS applications you use regularly so that Windows applications will get less CPU time when they run in the background. (Be aware that this decreases the performance of your Windows applications when the DOS application is running.)

- Don't use the shell option of your DOS applications to get to a DOS prompt. Many DOS applications provide an option to let you "shell out" of the application to a DOS prompt in order to perform DOS tasks such as file management. But, using this option when the DOS application is running within Windows is a waste of memory and resources. Switch back to Windows and use the Programs option of the Start menu to get to a DOS prompt.

I

10

Windows and Multimedia

This chapter covers multimedia-related topics. Included in this chapter are details on how multimedia is used with Windows, the definition of the MPC-2 standard, installing CD-ROM drives and sound cards, the installation and maintenance of drivers, the use of multimedia applets such as Sound Recorder and Media Player, and common multimedia-related problems and solutions.

10.1. What is multimedia?

Multimedia is any technology that uses more than one sense to convey information. A common example is television, which is a one-way form of multimedia because it combines both visual and aural mediums to get a message across. PCs have not historically lent themselves to multimedia; until the advent of graphical user interfaces such as Windows and the Macintosh operating system, PCs were pretty much limited to text as a way of getting information across. The graphical user interfaces did much to incorporate visuals, but PCs nevertheless remained a single-media environment.

With the addition of sound to a PC's existing capabilities, the PC can communicate using more than just the visual sense; hence, the PC becomes a multimedia device. In addition to the inclusion of sound capabilities, the increased use of video and the complexity of the software needed to implement multimedia has resulted in the need for massive amounts of data storage. This is why the CD-ROM drive is fast becoming a standard part of any true multimedia implementation.

10.2. What do I need to build a multimedia-ready system?

Multimedia data types are unlike other data types handled by Windows. The demands of handling multimedia data place special requirements on the operating system, the PC, and the attached peripherals. Therefore, the hardware needs to be up to the demands of handling multimedia. If you want to build a multimedia-ready system and take advantage of some of the multimedia software currently available, you need at least the following in the way of hardware:

- A Windows PC of reasonable power
- A sound card and speakers
- A VGA board and display capable of 256-color graphics

As mentioned, a CD-ROM drive is not technically a requirement to implement multimedia, but it is a virtual necessity due to the amount of multimedia software that is published in CD-ROM format.

10.3. What is the MPC-2 standard?

The multimedia PC marketing council sets the standards for the minimum hardware for multimedia systems. The beginning standards set by the council were a bit modest: a 386 PC with 150K per second CD-ROM drive and 8-bit video board. You can still use these specifications for a large share of the multimedia titles, but interest has increasingly gone to motion video. As a result, the introduction of a new advanced standard was implemented, the MPC level 2. Before, any manufacturer who thought its product met the original specification could place the MPC logo on its products. But, a manufacturer that stamps the MPC level 2 trademark on its products has proven to the council that it has met or exceeded the minimum specs of the MPC level 2 (not to mention paying a fee for the privilege of using the MPC logo).

The following are the level 2 specifications:

- 25MHz 486SX-based PC
- 4M RAM
- CD-ROM drive with a 300K per second transfer rate (commonly known as a double-speed drive), plus an XA and multisession capability
- 160M hard drive
- Sound card featuring 16-bit sampling
- Video board with 16-bit (6500 colors) color capability

These specifications were chosen because video is the most hardware-intensive and least-developed part of Windows multimedia. It was decided that an advanced multimedia computer should be able to display digitized video in a 320-pixel by 240-pixel window at 15 frames per second. This is a quarter-screen window and half the broadcast rate of 30 frames per second, which makes the motion somewhat jerky. The council decided on these specifications because if it had chosen to go with what was necessary to run 30 frames per second, too big a market would have been unfit for motion-video multimedia applications.

If you currently don't have a PC that meets MPC specifications, you still can enjoy some of the multimedia applications as long as your PC meets the specifications listed under question 10.2. But, remember the MPC specifications when you go to purchase any multimedia components that you don't have, and when you want to upgrade your PC. If you want to get into the motion picture aspect of multimedia, you should have MPC-2 hardware minimums or better.

In this time of rapidly improving hardware, the council's level 2 minimums for multimedia systems are a long way from being the best you can purchase. For example, the 486DX system offers more processing power for multimedia than does the SX mandated by the council, and the price difference is not very much. For the kinds of demands imposed by video, a Pentium-based system is not an unreasonable expectation.

Aside from the processor, there are four areas (money permitting) in which you should consider exceeding the MPC level 2 minimums:

RAM   The more RAM that you have, the faster your multimedia applications will run. This is because extra RAM permits more programs and data to run from fast memory, instead of being recalled from disk. More RAM also allows the allocation of some RAM to speed up the CD-ROM. Eight megabytes should be considered an acceptable amount, and 12M to 16M is a good idea in this area.

Video   For your video board, a 16-bit or 24-bit graphics accelerator is good to have. These perform the screen redraws with much more speed than the unaccelerated video board. Redraws are very essential for running smooth video.

Hard Disk If you limit multimedia activity to canned CD-ROM applications, 200M may be sufficient. But, when you begin to store multimedia files, you'll find that they take up an enormous amount of disk space. One minute of video can take up to 10M of disk space. There are ways to compress the files, but if you wish to engage in these types of multimedia activities, you need 500M or more of disk space.

Speakers   This aspect of multimedia is not mentioned in the MPC specifications, but you may want to purchase a pair of shielded speakers to listen to your sounds. These types of speakers can be bought for about $50.

> **TIP** Some speakers are magnetically shielded, so as to not interfere with the monitor. (The larger the speaker, the larger the chance that the speaker's magnet would interfere with the monitor.) If the speakers that you buy are not magnetically shielded, you may have to place them at a greater distance from the monitor.

10.4. What is a sound card?

A sound card is an add-in expansion board that makes it possible for a computer to produce quality sound via external speakers. Sound cards also provide an output interface for many types of media such as CD-ROM drives, direct voice recordings, or recordings from other external sources. Sound cards can also support Musical Instrument Digital Interface (MIDI). Many sound cards contain ports where electronic musical instruments can be connected, which allows communication between musical instruments and the computer.

There are two basic kinds of sound cards that are currently available: monophonic and stereophonic (some of these cards have MIDI capabilities and some don't). The basic difference between the two types of boards is in sampling capacity. Sampling is the board's process of converting analog sound signals into a digital format that can be understood by the computer.

The sound card sets the sampling rate for sounds that it records. This is done via the analog-to-digital converter (ADC). The ADC converts the analog audio from a microphone into a digital form that can be stored by the computer in RAM or saved to a hard disk. The sound card also has to change the digital signals back to analog signals that match the original sound. This is done by a digital-to-analog converter (DAC). This is where the sampling rate becomes important. The quality of the sound is directly dependent on the rate at which the card samples a sound, and the size of the sample. The sampling rate is measured in kilohertz and the sampling size in bits.

There are three standard rates of sampling available to you: 11.025KHz, 32.05KHz, and 44.1KHz. There are also three sampling sizes available: 8-, 12-, and 16-bit.

Monophonic cards are the least expensive of the cards, and are also the least capable. They only produce sound from a single source. If you just want speakers for games, voice annotation, or entertainment, these cards will be fine for you. However, if you wish to have higher sound quality and editing, you will need to go with a more expensive sound card.

Stereophonic cards, unlike monophonic, have the capability to produce many sounds at once, and do so from different sources. These cards also have more voices, which allows them to better reproduce the MIDI files. Because sampling in stereo mode doubles the size of the sound file, you'll find that most stereo cards come with a mono mode switch.

In choosing a sound card, it makes sense to look for the following: full compliance with the MPC-2 standard (16-bit stereo sound, with a sampling rate of 44.1KHz or better); compatibility with the Sound Blaster standard; wave-table lookup capability, which is better than the less-expensive FM synthesis method of sound reproduction; and the inclusion of a CD-ROM disk controller, which can spare you the expense of buying a separate controller for your CD-ROM drive.

10.5. How do I install a CD-ROM drive?

Installing a CD-ROM is much easier today than it was a few years ago, thanks to installation software that walks you through the installation process. There is one topic that can complicate your CD-ROM installation process: the method of connection that you choose. There are several options for connecting the CD-ROM to your system:

- A sound card with a CD-ROM interface
- An interface card that comes with the drive
- A SCSI adapter already installed in your system
- An IDE interface
- A parallel port

The easiest installation route is to connect an external CD-ROM to a parallel port, but performance suffers and the cost is higher. You may also purchase an internal IDE CD-ROM drive. This drive costs less but installation may be difficult and performance with video and other multimedia applications that are demanding may suffer.

If you are going to add a sound card too, and you don't have a SCSI interface card, your best choice is to find a sound card with a CD-ROM interface so that you don't waste a slot in your computer installing a separate CD-ROM interface card.

> **TIP** Usually, you can find a drive bundled with a sound card and a few multimedia programs. If you purchase the drive and sound card separately, get nothing less than a 16-bit sound card with a 44KHz stereo sampling rate and Sound Blaster compatibility. For your CD-ROM, get nothing less than double-speed operation, MPC-2 compatibility, and 350ms average access time.

For those of you who don't buy a kit but still want to hook the CD-ROM drive to a sound card interface, you need to be very careful when matching the drive and the card. The cards usually have a limited selection of drives with which they are compatible. The list of compatibility can be found in the card's documentation.

10.6. I've installed a CD-ROM drive and I can't get it to work. What do I do now?

Most installation problems are the result of conflicts between the card used as the interface and other cards in the system. Most cards today come with software to check IRQs, I/O addresses, DMA channels, and ROM BIOS addresses. This helps you to set the board correctly to avoid problems. If this software is not part of your package, you need to run the MSD utility that is shipped with Windows. This provides you with information on IRQs, which likely are the problem. Switch to your MS-DOS prompt by choosing Start from the Toolbar, then Programs | MS-DOS prompt, and enter MSD. When the program starts, click IRQ status. If No or a blank entry appears in the status detected column, the IRQ can be assigned to the card being installed.

When the board is configured and in the slot, you are ready to connect it to the CD-ROM drive. Provided you purchased an internal model, the board and drive should be connected with a ribbon cable. Next, connect the audio patch wire between the drive and sound card, if there is one. Now plug a power connector into the drive, and if it is fully mounted in the bay, the physical installation is completed.

The final thing you want to do is run an installation utility that permits the drive to talk to Windows. (This usually comes with the interface card or sound card.) These installation programs vary in operation, depending on the hardware manufacturer. But, virtually all manufacturers provide any needed software and the documentation necessary to tell you how to run the installation program from within Windows in order to complete the installation.

10.7. How do I install a sound card?

To install a sound card, follow these steps:

1. Turn off and unplug the electrical supply to your computer.

TIP	You may want to label all of your cables so that you don't become confused as to where they belong and how the cables should be oriented when you go to return them to their places.

2. Now unplug the rest of the cables from the computer. Be careful not to damage the cables; don't pull them off at an angle, pull them straight back. Also, check to see whether there are any screws or clamps that hold your cables in place before removing them.

3. Move your computer to a place that allows you to easily access all its areas. With a Phillips screwdriver, remove the screws that hold the case on the unit, and remove the casing.

4. When the cover is off, you will see about six or eight slots for expansion cards. Notice that some of the slots are 8-bit (room for one edge connector) and some are 16-bit (room for two edge connectors).

5. Choose a slot for the sound card. This is determined by whether the card is an 8- or 16-bit card. A 16-bit card forced into an 8-bit slot will not operate (yes, it can physically be done; it just won't work). However, you can put an 8-bit card into a 16-bit slot.

6. After you have chosen an expansion slot, remove the metal cover of the empty expansion slot.

7. After draining yourself of static by touching the metal frame of the computer, remove the sound card from its antistatic bag. Hold the card by its metal brackets or edges. Don't touch the gold connectors to prevent damage.

8. You may have to set some of the jumpers or DIP switches on the sound card so that it works as discussed in question 10.6. Also, as an example, if your sound card has a joystick port and you already have a joystick installed, you should turn off the joystick port on the sound card because the joystick is connected elsewhere. The documentation tells you which switches to change to do this or to prevent IRQ conflicts.

9. If you wish to connect an internal CD-ROM drive to the sound card, attach the cables. Sound cards are available that will run your CD-ROM drive; this is especially true if the sound card has a SCSI interface available. Connect the ribbon cable of the CD-ROM to the sound card. Next, connect the audio cable from the CD-ROM to the sound card.

10. Once again, drain yourself of static, hold the card by its metal edges, and put it into place. Apply force alternately on both ends to insert the card in the slot.

11. Tighten the screws, being careful not to strip them, and return the cover to the computer.

12. Now that the sound card is in place, turn on your computer. After Windows has loaded, click Start from the Toolbar, then click Settings and Control Panel. When Control Panel is open, click New Devices to open the New Devices Wizard. When the window appears, click Next. When asked whether the card is installed, click Yes. Next, a list box appears; choose Media Devices for the type of hardware being installed. Then, follow the instructions in the dialog box, and Windows will configure itself to match the settings of the sound card.

10.8. How do I add multimedia drivers?

In some cases, you may want to manually add new drivers for your multimedia hardware. (If the equipment you've added is plug-and-play compatible, Windows automatically configures itself to match the equipment when you turn the power back on.) But, in the case of equipment that's not Plug-and-Play compatible, you'll need to install any drivers that you want to add on your own. Windows comes with drivers for many types of multimedia accessories. In many cases, you can use one of the Windows-supplied drivers with your equipment. In some cases, you may need a driver supplied by the manufacturer (check the instructions that came with the equipment to determine whether you must use a disk supplied by the manufacturer).

Before attempting to install the driver, you should have your original Windows installation disks (or the disk that came with the multimedia device, if you are using a disk supplied by the manufacturer). After you've installed the hardware, perform these steps to add drivers:

1. Open the Start menu and choose Settings | Control Panel to display the Control Panel.

2. When the Control Panel appears, double-click the Add New Hardware icon. Doing so causes the Hardware Installation Wizard to appear, as shown in Figure 10.1.

Figure 10.1. *Hardware Installation Wizard.*

3. Click the Next button. The Hardware Installation Wizard now displays a list box with various devices, along with two options: Automatically Detect Installed Hardware, and Install Specific Hardware (see Figure 10.2).

4. Turn on the Install Specific Hardware option.

5. In the list box, select the specific hardware type from the list and click Next. The Hardware Installation Wizard dialog box now displays a list of manufacturers and models for the chosen type of hardware, as shown in Figure 10.3.

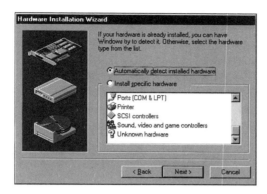

Figure 10.2. *Hardware Installation Wizard with list of various devices.*

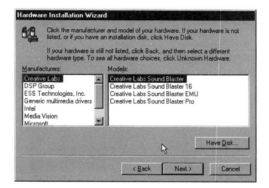

Figure 10.3. *Hardware Installation Wizard with list of manufacturers and models.*

6. If you are using a driver supplied with Windows, click Next. If you are using a driver supplied by the manufacturer, click the Have Disk button, insert the disk, select the appropriate drive from the next dialog box that appears, and click Next.

An additional dialog box may appear asking for configuration information (such as which port and/or interrupt the hardware is using). If you see such a dialog box, respond to the questions using the settings indicated by your particular hardware. (In the case of peripheral cards such as sound cards, you may need to refer to the documentation that came with the hardware to determine which settings should be used by the device.) If Windows needs any additional drivers to be installed with the one you've added, it will install them, and it may ask for additional setup information. Respond to any dialog boxes you see, and click OK.

When the driver's installation has been completed, Windows displays a dialog box advising you of that fact. You probably need to restart Windows before the changes will take effect.

10.9. How can I remove a multimedia driver I'm no longer using?

You can remove an unwanted driver by using the following steps:

1. Open the Start menu and choose Settings | Control Panel to display the Control Panel.

2. When the Control Panel appears, double-click the Multimedia icon.

3. When the Properties for Multimedia window appears, click the Advanced tab to display the list of multimedia devices (see Figure 10.4).

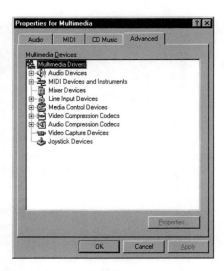

Figure 10.4. *Multimedia devices list.*

4. Click the plus symbol beside the type of device to open a list of all devices of that type, and then click the desired device to select it.

5. Click the Properties button to open a Properties window for the device.

6. Click the Remove Button. A dialog box appears asking for confirmation; click Yes in the dialog box to complete the process.

10.10. What is Sound Recorder, and how do I use it?

Sound Recorder is an application provided with Windows that supports the recording and playing of sound stored in files under the Wave (.WAV) format. If you've installed a sound card that meets the MPC standards, you can use Sound Recorder. With the Sound Recorder, you can play, record, and edit sounds having the Wave format. (To record sounds, you will need a microphone or other audio source connected to the appropriate jack on your sound card.) To start Sound Recorder, from the Start menu choose Programs | Accessories | Multimedia | Sound Recorder. In a moment, Sound Recorder appears, as shown in Figure 10.5.

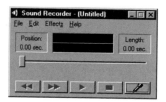

Figure 10.5. *Sound Recorder.*

To open and play a sound file, use these steps:

1. Choose File | Open from the Sound Recorder menus to display the Open dialog box.

2. In the dialog box, select the .WAV file that you want to play and click OK.

3. Click the Play button. As the sound plays, the status bar displays the word Playing. When you want to stop playing, you can click the Stop button; to resume playing, click the Play button again.

To create a sound, use the following steps:

1. Choose File | New from the Sound Recorder menus.
2. Click the Record button.
3. Use the microphone (or turn on your audio source that's connected to the sound card).
4. When done, click the Stop button. (If you want to save the file, be sure to use the File | Save command on the Sound Recorder menus.)

> **NOTE** Sound Recorder can record a maximum of one minute of audio. You should also be aware that the .WAV files created by Sound Recorder can be sizable; a minute of sound can routinely occupy a half-megabyte or more of disk space.

To edit a sound file, use these steps:

1. Choose File | Open from the Sound Recorder menus to display the Open dialog box.
2. In the dialog box, select the .WAV file you want to edit and click OK.
3. To merge the sound with sound from another .WAV file, open the Edit menu and choose Mix with File; then, select the desired .WAV file in the dialog box that appears.
4. To change the effects of the sound, open the Effects menu and choose the desired option. Your choices from this menu are Increase Volume and Decrease Volume (which make the sound 25 percent louder or softer), Increase Speed and Decrease Speed (which make the sound 100 percent faster or 50 percent slower, respectively), and Add Echo (which adds a reverberation effect to the sound).

10.11. How can I assign sounds to system events?

To assign sounds to system events, perform these steps:

1. Open the Start menu and choose Settings | Control Panel.

2. When the Control Panel opens, click the Sounds icon. When you do so, the Properties for Sounds window opens, as shown in Figure 10.6. In the list box under Events, you see all events that can be assigned to sounds.

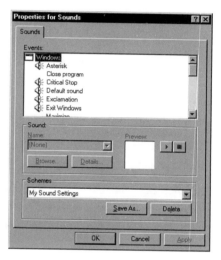

Figure 10.6. *Properties for Sounds window.*

3. Choose the desired event to assign a sound to by clicking on the event. To choose the sound, click the Browse button to open the Browse window, locate the desired sound file in the window, and click OK.

4. To test the sound, press the right-arrow button in the Preview portion of the window.

5. Repeat steps 3 and 4 for any other events that you wish to assign sounds to.

6. Click the OK button to activate the sounds.

10.12. What is Media Player, and how can I use it?

Media Player is a general-purpose multimedia player provided with Windows, which can be used to play Wave or MIDI-format based sound files, CDs with audio tracks (if an audio-compatible CD-ROM drive is installed), and animated video files. Although Media

Player plays a wider variety of formats than does Sound Recorder, it is limited to serving as a player only; you cannot record using Media Player. (As with Sound Recorder, before using Media Player you must have hardware that supports the MPC standard installed in your system.) To launch Media Player, open the Start menu and choose Programs | Accessories | Media Player. In a moment, the Media Player appears, as shown in Figure 10.7.

Figure 10.7. *Media Player.*

To play a file using the Media Player, perform these steps:

1. Open the Device menu and choose the type of device (such as Sound, MIDI Sequencer, CD Audio, or Video for Windows).

2. Choose File | Open, select the desired file in the dialog box, and click OK.

3. Click the Play button to play the file. You can use the Pause button to pause the playback and the Stop button to halt the playback. The Eject button ejects the media on devices (such as CD-ROM drives) that support this option.

To exit the Media Player when done, choose File | Exit from the Media Player menu. Note that if you're using Media Player to play the audio track of a CD, choosing File | Exit won't halt the playing of the audio track. You'll need to use the Eject button on your CD-ROM drive (or the Eject button within Media Player) to stop the music.

Working with the Registry

This chapter details the use of the Windows Registry Editor and how it can be used by advanced users to maintain Windows' configuration data.

11.1. What is the Registry?

The *Registry* is a hierarchical database used by Windows to store information describing user preferences, the hardware configuration, and the various system settings, as well as configuration information from individual 32-bit Windows applications. The Registry was designed to replace the proliferation of files used for those purposes under Windows 3.*x*, including AUTOEXEC.BAT, CONFIG.SYS, SYSTEM.INI, WIN.INI, and all the individual .INI files created by most 16-bit Windows applications. For example, when a 32-bit Windows application is installed, an entry regarding that application's settings and preferences is added to the Registry. When a Plug-and-Play-compatible hardware device is installed, Windows senses the device upon startup, and an appropriate entry is made in the Registry. When a Windows user changes colors or wallpaper, or chooses an international date format, this information is recorded in the Registry.

To understand how the Registry is used and how it must be used in combination with older configuration files, it helps to fully understand the system that the Registry will slowly replace. With prior versions of Windows, configuration data was stored primarily in four files: CONFIG.SYS, AUTOEXEC.BAT, WIN.INI, and SYSTEM.INI. The CONFIG.SYS file was loaded first, on startup of the operating system (MS-DOS). It set the basic parameters for the operating system, such as the number of files and buffers available, and set the loading of many device drivers. Once CONFIG.SYS had loaded as a part of DOS, the contents of AUTOEXEC.BAT were processed. Among other things, entries in AUTOEXEC.BAT would set environmental variables, and run any programs that needed to be executed after the startup of DOS (usually, a WIN statement was included here to immediately load Windows on top of DOS).

Upon the startup of Windows, the contents of SYSTEM.INI would be read to load basic Windows driver information (such as the display, keyboard, and mouse drivers). Then WIN.INI would load. It was used by Windows to control various hardware specifics; determine the available ports, I/O devices, and fonts; and control how Windows would appear on-screen.

The overall design of the system configuration for a machine running Windows 3.*x* developed in this manner for obvious reasons: CONFIG.SYS and AUTOEXEC.BAT were part of the design of DOS, and the .INI files came with the advent of Windows. But this scheme also had its obvious disadvantages. Information vital to the operation of the entire system was scattered in different locations, making it difficult at best to track changes. To add to the complexity, most Windows applications, when installed, would make additions to the WIN.INI file, and would add configuration files of their own with .INI extensions. Program Manager, an integral part of Windows 3.*x*, would add its own .GRP files to track the contents of program groups. This awesome proliferation of configuration files of different types made it a real challenge to find the source of the problem if something went wrong in the area of overall configuration; in a corporate setting, it was sometimes less time-consuming to reformat the hard drive and reinstall Windows all over again than to spend hours looking for an obscure compatibility problem caused by an error or corruption in one of these files.

The point of this dissertation is to help the power user/consultant/ support person (and assumed reader of this book) to understand Windows 95's mixed-bag approach to system configuration, with some data stored in the Registry, and some data possibly stored in WIN.INI or in other .INI files. Overall settings for Windows 95, all configuration settings that were formerly a part of DOS, and the hardware specifications (including those automatically added by Plug-and-Play compatible peripherals) are all stored in the Registry, along with configuration information for 32-bit Windows applications. But all 16-bit Windows applications, which have been written to run under Windows 3.*x* or earlier, will still make use of WIN.INI and their own individual .INI files. It's important to know this so that you have an idea of where to look as problems (or a need for custom configurations) arise. In the long run, the hope is that as 32-bit Windows applications replace the older applications written for earlier versions of Windows, WIN.INI and the other .INI files will be used less.

The Registry Editor is powerful as a tool, but fairly basic in terms of design. This is because Microsoft's intent was never for it to be an end-user tool. Most users never see the Registry; changes to it are made either through the Control Panel, by the software that is installed or modified, or through the interaction of Windows Plug and Play with new hardware that is installed.

11.2. How do I use the Registry Editor?

To start the Registry Editor, choose Run from the Start menu and enter REGEDIT in the Run Application dialog box that appears; then click OK. The Registry Editor appears, similar to the example shown in Figure 11.1.

The Registry Editor uses a dual-panel display, similar to that of Explorer. The right panel shows the details of whatever object is selected in the left panel. In a manner similar to the way you navigate with Explorer, you can double-click an object in the Registry Editor to reveal any additional objects contained within that object.

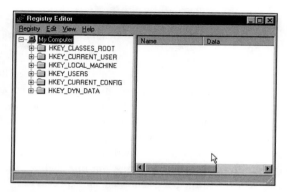

Figure 11.1. *The Registry Editor.*

To modify a value using the Registry Editor, double-click the value in the right panel of the Registry Editor. A dialog box will appear, which you can use to enter or edit the value. For example, Figure 11.2 shows the Edit String dialog box for changing a value string used by the HK_USERS value (the item selected for this example).

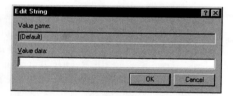

Figure 11.2. *The Edit String dialog box used to edit a value in Registry.*

The Registry Editor contains four menus: Registry, Edit, View, and Help. The options on the Registry menu let you connect to and disconnect from network objects, import or export an existing registry file, print the registry's contents, and exit from the Registry Editor. The Edit menu contains options for creating a new key within the Registry, and for deleting and renaming existing keys. The options of the View menu let you display or hide the Status Bar, change the size of the window's panels (using the Split window option and the cursor keys), or refresh the display based on the latest data available on a network. The Help menu accesses a help file for the Registry Editor.

Using the Registry Editor, you can read or write values directly into the User Profiles and System Settings portions of the Registry. You can examine and change the current settings, add new keys to the Registry, and delete current keys and values of your choosing.

11.3. Because configuration data is stored in the Registry, are the old AUTOEXEC.BAT, CONFIG.SYS, and various .INI files still used?

The contents of AUTOEXEC.BAT and CONFIG.SYS, if these files exist, are still read by Windows in order to provide full backward compatibility with older 16-bit applications. The .INI files also are read for the same reason: compatibility with older Windows applications. It's true that developers of 32-bit Windows applications are encouraged to use the Registry for all configuration data. However, most 16-bit applications routinely make changes to AUTOEXEC.BAT, usually adding to the existing PATH statement contained within it. Also, a number of older DOS applications routinely make changes to CONFIG.SYS on installation. The settings stored in these files will be taken into account by Windows as it establishes its environment during the startup process.

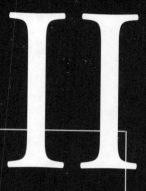

Maximizing Your Hardware

12	Upgrading Your Memory	189
13	Upgrading Your Hard Drive	205
14	Upgrading Your Video	223
15	Upgrading Your Processor	239
16	Upgrading Your Peripherals	253
17	Choosing and Upgrading Your Windows Printer	261

12

Upgrading Your Memory

This chapter presents the hardware considerations for your PC's memory, and details the ways in which you can expand your PC's memory. It's the first chapter in Part II, "Maximizing Your Hardware," for a good reason. As has been mentioned throughout this book, *nothing* improves Windows performance like a change from minimal to more-than-adequate memory. Even a new processor may not be as wise an upgrade as more memory. For example, if you already have 8M of memory and you're running a 386SX, a move to a 486 processor would add much in terms of performance. But if you have just 4M of memory, you'll get much more of a Windows performance boost by adding another 4M than you'll see by making one step up in processors.

Part of the common need to upgrade memory in so many computers running Windows is a direct result of the design specs for Windows. Knowing that a large number of sales of Windows 95 would be as upgrades for existing users of Windows 3.*x* running on existing 4M machines, Microsoft set an ambitious design goal of having Windows 95 run in a 4M machine. Hardware manufacturers are partly responsible for perpetuating the belief that 4M is plenty of memory—virtually all low-end machines (at the time of this writing) are sold equipped with 4M of RAM. But "minimum standard" doesn't mean Windows will run well, any more so than a subcompact car will haul the local elementary school soccer team around. If you're running Windows in a 4M machine, you definitely will need more RAM.

> **NOTE** The memory referred to in this chapter is system RAM, the kind that your machine's central processing unit (CPU) uses directly for data storage. Memory that's used for hard-disk caching or as video RAM isn't covered in this chapter. Hard-disk memory is generally not upgradable (outside of changing the hard disk) and is a function of the hard-disk controller design (see Chapter 13, "Upgrading Your Hard Drive," for more on hard-disk designs). Video memory, which may be upgradable, is a function of the design of the video adapter card (these are detailed in Chapter 14, "Upgrading Your Video").

12.1. I hear a lot about conventional RAM, extended RAM, upper RAM, and expanded RAM. Just how does my PC's memory work?

In some ways, Windows 95 has made things easier with its 4M minimum RAM requirement. The 4M that's mandated by Microsoft is made up of 640K of *conventional memory*. This 640K was designed as the total memory address space for the original IBM PC back in the stone age (early 1980s), and virtually all DOS programs were written to run in this address space.

The designers of the original IBM PC used a microprocessor (the Intel 8088) that had the capability to address up to 1M of RAM. But the PC's designers decided to use the top 384K of that available memory to control basic system functions, including the PC's video display. This 384K (sitting on top of the 640K of conventional memory) came to be known as *upper RAM* (or in some circles, *high DOS RAM*).

Extended RAM is the memory that physically starts at the 1M point, and extends up to the limit of your PC's installed RAM. The concept of extended RAM was introduced with the IBM PC-AT and other computers based on the 80286 processor. Extended memory is what made GUI environments such as Windows and OS/2 possible from a hardware standpoint; they can't run without it. All 80286-based machines (in theory) are able to access up to 16M of RAM, using extended memory addressing techniques. All 80386-based machines are theoretically able to address extended memory of up to four gigabytes (that's 4,000 megabytes). In practice, the amount of memory you can install in a PC is limited by how large a memory module you can install on your PC's motherboard and how many memory expansion slots exist. Many PCs shipping at the time of this writing reach a memory maximum at around 64M of motherboard memory. (At today's prices that's over $3,000 in memory chips alone, so this limit is not much of a problem—for now.)

Expanded memory is not actually a reference to any physical section of your PC's memory. Instead, it's a memory addressing technique, developed in the 1980s, that enables older programs (which were originally developed from a DOS point of view) to address large amounts of memory. Windows does not need expanded memory, and neither do any applications written for Windows. This type of memory is fast becoming obsolete, so there's not much of a need for Windows users to be concerned with it.

As far as types of memory relate to your hardware needs, assuming you are upgrading a machine that is already running Windows, extended memory is the only type that you need to be concerned with. Because any IBM-compatible that can run Windows in the first place will already have its full 1M of conventional RAM on the motherboard, extended RAM is all that you can add.

12.2. How much memory do I need?

Many "industry experts" will say to install as much memory as will fit in your PC, but those of us who live in the real world and put up with mundane things like budgets can't afford such luxuries. Because of the reality that memory is expensive, any Windows user should consider 8M a minimum. If your Windows work is with average word-processing documents, moderately large spreadsheets, and databases of a reasonable size, 8M should be sufficient. This will give your machine enough breathing space to run two major Windows applications and perhaps two or three small applets (such as Calculator) simultaneously, without constantly sending the CPU to the hard disk. Depending on your applications, you may need more than 8M. Some applications are known for being memory-intensive. These include any software that handles complex graphics, extensive use of multimedia (especially video), CAD/CAM applications, and, of course, any use of the PC as a network file server. For these types of applications, 12M should be considered a minimum, with 16M or more an ideal to shoot for.

> **TIP**   Adding memory is technically a fairly simple operation in most PCs. So if you're not sure how much you'll need, and cost is a major factor, increase your memory to 8M first, reassemble the PC, and run your applications. If you're still not satisfied with the performance, you can always add more memory later. Also, depending on the design of the system board, buying small SIMMs will max the system out at 8M or 16M of RAM. To go any higher in the future would mean scrapping this RAM. It is better to use the largest SIMMs you can afford to protect your investment in RAM futures.

12.3. I see many different types of memory chips advertised. Which kind will I need for my particular PC's processor?

There are so many different types of motherboards currently installed in computers that it is impossible to know precisely what kind you'll need without looking inside your PC or in the manual for your machine. About all you can be sure of is that the motherboards in virtually all modern PCs are populated with some type of user-installable RAM—usually SIMMs, SIPs, or DRAM chips. Precisely how memory is installed varies from system to system.

Many motherboards use SIMM holders (which are like miniature expansion slots), or SIP holders (which are like connectors into which the metal pins of SIPs are inserted). The memory types used by your particular machine actually depend on both the processor speed and the motherboard's design. There are a number of common designs for PC memory, including SIMMs, SIPs, chips, and proprietary. (No, these are not menu items at a snack bar.)

■ *Single In-Line Memory Modules* (SIMMs) are the type of memory most commonly used in PCs of recent build. SIMMs contain a group of memory chips mounted in-line on a small plug-in circuit board, similar to the illustration shown in Figure 12.1.

Figure 12.1. *Single In-Line Memory Modules (SIMMs).*

The SIMMs slide into special memory slots located on the PC's motherboard. The tiny boards on which the SIMM chips are mounted have one standard size, but the circuits on the SIMMs are configured to provide varying amounts of memory in different speeds. Common sizes of SIMMs include 256K, 1M, 4M, 16M, 32M, and 64M.

■ *Single In-line Packages* (SIPs) are designed just like SIMMs, but instead of having an edge connector that plugs into the motherboard socket, SIPs have rows of tiny metal pins that insert into a connector on the motherboard. SIPs are often found in machines built prior to 1992. SIPs are predecessors to SIMMs; the tiny metal pins on SIPs are easily damaged, and it is easy to insert a SIP in its slot backward (something that's difficult to do with a SIMM).

■ The term *chips* (also known as DRAMs, for Direct Random Access Memory) is used to refer to discrete (or separate) integrated circuits, like those shown in Figure 12.2. These are typically seen on older PCs, or on some memory expansion cards that are designed to plug into one of a PC's expansion slots. The chips plug directly into sockets located on the PC's motherboard or on a memory expansion card.

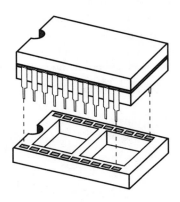

Figure 12.2. *Memory chips.*

■ *Proprietary* doesn't actually refer to a specific type of memory design; rather, it refers to the fact that the memory type must be obtained from the manufacturer. The three memory types mentioned previously are widely used in a variety of hardware, but proprietary memory designs work with one specific brand of PC. Proprietary memory designs are commonly found in laptop computers.

The most reliable method of determining which memory can be used by your PC is to consult your computer's documentation. If you can't locate the documentation (a rather common problem), the only reliable method is to open the PC and examine the existing memory. Most modern PCs contain banks of SIMMs; each bank contains two or four sockets, accommodating two or four rows of SIMMs. As an example, Figure 12.3 shows two banks of 1M SIMMs with four rows in each bank, making a total of 8M of installed memory.

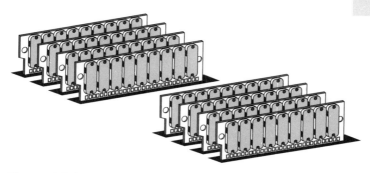

Figure 12.3. *8M of 1M SIMMs in two banks.*

If you're faced with upgrading memory in a PC that was built recently, there's a good chance your memory type is SIMMs or SIPs. With either type, here are some general rules you must keep in mind:

- In most PCs, you cannot mix SIMM sizes within the same bank. Many PCs will take different capacity SIMMs, but all the SIMMs that you install in any one bank of that PC must be of the same capacity. For example, in a bank of four slots, many PCs will accept either 1M SIMMs or 4M SIMMs. You could fill the bank with 1M SIMMs, and that bank would contain a total of 4M. Or, you could fill the bank with 4M SIMMs, and that bank would have a total of 16M. You could not, however, put two 4M SIMMs into two of the bank's slots and two 1M SIMMs into the other two slots to try to obtain a total of 10M of RAM.

- In many PCs, you can run into problems if you attempt to mix SIMMs of different speeds, even when they are of the same size. For example, you may have a computer with 4M of existing SIMMs rated at 70 nanoseconds (ns), and your documentation claims that your computer can get by with 85ns SIMMs. If you put new SIMMs rated at 85ns in

II

remaining empty banks of the motherboard, your machine
may refuse to boot, or may crash shortly after startup. You
can get away with mixing speeds on some machines if you put
the slowest SIMMs into the first bank. The computer will
then access memory at the speed of the slowest memory chips,
and the remainder won't have a problem keeping up.

■ Most PCs require you to completely fill a bank of slots. You
can leave a bank empty (unless, of course, it's the first bank),
or you can fill the bank; but you cannot partially fill a bank.

■ PCs will accept SIMMs up to a certain size. (The maximum
size for your PC is something you'll have to get from your
PC's documentation. If no documentation is available, the
only way to discover the largest size becomes a process of trial
and error.) We once sold a 386SX laptop through the
classifieds, partially because the machine (which looked like a
bargain back when it was bought) was designed with four
SIMM slots that would not take SIMMs any larger than 1M
each; hence, we could never install more than 4M of RAM in
the machine.

When you think about these rules, it may become obvious that in
some cases, when you upgrade memory you may have leftover
SIMMs that you can't use anywhere (except perhaps in someone
else's computer). Often, upgrading means that you put the SIMMs
you remove on a shelf and completely replace all of them with larger
SIMMs. This design, which unfortunately is the norm in the
hardware industry, can box you into a corner when it comes to
future upgrades. Most newer PCs have two banks of four slots each,
with the capability to accept 256K, 1M, or 4M SIMMs. If such a
PC came with 4M standard packaged as four 1M SIMMs, and you
wanted to upgrade it to 16M, you would have to shelve the 1M
SIMMs and go to 4M SIMMs throughout.

If you absolutely can't locate the documentation for your PC, you
can open the PC and count the existing SIMMs, then do the math
to determine what size SIMMs you have (based on what your
computer's power-on test tells you is installed as existing memory).
For example, if your PC has 8M of RAM and you see eight SIMMs
installed, they are obviously 1M SIMMs. If the number of SIMMs
you see doesn't match the installed memory reported by your

computer, look for additional memory, either inserted as chips into sockets on the motherboard or installed in a memory expansion card that's plugged into one of the slots.

Once you know the size of the SIMMs, you'll also need to know the speed at which your memory is running before you purchase additional SIMMs. Memory chips are rated in *nanoseconds* (ns), which are billionths of a second. The rating refers to the amount of time it takes the CPU to access the data that's stored within the chip. (The lower the number, the faster the memory chip's speed; for you technical freaks, a nanosecond is the time it takes light to travel about 11 3/4 inches.) The rated speeds of the memory chips already installed in your PC are chosen by the system's designers to match the rest of your PC's hardware. You should never try to use chips that are slower than those designed for your system. At best, they'll slow down your system, and at worst, your system will refuse to boot after you've installed the chips.

On each chip mounted on the SIMMs, you'll see a code that has a number as the last digit. If the number ends in a zero, take the last two numbers (including the zero) as the speed of the chip in nanoseconds. If the last number is a number other than zero, add a zero after the number, and you get the speed of the chip in nanoseconds. You can use Table 12.1 as a general guide to speeds needed by different processor chips. (The table specifications are by no means industry rules; the best guide is your computer's documentation, or what's already installed in your system.)

Table 12.1. Memory speeds.

Processor type	Chip speed needed
386SX/16 or 386SX/25	100ns
386SX/33 or 386DX/33	85ns
486SX/33 or 486DX/33	85ns
486SX/50 or 486DX/50	70ns
486DX2/66	70ns
Pentium/66	60ns
Pentium/99 or 100	50ns

Once you know the size and speed of the existing SIMMs, you can safely add more SIMMs of the same size and speed. If doing so won't get you the amount of memory you need (and you can't find the documentation for your system), you can try populating entire banks with SIMMs of the same speed and the next larger memory size. (For installation tips, see Question 12.8, "How do I install SIMMs or SIPs in my PC?") Obtain your memory from a vendor who's willing to provide a refund if the larger size can't be used by your system.

12.4. I've seen a memory board advertised; I can insert memory chips in the board, and just drop the board in an expansion slot. Can I go with this approach instead of adding SIMMs?

This will increase your memory, but if you have empty slots for SIMMs, adding a memory board has its disadvantages in terms of performance. A memory board that must send its data through the expansion bus is usually restricted by the speed of that bus; on the other hand, memory installed directly on the motherboard by way of SIMMs faces no such restrictions. The result is faster data transfer reading from and writing to memory that's installed on the motherboard. An important exception to this advice exists if your PC uses a local bus type motherboard design, and the memory expansion card you want to add is designed for use with the local bus. This design solves the problem of slower access through the expansion bus, so memory installed on such a card would be as fast as memory installed on the motherboard. (For specifics on local bus designs, see Chapter 15, "Upgrading Your Processor.")

12.5. Does it make sense to buy memory that's much faster in speed than the processor?

Doing so won't gain you anything now in terms of performance; the processor can't run any faster than it's doing already. But if you ever plan to upgrade your hardware by exchanging motherboards, it may make sense to buy faster-than-needed memory. Buying faster memory will only add 10 percent or less to the cost, and you'll probably be able to use the same memory with the faster motherboard when the time comes for your next processor upgrade.

12.6. How much will more memory cost?

Memory prices have an annoying habit of fluctuating, due to a wide variety of market factors: inflation, import tariffs (or a lack of them), shortages of raw materials, natural disasters in the countries where the plants are located; in short, nearly everything but ocean tides and phases of the moon. (To a small degree, prices also vary with how fast the memory must be; faster processor chips demand faster memory, and the price goes up somewhat with the speed.) In terms of mid-1990 U.S. dollars, memory costs are running between $40 and $50 per megabyte and show no signs of drastic drops anytime soon.

12.7. What are sources for additional memory?

You can purchase memory from your system's vendor, from local retail computer stores, from the national superstore chains, or from mail-order houses commonly listed in the computer magazines, to name a few common sources. The surest way of obtaining the correct memory is from your system's vendor, though prices tend to be higher when you go this route. The superstore chains and mail-order houses tend to offer the best prices, but it's hard to expect much in the way of support when you're performing a do-it-yourself upgrade and buying parts from these sources.

12.8. How do I install SIMMs (or SIPs) in my PC?

Memory installations will vary with system design, but you can use the following general steps as a guide for installing memory in PCs that use SIMMs or SIPs. (If you have your PC's documentation and it offers steps for memory installation, those steps are likely to be more specific than these.)

1. Open the PC (refer to Appendix B, "PC Assembly," if you're unfamiliar with the basics of disassembling your PC).

2. Locate the banks of SIMMs. Be warned that some systems with less than exceptional design have the memory banks obscured beneath hard drives or hidden behind the power

supply, so you may have to remove some items before you can get easy access to the memory.

3. Observe which way the existing SIMMs are facing—*this is important.* Most SIMMs are difficult to insert backward, but some early-design SIMMs and their predecessors, SIPs, can be inserted backward.

4. If you need to remove any existing SIMMs, release any edge clips that hold the SIMMs in place, grasp them by the edges, and, gently rocking them outwards at an angle, pull each SIMM out of its socket. Avoid touching any of the pins on the edge connectors of the SIMMs; static electricity from your body could damage the memory chips.

5. Continue to handle the chips by the edges and insert the new SIMMs, making sure that they face in the same direction as the existing SIMMs (or the ones you removed). Insert the SIMMs at an angle, aligning the leads on the edge connector with the pins within the connector that's mounted on the motherboard.

6. Gently push in on the SIMMs until they are firmly seated. (Never attempt to force a chip into a socket.) The SIMMs should easily engage firmly in their sockets, and if there are edge clips, the SIMMs should snap into place in those clips. The edge clips (and the holes in the SIMMs that align with them) ensure that the SIMMs are inserted completely, and that they are not in backward.

> **TIP**
> An inexpensive plastic tool designed for the removal and insertion of SIMMs is routinely available at most computer retail outlets and through mail-order firms that sell PC memory. The tool usually retails for around $10, avoids the danger of body static damaging the memory, and comes with instructions for SIMM removal.

Once you've installed the SIMMs, on older systems that don't employ Plug-and-Play, you must tell your hardware about their existence. With most PCs, you'll need to make a change in the basic configuration that's stored in special chips on the motherboard; you usually do this by pressing a special key combination, after turning your machine on, to get to a configuration screen. (Again, consult your computer's documentation for specifics. If your computer uses a variation on the popular "AMI" BIOS, you can get to the setup screen by holding down the Delete key when you start up the computer.) On some older computers, you may need to change switch settings or jumpers on the motherboard to use the additional memory; you'll have to get any information on this from your computer's documentation.

12.9. How can I install DRAM chips in my PC?

You can use the following steps as a guide to expanding memory in PCs that use DRAM chips in sockets:

1. Remove the PC's covers (refer to Appendix B, "PC Assembly," if needed, as a general guide). Also, remove any expansion cards that are in the way of the memory chips.

2. Locate the next empty memory banks to fill. (If the banks are on a memory expansion card rather than on the motherboard, you'll need to remove the card from its slot.) Memory banks on motherboards are usually numbered 0 through 3 or 0 through 7, with at least bank 0 being filled with existing chips.

3. Locate pin 1 on your DRAM chips (remember to handle the chips by the edges, never by touching the metal pins, because the chips can be damaged by static electricity). DRAM chips have an orientation dot or notch on one edge of the chip. In some PCs, you can look at the existing chips on the motherboard to determine where pin 1 is located. At least make sure any chips you install face in the same direction as the existing chips.

4. Insert the additional DRAM chips one at a time, with the pin 1 markers or orientation dots aligned with pin 1 of each socket. Gently insert the pins in one side of the chip into the holes in one side of the socket. Then, gently apply lateral pressure to align the pins on the other side of the chip with the holes on the other side of the socket, and press the chip down into the socket. Make sure that you don't bend any of the pins during insertion, and be careful not to misalign any

II

of the chips with their sockets. If a chip appears misaligned (two pins are completely out of one side of the socket), you'll need to remove the chip and reinsert it correctly.

5. Repeat step 4 until all the necessary DRAM chips have been installed.

> **TIP** You can avoid static damage and possible mishandling or bending of the chip pins by using a chip puller/insertion tool. These are commonly available at electronics supply outlets such as Radio Shack.

12.10. How do I install a memory expansion card?

Adding memory by means of memory expansion cards is similar to installing separate DRAM chips or SIMMs, because the memory cards are designed to accept either SIMMs or DRAM chips. You can use the following steps to install memory using an expansion card:

1. Place the memory expansion card on a flat surface and set any switches or jumpers on the card according to the amount of memory that you plan to add. The memory expansion card should come with full documentation detailing how any switches should be set. If you are given a choice of switch settings for expanded memory and different settings for extended memory, set the switches to read all of the memory as extended memory.

2. Insert the memory into the expansion card. (Use the SIMM or DRAM chip installation steps detailed in the previous procedures as a guide to memory installation.)

3. Refer to your computer's documentation, and set any switches on the motherboard to reflect the amount of newly installed memory.

4. Grasp the adapter by the card edge and the slot connector on the rear of the card, and insert the card into the expansion slot, aligning the edges of the card's connector into the motherboard slot. Gently insert (don't force) the card into the slot, then replace the screw at the top of the slot connector.

12.11. I've installed new memory and my PC doesn't work. Now what?

There are a number of possible pitfalls that may occur when you install memory upgrades. A chip that you purchased could be bad (this happens more often than you might suspect), a SIMM or DRAM could be installed incorrectly, there could be a memory size or speed mismatch, or your machine might be lacking the required change of settings to properly recognize and work with the installed memory. Try to get a clue as to what's wrong from the way that your system behaves when you start it. Here are some common symptoms and possible solutions:

- *System beeps in an odd manner, and* CMOS mismatch *or some other type of memory error appears on the screen:* This usually means that you must manually change your PC's CMOS setup to recognize the newly installed memory. (See your PC's documentation for instructions on changing the setup; on many PCs, you can get to the setup screen by holding down the Delete key as you turn the power on.) On some older computers, you must press a key to get past the memory error, load DOS from a floppy disk, and run the setup utility from a floppy disk provided with the computer.

- *System will not boot:* Look for SIMMs or SIPs that are installed incorrectly or installed in the wrong banks, or DRAMs that are improperly inserted in their sockets. If you've mixed SIMMs or SIPs with regard to speed (not a recommended practice), make sure that the slowest-speed SIMMs or SIPs are installed in bank 0.

■ *System displays "parity error" message followed by a specific alphanumeric code:* This can indicate that one or more of the chips that you have installed is defective. Try rearranging the SIMMs or DRAMs, and see if the error code changes; this technique can help you isolate a defective memory chip. Note that with some older 80386-class systems, this type of error occurs if certain motherboard switch settings are not set to match the speed of the installed memory.

Upgrading Your Hard Drive

This chapter covers the specifics you'll need to know if you are considering an upgrade in basic storage capacity (to put it bluntly, you need a larger or faster hard drive). Windows has shown a clear tendency to put a continuing squeeze on hard disk space, and the jump from Windows 3.*x* to Windows 95 hasn't done anything to get away from this tendency. At one time, 120M or so may have seemed like more disk space than most Windows users would ever need. But progressively more complex versions of Windows and Windows applications have reduced a drive of that size to little more than a minimum for Windows itself and two or three full-blown applications.

As an example of the increasing need for disk space, Microsoft's Word 6.0 for Windows and Excel 5.0 both consume in excess of 20M each; if you install the full suite of applications in Microsoft Office with all the options included, you'll need about 120M of disk space. (And that doesn't include Windows itself, which needs over 20M of space, or storage space for the files you'll work with on a daily basis.) Large hard disks, often in the range of 300M to 1 gigabyte, are becoming the rule for serious work in Windows. And because most Windows PCs more than a year old shipped with

drives 200M or smaller, the need for an upgrade is taking place in
all too many situations. Unfortunately, upgrading a hard drive is
often one of the more technically challenging types of upgrades you
can attempt; there's more involved than just pulling off a cover and
plugging in a card. This chapter details the topics you should be
aware of and the techniques that you can use to upgrade your hard
drive's capacity.

> **NOTE**   If you already have one hard drive installed in
> your system and you plan to install another, you'll
> need to be careful in selecting the type of hard
> drive that you want to install. It can be difficult to
> get a second hard drive to coexist with an
> existing one. Even in PCs with relatively standard
> IDE interface cards and cables that are ready for
> a second drive, you'll need to configure jumpers
> on the hard drives so that the drives work
> correctly.

13.1. What features can I look for to get good drive performance under Windows?

Getting the highest performance from any hard drive that you
install will involve making decisions in three areas: drive type,
speed, and transfer rate. And because every hard drive requires some
interface circuitry, any upgrade decision has to take both the drive
and the interface into account. Regarding drive types, in many older
PCs, you'll find drive and controller card combinations that make
use of what are known as MFM, RLL, or ESDI standards. All of
these standards are virtually obsolete, and none are worth serious
consideration for an upgrade at the time of this writing. Your basic
choices among available drive types are IDE (Integrated Drive
Electronics), Enhanced IDE, and SCSI (Small Computer Systems
Interface). Their pros and cons are discussed under the following
question.

The speed of the hard drive will have a direct impact on Windows
performance. Hard drive speeds are measured in terms of access
times, transfer rates, and to some degree, rotational speed. Access

time, expressed in milliseconds (ms), is a measurement of how long a hard drive takes, on average, to find a sector on the disk. For good performance under Windows, you should look for an access time of 15ms or better. If you can get a drive in the 10ms to 12ms range, you'll do much toward reaching a goal of ultimate Windows performance.

Transfer rates measure how fast the drive can transfer its data back to the motherboard. These rates generally aren't published in advertisements for drives, so your best bet is to look for a drive with a 16-bit controller (or a local bus controller if your motherboard uses a local bus style design). Don't settle for any kind of an 8-bit hard disk controller card; using a 16-bit or better controller assures you of getting a good data transfer rate. (As discussed shortly, if you plan to use a SCSI-type drive, there's no need to worry about looking for a good data transfer rate; by design, all SCSI drives boast great transfer rates.)

Hard-drive rotational speeds also aren't widely published, but because all high-capacity hard drives currently made use a design known as one-to-one interleaving, the faster a drive spins, the faster it's able to read data off the disks.

One feature that has absolutely nothing to do with Windows performance but should always be considered nevertheless is the warranty offered on the drive. Obviously, the longer the warranty, the better. Today's hard drives are very durable, with typical mean times between failures in the hundreds of thousands of hours, but vendor warranties do vary widely. Some drives are warranted for as little as a year, some for as long as five years.

13.2. Which drive types should I use?

The first question you'll face when you consider adding a new hard drive is whether you want to use the Integrated Drive Electronics (IDE) standard, or the Small Computer Systems Interface (SCSI) standard. Both have their advantages and disadvantages. IDE is by far the more popular of the two as far as Windows PCs are concerned; the overwhelming majority of PCs shipped as of this writing use either IDE drives or a newer variation of the technology known as Enhanced IDE. IDE drives have virtually all of the drive controller circuitry built onto the drive itself. And compared to SCSI drives, IDE drives are a less expensive technology to implement. Most PCs already have an IDE interface either built into the motherboard or mounted on a card that also contains electronics for the floppy disk drive. If an interface card is needed to connect an IDE drive to a PC that's never had one before, you can obtain one for under $30 from a variety of sources. This fact makes upgrading using IDE a less expensive proposition. And IDE drives offer reasonably good to excellent Windows performance.

In comparison to IDE, SCSI drives cost more to implement initially, but offer better performance and very fast data transfer speeds when compared to IDE technology. SCSI drives run faster because by design they are able to bypass the PC's CPU and send data directly to system memory. For this reason, SCSI drives are increasingly becoming a sought-after option in high-performance file servers. SCSI drives are designed to connect to the SCSI interface, which (unlike initial implementations of IDE technology) can allow connections to other peripherals. One SCSI adapter can support SCSI hard drives, SCSI-compatible CD-ROM drives, or tape backup devices. Up to a total of seven SCSI devices can be daisy-chained through SCSI cables, all connected to the same SCSI interface card that's inserted into one of the PC's expansion slots. (Note that this isn't always the connectability panacea that it sounds like because SCSI cables can in some cases be more expensive than you expect.) SCSI drives also have the advantage of offering very big hard disk sizes (up to 2 gigabytes), though IDE drives are catching up in this area because of the Enhanced IDE specification (see Question 13.3 for details).

In general, your choice of which system you go with will be directly driven by what hard drive technology is already in your system. If you already have a SCSI adapter and a SCSI hard drive, adding another SCSI drive (or a larger one) is the only option that makes real sense. If your PC uses an IDE drive now, the most sensible upgrade would be a replacement or additional IDE drive. (And if by some slim chance your PC uses a drive controller technology older than IDE, the computer is probably a little old to consider adding significant amounts of storage capacity; see Question 13.5, "Does upgrading a hard drive make sense?," later in this chapter.)

To a degree, the bus on which your PC hardware is riding also affects how much of a performance increase you will get from a hard disk upgrade. As Chapter 15 discusses, PCs use a variety of expansion buses. These include the popular (but dated) ISA bus, the Extended ISA (EISA) bus, and the newer, faster standards such as local bus and VL-bus. Many of today's high-speed IDE drives will outrun an ISA bus in terms of data handling capacity. And SCSI drives can move data faster than an EISA bus can keep up with. (There's no chance of a hardware incompatibility here; the drives just have to wait for the motherboard to catch up before proceeding to the next data transfer operation.) If getting the most in terms of performance is important to you, you can get around this performance drawback by taking both the motherboard and the drive interface card to local bus standards.

NOTE Many newer PCs use one interface card to support both the hard drive and all floppy disk drives. If you upgrade the hard disk and disk controller in such a system, make sure that the new controller supports your floppy drives, or purchase a separate floppy drive controller card. (Floppy controllers are inexpensive, generally retailing for around $20.)

13.3. What's the Enhanced IDE specification?

Enhanced IDE is a newer drive technology designed to offer the low costs of IDE and the higher data transmission speeds of SCSI. The Enhanced IDE standard is a result of the IDE drive makers reworking the older IDE specification so that IDE drives could keep up with their SCSI counterparts. If you're serious about getting the most for your drive dollar, look for the following technical features of the new drives and controllers:

- *Multiword Direct Memory Access:* This design is what gives Enhanced IDE drives the kind of data transfer speeds that were once the province of SCSI drives. The design enables the drive to transfer its data directly to memory, without having to tie down the CPU in the data transfer process.

- *Logical Block Addressing:* This is a method of addressing data that permits the PC to get past the older 528M limit and address drives with partitions up to 8.4 gigabytes. (This method is reliable when done by means of the hardware design; it can be problematic when done by means of TSR programs or device drivers.)

- *I/O Channel Ready:* This term describes a data line that, along with a data-sending protocol called Mode 3 PIO, controls the data output of the drive, enabling the drive to pump more data into the system when the data bus can handle it.

- *Multiple Device Support:* The design of Enhanced IDE circuitry lets you connect other enhanced IDE-compatible devices, such as CD-ROMs and tape drives, to the same controller electronics.

If you're looking to upgrade your hard disk capacity past 528M, you should look for these features in the drive that you buy. Keep in mind that using Enhanced IDE requires newer ROM BIOS chips in your motherboard than can support the standard; hence, it often makes sense to upgrade to a newer motherboard and an enhanced IDE drive at the same time. (You'll find techniques on motherboard upgrades in Chapter 15, "Upgrading Your Processor.")

NOTE If you plan to install a drive in excess of 528M in a PC that does not have a newer ROM BIOS compatible with the Enhanced IDE standard, you'll need to use an Enhanced IDE interface card with the drive rather than your existing IDE electronics, or you'll need a driver that enables Windows to recognize all of the drive space. (Check with the vendor to be sure that the driver supplied works with Windows 95.)

13.4. What's drive caching, and do I need it?

Drive caching, when built into a hard drive, is a design technique whereby the drive stores commonly needed data in memory that is part of the disk drive electronics. As the CPU needs this data, the drive can send it from its own memory, reducing the number of physical accesses to the hard disk. Hardware caches work along with the drive to read-ahead the outgoing data requests—or store incoming data requests—and hold them in the memory on the drive until the drive is ready to process the data. In theory, this sounds like the source of a magnificent performance gain. In practice, how much performance is gained varies widely with how large and how effective the cache design is. The electronics that control the cache have to be smart enough to anticipate what data will most likely be accessed repeatedly by the CPU, and the cache has to be big enough to be useful.

All Windows PCs do the same job with the caching that's built into Windows, but a natural advantage to hard-disk caching is that it doesn't consume any of that valuable system memory that Windows needs so badly. A trade-off is that disk caches are slower than Windows built-in software caching, because the data stored in a disk cache has to travel through a disk controller and an expansion bus to get to the CPU. With a software-based cache, the data is already in memory, and can be retrieved faster by the CPU. In general, hard-disk caching is a desirable feature to look for when upgrading your hard disk. Try to look for a drive with the largest cache you can find. Caches range from 32K to 512K; try not to settle for one that's less than 64K in size.

13.5. Does upgrading a hard drive make sense?

Of course, this isn't a question to which you will get a canned answer. Perhaps a better way of phrasing the question should be, "In view of the age of the existing hardware, does it make economic sense to upgrade the hard drive?" You can run into real problems trying to mix new components with aging technology; you may run into strange incompatibilities and unpleasant surprises (like an old motherboard ROM BIOS that conflicts in some way with modern drive technology).

A good example is taking an older, minimal Windows platform such as a 386SX/16, with a maximum RAM capacity of 4M (don't laugh—the industry built thousands of these boxes in the early 90s). The system has a pitifully inadequate 40M hard drive based on the old MFM technology. You could add an IDE interface card and a big IDE hard drive, and, yes, system performance would improve significantly (due to the much faster access time of the hard disk, if nothing else). But the basic platform is still seriously inadequate for good Windows performance; the upgrade would be analogous to hanging modern jet engines under the wings of a DC-3. The result might fly, but does it make economic sense?

In general, anything slower than the recommended minimum platform for Windows 95 (a 386DX/33 or better) should not be upgraded just in terms of hard disk capacity—you should move to a better overall platform. Consider a simultaneous motherboard and hard drive upgrade for such situations—you'll find motherboard upgrade tips in Chapter 15.

NOTE	Some very fast drives (particularly those with some or all of the features of Enhanced IDE) may not run correctly in older PCs. As an example, drive maker Western Digital cautions buyers to test their 541M Caviar model in older (non-local bus) PCs before buying that particular model for use with such systems.

13.6. Must I upgrade my motherboard and drive controller (or entire system) to local-bus technology to get really impressive hard drive performance under Windows?

In general, no. Under speed tests with typical Windows software, there's not a significant difference between the performance of a modern Enhanced IDE drive connected to a local bus interface card in a local bus PC, and the same drive connected to a 16-bit adapter in a non-local bus PC. The one area where you will see a speed difference is with large database applications, or where the PC is used as a network file server.

13.7. I already have one hard drive in my system, and I want to add another. Is this feasible?

In a nutshell: *maybe.* There are a number of possible pitfalls you'll want to carefully consider before you try to install a second hard drive in an existing system. Make sure that the new hard drive is compatible with the existing one. (If your computer is an older model that uses a hard drive based on the old MFM or RLL technology, you probably can't install an IDE drive in the same machine, though you usually can remove the old drive and controller and replace them with an IDE drive and interface card.) You'll want to check the existing hard drive interface card to make sure it can handle a second hard drive. Most IDE interface cards are designed to handle two drives. If your computer uses SCSI drives, be sure it's possible to connect multiple drives. One reason for the design behind SCSI technology was to enable multiple drives to be connected to the same controller.

If at all possible, make sure that the computer's ROM BIOS (installed in chips on the motherboard) is compatible with any type of hard drive that you install. Unfortunately, the only way to be sure about this is to check with the hard drive vendor. For most PCs, you can obtain a designation that indicates the level of your installed ROM BIOS by looking at the screen after you first turn on the system. Usually, you'll see the name of the BIOS and its revision level among the first messages that appear on the screen.

Finally, keep in mind that you may need to buy a new set of hard drive cables in order to connect two hard drives to the interface card. Even when PCs are shipped with interface cards that are designed to work with more than one drive, the cable attached to the card is often of the single-drive variety, and you'll need to replace the cable with one containing connectors for the two drives.

II

TIP
One nearly foolproof way of installing a second drive in a machine with an existing drive is to add Quantum's HardCard, a hard drive mounted to an expansion card that's designed to drop into

an existing expansion slot. This approach is more expensive than buying an IDE drive and a connector cable, but in return for the expense, you get a relatively easy installation that's unlikely to conflict with an existing drive. For more on the subject, see Question 13.10, "What's a HardCard, and how can I install one?" later in this chapter.

13.8. How much hard disk space is enough?

This is the perennially impossible question, akin to asking the meaning of life or the size of the physical universe. But for serious users, a good rule of thumb for planning purposes is to obtain 150M of disk space for every year that you plan on keeping your current system.

13.9. How can I install an IDE hard drive?

The precise steps for installing a hard drive will vary due to the design of your particular PC. For that reason, it's a good idea to check your PC's documentation for any specifics relating to hard drive installation. You can refer to the following steps as a general guide to hard drive installation:

1. Perform a complete backup of all the data on your existing hard disk.

2. Turn off the machine and remove the cover. (Refer to the general guidelines in Appendix B, if needed.)

3. Visually examine the existing hard drive and make a note of all jumper settings and the general layout and arrangement of the power cables. These settings are important because they indicate which drive is a master (the first drive in the system), and which drive is a slave (the second drive in the system). Figure 13.1 shows a typical arrangement of a system; yours may look like this, or may vary significantly, depending on the system's design.

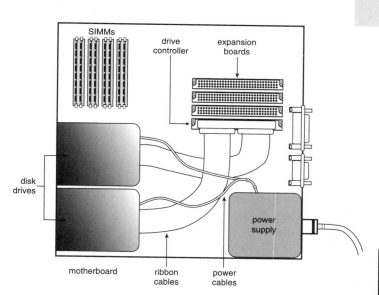

Figure 13.1. *The internal layout of a typical system.*

4. Remove the old drive and controller, if needed.

5. Install the new controller card in the same way you would install any expansion card. (Visually check the length of the ribbon cable supplied to connect the card to the drive. If it is rather short, you may need to install the card in a slot that's close to the drive bays, so the cable will reach the drive.)

6. Determine which pin on the drive's connector is pin 1. (The drive should have a number stamped or etched on the printed circuit board near the edge connector, indicating which pin is pin 1.)

7. Install the drive into the desired drive bay, using the mounting hardware that was included with the drive. If you are installing one drive, you should not need to make any changes to the jumper settings on the drive. If you're installing a second drive in a system with an existing drive, you'll need to change jumpers on both the drives to indicate that the first drive is a master drive and the second drive is a slave drive. (Neither drive will operate properly without this step.) Refer to the documentation that accompanied the drive (or your PC's documentation) for the correct jumper settings; if

you have any doubts about the jumper settings, call the drive maker's technical support line for assistance. (The phone number is usually included in the documentation that came with the drive.)

NOTE   If the drive is too small for the drive bay in which you're trying to install it, you'll need to assemble mounting brackets or mounting rails supplied with the drive to fit the drive bays of your particular computer.

For example, most IDE drives currently manufactured are designed to fit into the physical space like that occupied by a 3.5-inch floppy disk drive. You can't mount such a drive in the drive space for a 5-1/4 inch floppy disk drive unless you have an adapter kit with the mounting hardware necessary to install the drive. If you don't have the needed hardware, look around for an alternative mounting arrangement before you run out and buy more hardware.

Many recently manufactured computers contain additional small drive bays located beneath the standard-sized ones to accommodate smaller IDE drives. As an example, Figure 13.2 shows typical mounting hardware that's supplied with a hard drive.

---

8. Attach one end of the ribbon cable to the controller card (or to the motherboard for PCs with IDE interfaces built into the motherboard). Then attach the other ends of the cable to the drive (or drives). The connector on the controller card differs from the design of the connectors on the drives, so it's not possible to mix them up. With two drives, you'll use both drive connectors on a cable containing a total of three connectors (one for the controller or motherboard, and two for the drives). The drive connectors are identical, and it does not matter which connector goes to which of the two drives. Note that it is important that you connect all the cable's connectors to the correct *pin numbers*. (The pin numbers are

etched or plated on the controller card by the connecting pins, and on the drive by the edge connectors.) Make sure the red or blue-striped side of the cable always connects to pin 1 of the drive or controller connectors.

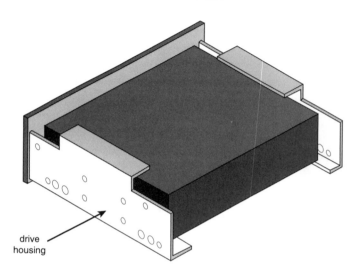

drive housing

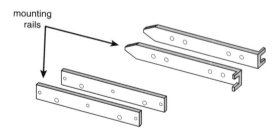

mounting rails

Figure 13.2. *Mounting hardware typical of hard drive installation.*

9. Attach the four-pin power connector to the drive. Don't be concerned with attaching this cable backward; it is keyed, and can only be inserted one way.

10. If necessary, connect the wires from the drive activity lamp on the PC's case to the matching pins on the drive.

11. Tighten all the screws holding the drives in their respective bays, and the screw holding the controller card (if there is one) in its expansion slot.

12. Reconnect any other components you disconnected in order to install the hard drive.

13. Turn on the computer. Don't expect it to run normally; most likely, you'll see a delay due to the machine's failure to recognize the newly installed hardware.

14. Refer to your computer's documentation, and enter the configuration setup (or boot the system with a DOS disk and run the setup program supplied on disk with your computer) to configure your machine to operate with the hard drive.

> **NOTE** With most IDE drives and configuration setup programs used by PCs, you'll need to know a number of specifications for the new drive, including the number of heads, the number of cylinders, and the drive type. You'll find these specifications packaged with the drive's documentation, or on a label that's attached to one side of the drive.

15. Exit the CMOS setup utility and reboot your computer. Your PC will now recognize the drive from a low-level hardware standpoint, but you will still need to format the disk before it can be used by Windows.

> **WARNING** In days past, with drives that used the older MFM or RLL technology, a low-level format was performed on newly installed drives. You should never attempt to perform a low-level format on an IDE drive unless the manufacturer specifically recommends it. With most IDE drives, any type of low-level formatting will destroy important track information that's needed by the drive.

16. Boot the system using a DOS disk. Run the FDISK utility from your DOS disk.

17. If you've installed a second drive, from the FDISK menu select the option for changing drives, and change to Drive 2.

18. From the FDISK menu, choose the option for creating a partition. If Windows is the only operating system you plan to use, the partition you create should be the maximum size available. When FDISK finishes adding the partition, the system will reboot.

19. When DOS again loads from the floppy drive, run the DOS FORMAT utility to format the new drive. Enter

    FORMAT x:

    where *x* is the letter representing your new hard drive. (If you plan to start the computer from this hard disk, add the /S option at the end of the FORMAT command (for example, FORMAT C: /S).

20. When the formatting process is complete, turn off the system, and reinstall the covers. If you've replaced your original drive with a new, larger one, you'll need to reinstall Windows and restore your files.

13.10. What's a HardCard, and how can I install one?

HardCard is Quantum Corporation's brand name for a hard drive that's mounted on an expansion card; you install the card in an expansion slot, run some installation software, and you have instant hard disk. Quantum Corporation, a major hard-drive manufacturer, was the first to come up with the design that places a hard drive and all the associated electronics on one expansion card. But other vendors have imitated the concept, and many PC users generically refer to this type of drive design as a *hard card*.

Installing a hard card is about as straightforward as with any type of expansion card. Find an empty slot, remove the slot cover from the PC, slide the hard card into the slot, and replace the mounting screw and the PC's covers. The switch settings or jumpers on most drives of this type (including Quantum's HardCard) assume that you are installing the card in a system that already has an existing drive. If you are using a hard card to replace an existing drive, you should refer to the documentation that's packed with the drive to reconfigure the switch settings or jumpers.

After you've installed the card, you will need to run the installation software that accompanies it. In most cases, you should use the automatic option displayed by the software; this option will format the drive and prepare it for use along with Windows.

13.11. How do I install an internal SCSI drive?

The installation of a SCSI drive and controller card are similar in many ways to the installation of an IDE drive and its interface card. The major difference is that with SCSI devices, you must be concerned with *terminators*. The design behind SCSI consists of a chain of items made up of an interface card, up to seven devices (such as hard drives, CD-ROM drives, or tape backup units), and terminators. The terminators must be connected at each end of the chain. (Terminators are usually small resistor packs that connect to a plug on the host adapter card, or to a connector on the rear of the peripheral device.) You also need to assign SCSI ID numbers, from 0 to 7, to each of the devices (7 is usually reserved for the host adapter). You'll need to assign a unique SCSI ID number to each SCSI device in the chain. You must refer to the documentation for each SCSI device that you add, to determine how to set its switches to establish the SCSI ID number, and to ensure that the device is properly terminated when the device is located at the end of the chain. Keeping those rules in mind, you can perform the following general steps when installing a SCSI drive:

1. Perform a complete backup of all the data on your existing hard disk.
2. Turn off the machine and remove the cover. (Refer to the general guidelines in Appendix B, if needed.)
3. If the SCSI card isn't already in your system, install the card in an available expansion slot.
4. Install the drive in the desired drive bay, using the mounting hardware that was included with the drive.
5. Attach one end of the supplied ribbon cable to the host adapter, and attach the other end to the drive. Note that it is important that you connect all the cable's connectors to the correct pin numbers. (The pin numbers are etched or plated

on the controller card by the connecting pins, and on the drive by the edge connectors.) Ensure that the red or blue-striped side of the cable always connects to pin 1 of the drive or controller connectors.

6. If you need to connect any external SCSI devices to the host adapter, do so. Remember to add the required terminator at the end of the chain of devices, and to assign different SCSI ID numbers to each device using appropriate jumper or switch settings for each device.

7. Attach the four-pin power connector to the drive. Don't be concerned with attaching this cable backward; it is keyed, and you can only insert it one way.

8. If necessary, connect the wires from the drive activity lamp on the PC's case to the matching pins on the drive.

9. Turn on the computer. Don't expect it to run normally; most likely, you'll see a delay due to the machine's failure to recognize the newly installed hardware.

10. Exit the CMOS setup utility, and reboot your computer. Your PC will now recognize the drive from a low-level hardware standpoint, but you may still need to format the disk before it can be used by Windows.

11. Boot the system using a DOS disk. Run the FDISK utility from your DOS disk.

12. From the FDISK menu, choose the option for creating a partition. If Windows is the only operating system you plan to use, the partition you create should be the maximum size available. When FDISK finishes adding the partition, the system will reboot.

II

> **NOTE** Some SCSI controllers use their own disk-formatting routines. For such drives, the use of FDISK isn't appropriate. Check your drive's documentation to determine whether the drive uses its own disk-formatting routine.

13. When DOS again loads from the floppy drive, run the DOS FORMAT utility to format the new drive. Enter

```
FORMAT x:
```

where *x* is the letter representing your new hard drive. (If you
plan to start the computer from this hard disk, add the /S
option at the end of the FORMAT command (for example,
FORMAT C: /S).

14. When the formatting process is complete, turn off the system
and reinstall the covers. Assuming you've replaced your
original drive with a new, larger one, you'll need to reinstall
Windows and restore your files.

13.12. I've installed a new drive and it doesn't work. Now what?

Pray. No, seriously, there are a large number of possibilities as to
why your newly installed hard drive doesn't operate. These are some
general guidelines that you can follow when troubleshooting a hard
drive installation. They are general out of necessity because there are
so many possible combinations of hard drive and controller
combinations that it's impossible to be specific.

- Make sure that you run your SETUP utility, per your
computer's documentation, so that the CMOS memory in
your system is set up to recognize the new hard drive.

- Make sure that the interface card is completely seated in the
expansion slot, and that all cables are completely seated on all
the edge connectors.

- Make sure that all jumpers on the drive interface cards and on
the drives are properly set. In particular, if you've installed a
new IDE drive in a system that has an existing IDE drive,
you'll need to set the jumpers on the drives so that the first
drive is seen by the system as a master (or first) drive, and the
second drive is seen as a slave (or second) drive in the system.

If you see a message such as non-system disk, replace and press
any key, don't be too concerned. This message will appear if you
replaced your existing drive with a new one, and you formatted the
new drive but forgot to include the /S switch with the use of the
FORMAT command. Put the DOS disk in your floppy drive and enter
the command SYS C: at the A:\ prompt, to add the system files to
the hard disk.

14

Upgrading Your Video

This chapter examines how you can upgrade the performance of your system's video, with both the video card and the monitor you use. It begins by covering basic video concepts and video standards, and then provides information to help you understand what is available to you in the market of video cards and monitors. It also provides guidelines for installing new cards and monitors. It ends by providing troubleshooting tips for your new video setup.

Video Basics

Before you can effectively upgrade your video, however, you need to know some of the particulars of video so that you can make a better choice as to what you will upgrade to.

14.1. What exactly is monitor resolution, and how do the different resolutions affect what I see on the screen?

At some point, you probably have wondered about the confusing array of specifications presented when vendors advertise video cards and monitors. Resolution is measured in picture elements called *pixels*. As you ponder which monitor to buy, you should consider the resolution specifications. These specs describe the pixels. In the specification 640×480, for example, the first number describes the number of pixels across the top of the screen, and the second number describes the number of pixels down the side of the screen. A standard VGA monitor of 640×480 uses 307,200 pixels to display a full-screen image.

Currently, for those of you who really like high resolution, you can have monitors with a resolution of up to 1600×1200. An important point to keep in mind—especially if you have a small- to mid-size monitor—is that the higher the resolution is, the smaller the elements on your screen appear. This fact points out one of the benefits of having a larger monitor. If you choose 800×600, you may want to have a monitor that is 17 inches or more (measured diagonally). If your preference is the higher 1600×1200, you probably will not be satisfied unless your monitor approaches a size of 22 inches or more.

14.2. What do I need to consider regarding the amount and type of video RAM for my system?

Whether your system uses a video card installed in an expansion slot or video adapter circuitry built into the motherboard, the video circuitry has its own memory dedicated to the display of video that eventually winds up on your screen. The higher the video resolution, the more video memory, or *video RAM*, is used.

To see how higher resolutions require more memory, consider these examples:

■ A monitor with a resolution of 640×480; 16-bit color; and 65,536 colors needs one-half megabyte of RAM.

■ A monitor with a resolution of 1600×1200; 24-bit color; and 16,777,216 colors needs 6M of RAM.

You can see that there is quite a variation in the amount of memory you need for different resolutions. Memory needs can range from 512K for lower resolutions to 6M RAM for higher resolutions.

The video card you install has everything to do with supporting the colors and resolution your screen has. Here is a good tip as to the amount of memory your card should have. For the standard 256-color, VGA screen with a resolution of 640×480, your card should have no less than 512K of memory. If you have a resolution of 1600×1200 and 24-bit color, your card should have no less than 6M memory. True color requires much more RAM than other forms, such as 256-color or 65,536-color monitors.

You also need to consider the type of memory you want on your video card. Video cards usually come with a type of memory called VRAM (Video Random Access Memory). Regular RAM used to be significantly slower than VRAM, which meant that VRAM was the preferred choice. As so often is the case with faster, however, VRAM is more costly. However, recent advances in technology have changed this fact. Now some cards that use RAM can perform as well as cards that use VRAM. But, if money is not an object, choose VRAM for better performance. You will notice a difference in the speed with which your card performs.

14.3. How does refresh rate affect what I see on the screen?

Refresh rate refers to how often the image is repainted on your screen. This refresh rate is measured in Hertz. Hertz measures the number of times a screen is repainted per second. The higher the refresh rate, the more stable the image is.

It is recommended that you have a refresh rate of 70 Hertz at 800×600 resolution. The high refresh rate has the benefit of cutting down flicker on-screen. With the lower refresh rate, flicker is noticed between repaints. (The constant flashing from the repainting of the screen can give some users whose eyes are sensitive to such movements a headache.) The higher refresh rate helps reduce this eyestrain and increase productivity because you can spend longer periods of time in front of the screen without taking breaks to rest your eyes.

14.4. What is the difference between an interlaced and a noninterlaced monitor?

Interlacing describes the way a video card and a monitor together draw an image onto the screen of your monitor. A *noninterlaced* monitor creates your image by painting every line on the display. You cannot see the computer painting the screen, because this is done many times per second. The *interlaced* display creates the image on your screen first by painting the odd lines of the image onto the screen, and then the even lines of the image. Because the image is painted in two passes, some people can notice a flicker in the screen with this process and prefer a noninterlaced screen for less eye stress. If you want to cut down on the flicker, purchase a noninterlaced card and monitor combination. When you do purchase these, be sure the video subsystem has a high rate of refresh and that the two are compatible.

Video Standards

Many video standards exist—some of which are nearly obsolete. Some home PCs still use some of the older hardware. However, to show you what is needed in terms of an upgrade, these standards are listed under Question 14.5 to show you the difference between what a PC has and what it could have.

14.5. What are the different video standards, and what do they mean in terms of an upgrade?

Here are some of the prevalent standards and what they mean:

- *CGA and EGA:* These standards were used with early versions of IBM-compatible computers; they have been included as a historical reference, but neither is acceptable for use with modern versions of Windows.

- *VGA—Video Graphics Array standard:* This standard was introduced when IBM unveiled the PS/2 computer. Its standard resolution is 640×480 pixels with 16 colors and 320×200 with 256 colors. The VGA standard represents the minimum video standard for any machine running Windows 95.

- *Super VGA—Super Video Graphics Array standard:* This standard quickly surpassed the IBM VGA standard. This standard supports the following resolutions: 640×480 pixels at 256 colors; 800×600 pixels at 16 and 256 colors; and 1024×768 pixels at 16 and 256 colors. Currently, this is the best reasonably priced monitor type that you can purchase.

- *XGA—Extended Graphics Array standard:* This standard is the newest of all the standards. It supports only 1024×786 pixels at 256 colors. There is one problem with this standard, however; XGA is interlaced. You may remember that this means headaches and reduced productivity for some people. You can purchase a noninterlaced XGA card that reduces the flicker, however. The other drawback is the cost of monitors needed to support the high resolution rates; they are the most expensive of the VGA, Super VGA, and XGA standards.

II

14.6. What is local bus video?

Bus refers to the slots inside your computer used to plug in expansion cards for other devices such as modems, video cards, disk controllers, and so on; and the hardware pathways, or wires leading to and from those slots and connecting various parts of the system. Virtually all communication between the computer and its disks, video, and other cards is done via the bus.

Local bus video is what enables you to connect the video system directly to the CPU, as opposed to the moving of data via the slower bus speed of the expansion bus. Instead of bus speeds of 8 MHz or 10 MHz, you can get bus speeds of 20 MHz, 25 MHz, 33 MHz, or better, in conjunction with the speed of the system's CPU. Local bus video significantly increases your computer's video hardware performance.

Because local bus video improves your computer's performance, it is an important consideration in the upgrading process. Be sure that you purchase products that conform to popular standards; if you buy into a niche market, you may be stuck with a certain vendor.

> **NOTE** Buying products that do not conform to popular standards may cause you to pay significantly more for your video parts if you need to replace some part of your video hardware.

The most popular of the two local bus standards is the VL bus standard. Only three VL bus slots are on a motherboard; the rest are ISA slots.

> **NOTE** ISA is an older and slower bus. It is still popular, however, because many cards are made for it and it is inexpensive.

VL bus graphics cards are common, relatively inexpensive, and fast. In addition to the use of VL bus to support video, VL bus increasingly is used to support hard disk drive controllers.

> **NOTE** Often, it is hard to get more than two VL bus devices to coexist, and once in a while you will find that a VL bus card doesn't work in a VL bus slot.

The other standard, the PCI bus (or Peripheral Component Interconnect bus) was Intel's answer to the VL bus. Systems with motherboards that use the VL bus boards still accept common ISA cards, but VL bus slots are included for use by video graphics adapter cards and hard disk controllers that are compatible with this specific local bus standard. One significant advantage of the PCI bus design is that it supports the plug-and-play technology built into Windows 95. This feature makes the installation of VL bus components much easier, because Windows can automatically configure itself to the device after the device has been added and the system turned on.

Because the VL bus was first on the market, you will find a wider array of products for this standard than for the PCI bus. This is simply because more motherboards were designed to the VL bus standard first; as time passes, you will see an equal amount of products for the two standards.

14.7. What is a graphics accelerator card?

A graphics accelerator is used to improve video performance. Think of it as a video card in warp drive. These graphics cards perform some graphics chores normally performed by the CPU. As a result, the load on the CPU is not as great, which enables it to handle other things. The addition of a graphics accelerator card is perhaps one of the best ways to improve the video performance of your computer. Also, the coprocessors on an accelerator card can perform certain common windows screen-drawing tasks faster than the CPU can, again improving the performance of your video system.

Purchasing and Installing a Video Card

This section provides you with considerations to make before purchasing a video card, and then provides guidelines for installing a new card in your system.

14.8. What do I need to know before I commit to buying a particular video card?

Before you start, there are some things you want to look out for. First, make sure that you don't purchase a PCI or VL bus card unless you are sure that you have a PCI or VL bus slot on your motherboard to begin with; it is wise to check before you purchase. (Refer to the documentation that came with your system to determine which, if any, variation of local bus your system supports.)

If you are upgrading your existing system, you probably will want to purchase a standard ISA-compatible card. This will give reasonably good performance on your existing PC. If you have a slot for a VL bus card, however, purchase one. These cards are fast, cost-effective, and common.

14.9. Are there any alternatives to installing a new video card?

For those of you who want an alternative to a new video card, there aren't too many options. Upgrading your video card is mostly a hardware decision, and there aren't any practical or effective ways around it if you want increased video performance. You do have one option, however, if you want to keep a number of windows open on your screen and your screen is small. You can try a program that provides *virtual desktops* to provide you with more space on a limited desktop. Think of it as having several screens and being able to switch between them while they are running. Currently, some commercial programs have virtual-desktop software included with a host of other helpful utilities. Central Point's PC Tools for Windows and HDC's Power Launcher are two programs that offer this kind of software.

14.10. How can I match my card and my monitor?

Probably the most important thing to consider is whether the graphics board and monitor both support the resolution you want. Unlike in past years, most monitors today accept a wide variety of input signals. If you purchase your monitor and video card separately, verify with each vendor that the two will work together. Also, when buying the monitor and board, be sure that the monitor is able to support the refresh rate of your board. Some vendors give you the choice of purchasing video card and monitor combinations. This offer makes the matching process easy, because it is done for you; don't expect that luxury from some vendors, however.

Most monitors today are *multiscanning*—they match themselves to the scan and refresh rates of your board. If you purchase this type of monitor, you need to be sure only that your monitor's top vertical scanning rate meets or exceeds the board's top rate. These monitors also are among the more expensive monitors. You can find cost-effective, multiscanning monitors, however. (These monitors are described in detail next in the Monitors section.)

If you purchase a multifrequency monitor, be warned that it supports only a few specific rates; be sure that it supports your video board's rates. (Again, these monitors, also called multifrequency monitors, are described in the following section.)

14.11. How do I install a video card?

First, you need to decide where you are going to put your card. If you are using a card that is compatible with a local bus (VL bus or PIA), the card must go into one of the local bus slots available on your system. Graphics cards that are compatible with the ISA standard can be installed in any 16-bit slot.

If your PC has VGA circuitry built into the motherboard, you must disable the motherboard's video circuitry to use a graphics accelerator card or another video card in place of the video circuitry already on the motherboard. You can find out how to perform this task by reading the system manual or by asking your vendor. Usually, it is a matter of changing some jumpers or DIP switches to let the motherboard know that a video card is now in the computer. Some motherboards, however, are able to sense when a new display adapter has been added. Don't assume that your motherboard is one of these; check your documentation to be sure and to save yourself from possible problems.

After you consider these points, you can use the overall steps listed here as a guide to installing a video card. Remember that specifics can vary depending on the card's maker; if documentation accompanies your video card, it may offer installation details more specific than these.

1. After opening your box, slide the card into the 16-bit ISA slot you have chosen. Make sure that the card is placed firmly into the slot. After you insert the card, replace the screw used to hold the card in place. Also be sure that the card doesn't touch another card in your system.

2. Now plug the monitor into the output connector for your video card. Be sure that you use the correct connector; some video cards have multiple connectors for supporting different monitor types.

II

3. When everything is in place, turn on your computer. If the card is properly driving the monitor, you see the usual startup messages displayed on-screen. This doesn't mean that Windows' resolution is any better. If you installed a new card to take advantage of higher resolutions, you need to go into Windows, right-click at any blank space on the desktop, and choose Properties. Then choose the Settings tab in the dialog box that appears in order to change the resolution under Windows.

4. If your card included a disk with installation software for use with Windows 95, follow the instructions provided with the disk to install the drivers.

Purchasing and Installing a Monitor

Adding a new monitor to your computer causes you to consider several things; you need to consider the bus system you have, the video card you purchase or currently have, and whether it will work with the new monitor to which you will upgrade.

14.12. What should I consider regarding resolution as I look at different monitors?

If you like to run more than one Windows application at a time, all too often you find that your screen is not the spacious desktop you wanted. If you have a 14-inch monitor and you are running a resolution of 800×600, you will notice that you have more room on the screen than if you were running a resolution of 640×480. The one difference you will notice with the higher resolution monitor is that the icons are smaller. This is an advantage for some people, but for others, smaller icons are less legible, so they stay with the lower resolution to have the larger icons. The advantage of a larger monitor is that you can run a higher resolution without having to look at smaller icons.

When you purchase your monitor, you probably will get one with at least VGA resolution—it is not wise to buy anything less. Beware of the different monitor types. Not all monitors support all resolutions. Remember also to be sure that the new monitor supports the card you have.

14.13. What is dot pitch, and how does it affect what I see on the screen?

Dot pitch is another thing you should consider when purchasing a new monitor. Each pixel on a color monitor is composed of three phosphor dots. When struck by an electron beam from the electron gun in the back of the monitor tube, these dots glow red, green, or blue. *Dot pitch* is the measure of the distance between a phosphor dot and the nearest dot of the same color on a line above or below it. The closer the dots are, the sharper the picture will be. For a good sharp image, you will want a monitor with a dot pitch of .28 millimeters. If you use graphical software often, or you just like a very sharp picture, you may consider a monitor with a .25 millimeter dot pitch.

14.14. What types of monitors are there, and what are some key things to consider?

Three types of monitors exist: fixed frequency, multifrequency, and multiscanning. The following is a description of each of those monitors:

- *Fixed frequency:* These monitors only display one frequency (which may or may not be the one you want). Most of these monitors support VGA resolutions only. Buy this type of monitor only if you want to run a specific VGA resolution and don't intend to upgrade your video hardware in the future.

- *Multifrequency:* This type of monitor often is confused with multiscanning. This monitor supports only a few specific frequencies such as 800×600. These monitors are less expensive than true multiscanning monitors, and sometimes they are referred to as multiscanning in hopes of confusing the buyer with terms and specifications. If you want a true multiscanning monitor, be sure not to be confused by this type of monitor. If you want a multifrequency monitor, however, make sure that it supports the frequencies of your video card. Larger monitors of this type can cost up to $1,000. For those who need the support of only a few resolutions, this is definitely a cost-effective way to get a good monitor. You can get the benefits of a monitor that supports the high resolution of the card you are using, and not have to pay the price of a true multiscanning monitor.

■ *Multiscanning:* This type of monitor (also known as a *multisync* monitor) can display a number of resolutions in a range of frequencies. These monitors have a broad price range. You can buy one of the smaller multiscanning monitors for about $400. If you want something like a 30-inch, multiscanning monitor, however, be prepared to pay; large-screen, multiscanning monitors can cost well in excess of $2,000.

When buying a monitor, you definitely should consider monitor controls. This may seem like a small thing, but the little things make a difference. In some cases, the controls for the monitors are on the side or in the back, making them somewhat bothersome to reach. Also, if the controls are twist knobs, they can be extremely inconvenient when you need to adjust them. Many of the newer monitors place all controls in the front of the monitor for easy access.

Before you decide to take a monitor home, try using the controls. The capability to adjust both the horizontal and vertical edges of the image is good to have. Some monitors do not enable the user to make these adjustments; a technician must remove the cover to make such adjustments.

There are two kinds of controls for a monitor: analog and digital. *Analog* controls enable you to adjust the image to the various image parameters via knobs or switches. *Digital* controls, on the other hand, almost always are push buttons and give you greater control over the image on your monitor.

As a minimum requirement, you should have several controls:

■ *Brightness:* This control enables you to adjust the brightness of the image. With a blank screen, under ideal conditions, you can turn down brightness until the screen goes black; when programs are run, you still should see bright and contrasting images. You should not be able to wash out the image by turning up the brightness.

■ *Contrast:* This control adjusts the contrast between the dark and light parts of your monitor.

- *Vertical Position:* This control adjusts the position of the image. If you lose part of an image at the top or bottom of the screen, you can adjust this control to bring back the image.

- *Vertical Size:* This controls the size of an image vertically, from the top of the screen to the bottom. Use this control if you lose part of your image at the top or bottom of the screen.

- *Horizontal Position:* This control is similar to the Vertical Position control, but it functions from the left of the screen to the right of the screen. Use this if you lose part of your image at the sides of the monitor.

- *Horizontal Size:* This controls the size of an image horizontally, from the left side of the screen to the right side. Use this control if you lose part of your image at the left or right sides of the screen. (Not all monitors offer this control; many have the horizontal size preset internally.)

You also may want to consider some optional controls to make life with your monitor easier:

- *Convergence:* This contracts (or shrinks) the pin-cushioning effect. *Pin cushioning* is distortion that makes the image take on an hourglass appearance.

- *Color Difference:* This control compensates for the difference between the colors seen on-screen and the colors produced by the output device you choose.

14.15. How do I install a monitor?

After you follow the steps outlined in Question 14.3 to install a video card (assuming that you also were upgrading your video card), use the following steps to install the monitor:

1. Remove the monitor from its packaging in a place where it will not fall and be damaged.

2. Connect the power and signal cable to the back of the monitor. Note that some monitors may have more than one signal cable connector to support their use with multiple types of computers (such as with IBM-compatibles or Apple Macintoshes). On such monitors, be sure to connect the

signal cable to the monitor connector that is designed for use with IBM-compatibles.

3. Plug the monitor's signal cable into the back of your computer, on the video card.

These steps are basically all there is to a monitor installation; this type of upgrade is a relatively simple task. As stated earlier in this chapter, remember to match the video card and the monitor to avoid problems. If you have questions about this, see Question 14.4 on matching your card and your monitor.

Video Troubleshooting

This section outlines some common problems associated with a video adapter and monitor installation.

14.16. When it comes to video troubleshooting, what are some common things to check?

■ Make sure the adapter is placed firmly in its expansion slot. If the card is not seated correctly in the slot, it will not function. Don't be afraid to apply moderate pressure to the card when installing it in the bus slot of the motherboard.

■ Most monitors have two cables: a video cable and a power cable. Be sure that the two cables are plugged in firmly. (Sometimes a loose plug is the answer to a problem thought to be caused by a more serious defect.) One quick way to tell whether the power cord is plugged in properly is to check the LED light. Most monitors have this light located on the front of the monitor, and it can serve as a quick, painless way to check to see whether power is reaching the monitor.

■ Check the controls: contrast, brightness, horizontal, and vertical. Be sure that these are not set improperly. If you get no picture on the monitor, for example, the brightness may be turned down, causing the screen to appear black. This often happens when the monitor is shipped.

■ Be sure, in cases of adapter replacement, that the old adapter is removed (or if the old video circuitry is on the motherboard, make sure that any switches that should be changed to disable it are set properly). If there are two adapters in your computer, your system will not know which adapter to use.

■ Check to see whether your motherboard has its own built-in video circuitry. In order for the installed video card to work, the built-in video circuitry must be disabled. Look in the documentation for your system to find out whether it has such circuitry and, if so, how to disable it to enable the installed video card to function. The documentation specifies any switches that need to be flipped or any jumpers that need to be changed.

■ Be sure to look at the documentation for the installed video card, if one was installed, to see whether you need to change the IRQ address. You may have some other expansion cards installed that use the same IRQ your video card is set to, which will cause an IRQ conflict.

■ If the card still is not functioning properly, you may have to reinstall it in a different slot. (For reasons known only to the PC gods, a card that will not work in one slot of a PC occasionally will work in another.)

■ A good rule of thumb is to keep track of the IRQ addresses for all the other expansion cards you install if you are the type who installs a lot of hardware in your system. This practice helps you to prevent IRQ conflicts. (A good place to write down this information is in the manual that accompanies your system; that way you are less likely to lose it.)

This chapter covered some of the possible problems you could run into when installing a monitor and video card. Of course, all the possible problems could not be addressed, but these were some of the more common ones. The answers provided here should be helpful in your installation process. If you try all these suggestions and you still cannot get your monitor to run, try looking at some of the suggestions made by the manufacturer in the documentation that came with the monitor and card. This documentation sometimes provides specialized suggestions that general-help sections like this one may not be able to present. As a last resort, you could return to the vendor and see whether there is a compatibility problem with your hardware. Fortunately, most vendors are relatively cooperative in this regard.

Upgrading Your Processor

This chapter tells you how to upgrade the processor, or CPU (Central Processing Unit), in your PC. A CPU upgrade is second only to added memory in terms of what it can accomplish for your computer's speed. Depending on what is already in your existing system, you may be able to take two different routes when it comes to processor upgrades, both of which are presented in this chapter:

■ In virtually any PC using a standard design, you can replace the entire motherboard. When you take this route, the replacement motherboard contains the faster processor and corresponding memory. You can insert all your existing expansion cards into the expansion slots of the new motherboard.

■ In some PCs with upgrade capabilities, you can replace the existing microprocessor chip with a faster chip, or you can insert a special type of processor (usually called an *OverDrive* processor) into a special socket on the motherboard.

Q 15.1. What considerations should I keep in mind when upgrading a processor?

Given the complexity of this type of upgrade, you need to remember that there are a number of other components dependent on your processor. In particular, each time you upgrade a processor, you may need to consider a memory upgrade. This is true particularly if you plan to perform the processor upgrade by replacing the motherboard; chances are that you will need to use a faster type of memory on the motherboard, so you often are required to do both types of upgrading at the same time.

Another aspect you need to consider is speed or, more precisely, how much speed you want to buy. When the old 80286 chip used in the IBM PC AT was being replaced in the marketplace with the first of the 80386-based systems, upgrade decisions were much less complex. About the only questions PC users faced were when to upgrade from their old 8088 to an 80286 or 80386, or when to upgrade from the 80286 to the 80386. Now, anyone facing an upgrade decision has a much wider (and potentially confusing) array of choices. Part of the confusion is due to the fact that chip maker Intel has been joined in the IBM-compatible microprocessor business by competitors who manufacture their own Windows-compatible microprocessors and upgrade kits. Also, although CPU speeds are measured in megahertz, there are chip manufacturing designs other than speed ratings that also affect the performance of the CPU. Table 15.1 shows, in overall increasing order of performance, the CPU chips used by IBM-compatible manufacturers.

Table 15.1. Popular chips used in IBM-compatible PCs.

CPU Chip	Description
8088	CPU used in the original IBM PC. Still used in some hand-held PCs. Included here for a historical perspective; cannot be used by any version of Windows.
80286	CPU first used in the IBM PC AT. Still used in some hand-held PCs. Irrelevant as far as the use of Windows 95 is concerned.

CPU Chip	Description
80386SX	Minimum level of chip that can be used with Windows 95. Internally, this chip is identical in design to an 80386DX, but its external design of a 16-bit data bus connecting the chip with system memory made it less expensive to manufacture (and purchase) than the 80386DX. A large number of these chips rated at a speed of 16 MHz were shipped (they carry the 386SX/16 designation). Although machines equipped with this chip can run Windows 95, performance often is slow or abysmal, particularly on machines with 4M of RAM.
80386DX	This chip was Intel's first CPU with true 32-bit data buses, both internally and externally, which gave it (in theory) the capability to address up to 4 gigabytes of system RAM. A system with this processor rated at 33 MHz, along with an installed system RAM of 8M, should be considered the minimal configuration that is capable of reasonable performance when running Windows 95.
80486SX	This chip is a scaled-down version of Intel's 80486DX. Like its larger cousin, the 80486SX uses true 32-bit data buses internally and externally. In terms of performance when compared to its predecessors, the chip is roughly twice as fast as an 80386SX. The big difference between the 80486SX and the 80486DX is that the SX chip does not have a built-in math coprocessor, which the DX version of the chip has.
80486DX	This chip has an internal and external 32-bit data bus design like the 80486SX, but it also includes a math coprocessor built into the chip. The chip also has 8K of internal memory built in as a software memory

II

continues

Table 15.1. continued

CPU Chip	Description
	cache. In terms of performance when compared to its predecessors, the chip is roughly twice as fast as an 80386DX.
80486DX2	Any chip with this designation is identical to an 80486DX, but the chip runs at twice the speed rating internally. A chip with the internal design of an 80486DX/33 that runs at double the speed internally is an 80486DX2/66, for example. These types of processor chips commonly are known as *clock-doubled* processors.
Pentium	At the time of this writing, this is Intel's most advanced processor. Architecturally, the chip uses dual 32-bit internal data buses and an external 64-bit data bus. The Pentium also has dual 8K memory caches built into the chip. The Pentium originally was intended for file servers and desktop systems performing advanced calculations (like CAD/CAM), but it is increasingly coming into use with desktop machines aimed at everyday users. If you can afford the cost, a Pentium machine makes an ideal platform for running Windows 95.

In addition to these designations (all introduced by Intel), you probably will see chip designations from Intel's competitors. Cyrix Corp., for example, makes a 486DRX/2 processor that is designed to provide a plug-in upgrade to memory motherboards with 386DX processors.

Besides falling into different classes as far as design is concerned, processors also are rated at different speeds. Speed ratings for CPU chips are given as *megahertz (MHz)*, a term meaning millions of cycles per seconds; hence, a Pentium rated at 100 MHz can process 100 million instructions per second. A 486DX/33 runs at 33 MHz (or 33 million instructions per second), and a 486DX/50 runs at 50

MHz (or 50 million instructions per second). A 486DX2/50 runs at 50 MHz internally (inside the chip) and 25 MHz externally, and a 486DX2/66 runs at 66 MHz internally and 33 MHz externally.

With so many designations and the existence of clock-doubler design, you quickly can get an idea of why it's important to be familiar with available motherboard designs and options. A 486DX2/50 and a 486DX/50, for example, may sound like systems with the same level of performance; or, if anything, to the uninitiated, the DX2 might imply a higher level of performance. In reality, the opposite is true, because the motherboard containing the DX2 chip is running at half the speed of the motherboard containing the DX chip.

If you plan to use the motherboard replacement method of processor upgrade, two additional considerations remain: what motherboard size your system will accept, and how you can handle possible added heat from a newer (and faster) processor. Before you buy a motherboard, you should be sure that the board you buy will fit into your existing system. Motherboards are sold in two basic sizes: XT (measuring about 14 inches by 8.5 inches), and AT (measuring about 13 inches by 12 inches). In some circles, the XT-sized motherboard is referred to as the *Baby-AT* size. Some PCs accept motherboards using only one size or the other, and some accept motherboards in both sizes. Because there is a significant difference between 14 by 8.5 inches and 13 by 12 inches, a quick visual check of your system with the covers removed should confirm which type of motherboard you have.

A final consideration when replacing a motherboard is whether the additional heat generated by the newer chip will be detrimental to the system as a whole. In most cases, PCs have adequate ventilation to deal with the level of heat generated by whatever chip was installed on the motherboard, because the motherboard was designed to operate with the chip that is installed on it. If you have a large number of heat-generating components packed within the case (like multiple hard disk drives and CD-ROMs), for example, you may want to consider adding more ventilation. The same vendors that provide replacement motherboards can supply heat-sink and fan combinations that mount on top of a processor to keep the CPU from running hot.

15.2. When upgrading motherboards, what is local bus, and is it worth the cost?

Local bus is a standard of design that increasingly is used in modern PCs to speed up performance. With the ISA (Industry Standard Architecture) design that was introduced with the IBM PC and later refined with the PC AT, all data had to move between peripherals using the 16-bit bus that was a feature of the design. This bus was perfectly adequate for the 80286 CPU used in the PC AT. With the advent of faster, better processors, however, it quickly became evident that the ISA bus no longer was adequate. The big bottleneck was with hard drives and video controllers; the improving adapter circuitry in hard drive and video controllers had outpaced the capability of the ISA bus to handle the data.

To get around this bottleneck (and to offer customers the increased performance that hardware purchasers always want), manufacturers began to engineer additional slots that would provide direct or "local" access to the PC's CPU and memory subsystems. Systems designed with local bus slots could be recognized easily by the presence of one or more slots on the motherboard that had more than the usual two connectors offered by a standard 16-bit slot in an ISA bus machine.

A problem quickly arose with each manufacturer's design; each design was proprietary, and only the manufacturer could be relied on to provide memory, video, or other expansion cards that would take advantage of the local bus slots. To overcome this incompatibility between systems, manufacturers began to cooperate to develop local bus standards, which they hoped a variety of aftermarket suppliers would support. At the time of this writing, two popular local bus standards exist: VL bus (also known as VESA local bus) and PCI local bus. VL bus is a local bus standard developed by the Video Electronics Standards Association. PCI local bus is a standard developed by a consortium of manufacturers led by Intel. Both standards have their proponents, and endless hours could be spent discussing the technical advantages of each.

In a nutshell, when upgrading motherboards, it makes sense to spend the extra money involved for a motherboard that meets one of these two standards. Remember that a local bus motherboard is

Don't think that you get the advantage of two processors working at once; the older CPU becomes dead weight.

Some motherboards that lack OverDrive sockets still can take advantage of this type of upgrade. If the current CPU is installed in a socket (nearly all are) and is a 486SX/16, 20, or 25; or a 486DX/ 25 or 33; you can remove the current processor and replace it with an OverDrive processor. (Intel provides a special chip-removal tool to help you get the existing processor out of its socket.) You can purchase OverDrive processors through retail computer outlets or mail-order suppliers.

> **NOTE** If you are considering an OverDrive processor, you should check your PC's documentation to determine which OverDrive processor can be used with your system. Some systems (specifically 486SX-based machines with 168-pin CPU sockets and no coprocessor socket) cannot use OverDrive chips. If you cannot find the information in your system documentation and you have trouble reaching your vendor, you can contact Intel to get a list of systems that are compatible with OverDrive.

15.4. I've seen advertisements that claim I can upgrade my 80386 system by replacing the processor. Is this possible?

You can purchase upgrades to replace 80386SX and 80386DX chips with faster processors. Intel does not support this type of upgrade, but another chip maker (Cyrix Corp.) manufactures processors using a special design based on the 80486 chip architecture, designed for this type of upgrade. The Cyrix chips use an internal design similar to the 80486, but are pin-compatible with the 80386 chips that they are designed to replace. You also can get upgrade kits for upgrading 80386s to 80486s sold by Kingston Technology. All these upgrades suggest different steps to the upgrade process, but they all involve the removal of the existing 80386 CPU with a chip puller tool, and the replacement of that chip with the upgrade chip. (On some computers, the ROM BIOS chips also must be replaced so that the motherboard will work with the new processor.) These types of upgrades are available from the usual computer retail outlets.

15.5. There is a socket for a math coprocessor in my system. How much of a performance gain can I expect if I install one?

Math coprocessors (also called numeric coprocessors) can provide significant performance gains *if* you make use of software that depends on intensive math operations, and the software was written specifically to make use of a math coprocessor. Good examples of such programs are Windows spreadsheets and computer-aided design (CAD/CAM) programs. If you use this kind of software, a math coprocessor is a good idea. If you don't use software designed to take advantage of a math coprocessor, adding the coprocessor is a waste of money. Sockets for math coprocessors exist in most 80386DX- and 80386SX-based machines and in some 80486SX-based machines. Any machines using more powerful processors than these already have the math coprocessor circuitry built into the CPU.

II

15.6. How do I install a new motherboard?

A motherboard replacement is about the most complex hardware operation that you can perform on a PC. Still, only a limited number of components are involved, and it's the kind of job that most persons with a minimal level of dexterity can complete in less than two hours. Before beginning, make sure that you have the following tools:

- One regular and one Phillips screwdriver
- One 1/4-inch and one 3/16-inch nutdriver
- One pair of needle-nosed pliers (usually needed for removing any plastic standoffs that are installed in holes in the motherboard)

Armed with the tools and a desk surface with plenty of work space, you can use the steps here as a guide to motherboard replacement:

1. Before disconnecting any components from your PC, write down the appropriate information that is stored in your existing system's CMOS memory (such as the number of drives, cylinders, and sectors installed; hard disk drive types;

and so on). You need to enter this information at the setup screen of the CMOS configuration utility for the new motherboard. (If you are replacing the hard disk drive at the same time, you don't need to use the old hard disk configuration information; instead, you can use the configuration information that is packaged with the new drive.)

2. Unplug your PC and remove the cover (refer to Appendix B, "PC Assembly," if needed, for guidelines concerning cover removal).

3. Make notes about how all your system components are connected. In particular, pay attention to how your hard drives are connected to the disk controllers, because you will need to reinstall them in the same manner.

> **TIP** You can make the job of reassembly easier if you place easily removable adhesive stickers on cables that attach between your various devices (like your disk drives) and their respective expansion cards. You then will be able to note where the cables should align with the connectors on the devices during the reinstallation process.

4. Disconnect all cables (including the power connectors) and remove the expansion cards from your PC, along with all hard drives and floppy drives. Be sure to handle the expansion cards by their edges, and be careful not to touch the pins on any of the connectors or edge slots.

5. If the power supply blocks access to the motherboard, remove the power supply (it usually is mounted to the rear of the PC's frame with 1/4-inch hex head screws).

6. Remove the mounting screws from the corners of the motherboard, and remove the old motherboard.

7. If any memory must be added to the motherboard, install the necessary SIMMs or DRAM chips before installing the motherboard; it's easier to gain access to the DRAM or SIMM slots when numerous expansion cards, cables, and disk drives are not in the way. (See Chapter 12, "Upgrading Your Memory," for tips on installing memory.)

8. In some cases, vendors include plastic standoffs mounted in holes on the motherboard, usually added as insurance against the underside of the motherboard touching any part of the PC's metal frame. If these standoffs have been included, you can use your needle-nosed pliers to remove them and reinsert them into any corresponding holes in the new motherboard.

9. Insert the new motherboard in the space vacated by the old motherboard, aligning the holes in the corners of the motherboard with the mounting holes in the PC's case. Install, but don't yet tighten, the motherboard's mounting screws.

10. Install one of the expansion cards into an expansion slot of the motherboard to make sure that cards in general can line up with the slots on the rear of the computer. When the general alignment looks OK, tighten the mounting screws that hold the motherboard to the PC's frame.

11. Reinstall the power supply (if necessary).

12. Connect the power supply connectors to the motherboard.

13. Connect any wires from the case's power indicator lamp to the motherboard.

14. Reinstall the floppy and hard disk drives.

15. Reinstall the floppy and hard drive interface cards in their expansion slots. (Many PCs use the same interface card to connect to both the floppy and the hard disk drives.)

16. Using the ribbon cables you removed in step 4, reconnect the drive interface cards to the floppy and hard drives. In all cases, make sure that pin 1 on any of the drive edge connectors aligns with pin 1 on the cables (usually marked by a red or blue stripe along the wiring).

17. Reinstall all remaining expansion cards and reconnect any peripherals (such as monitors) to the expansion cards.

18. Replace the covers, and plug in and turn on the PC. Immediately after turning on the PC, you should hear the power supply fan and see a message on-screen indicating the system's level of ROM and the start of the memory test. If you get an abnormal indication (such as a series of constant beeps or a black screen), turn off the power and recheck all your connections.

II

Because the motherboard is new, you have to configure its CMOS setup to match the hardware you have connected (particularly in terms of the type and number of drives connected). Refer to the instructions that came with the motherboard for specifics on how to do this.

15.7. How can I install an OverDrive processor?

The precise steps you follow depend on whether your PC has an empty OverDrive socket. If your PC does have an empty OverDrive socket, the OverDrive processor simply goes into that socket. If there is no empty socket, you must remove the existing processor and install the OverDrive processor in its place. If your system has an empty OverDrive socket (usually it's located beside the existing CPU), follow these steps:

1. If the socket has a ZIF (Zero Insertion Force) handle on its edge, lift the handle and drop the OverDrive processor into the socket, making sure that the pins line up correctly. When the OverDrive processor is seated fully in the socket, release the ZIF handle.

2. If the socket has no ZIF handle on its edge, insert the OverDrive processor partially into the socket, making sure that all the pins are correctly aligned. After checking on the alignment of the pins, firmly press the OverDrive processor fully into the socket.

If your system does not have an empty socket, use the following steps to install an OverDrive processor:

1. If the socket has a ZIF (Zero Insertion Force) handle on its edge, lift the handle and pull the old processor out of the socket. Drop the OverDrive processor into the socket, making sure the pins line up correctly. When the OverDrive processor is seated fully in the socket, release the ZIF handle.

2. If the socket has no ZIF handle on its edge, use the chip puller/insertion tool provided with the OverDrive processor to remove the existing processor from the socket. Insert the OverDrive processor partially into the socket, making sure

that all the pins are aligned correctly. After checking on the alignment of the pins, firmly press the OverDrive processor fully into the socket.

After the OverDrive chip is installed, you can reassemble the covers and turn on your system. With an OverDrive upgrade, you do not need to change any configuration settings; the new processor begins working immediately, providing a speed boost to your system.

II

16

Upgrading Your Peripherals

This chapter examines peripherals (including keyboards, mice, trackballs, and graphics tablets) that can be used with your Windows setup. It also provides troubleshooting hints for mice, which are among the most potentially troublesome rodents (pardon the pun) in the peripherals lineup.

Keyboards

Keyboard layouts are about as varied as shells on a seashore. The original IBM keyboards had the Esc key on the left of the 1 key in the numeric row. The 84-key keyboard moved the Esc key to the top row of the keypad. The tilde (~) and grave (^) keys were moved to the original Esc position to the left of the one (1) key. In the past, most keyboards had generally the same layout with minor differences in the placement of the Alt keys and function keys. It's these minor differences that cause different people to buy different keyboards.

Another quality that makes keyboards so varied is their feel. *Feel*, or touch, is used to refer to how much pressure one has to apply to the keys and how it feels to actually press and release the key. Some people like to hear their keyboards as they type; others don't and want a keyboard that is quieter. Therefore, there are a variety of keyboards because there are a variety of ways people like them.

Recently, Microsoft, Kinesis, and other companies have introduced a new generation of keyboards, the *ergonomically designed* keyboards. These keyboards take into account the stress and strain on the hands as you type. Ergonomic keyboards split the standard keyboard down the middle, placing the keys commonly pressed by each hand on the two separate ends of the keyboard. The idea behind this design is to have the keyboard imitate the natural contour of the arms and hands, making typing more comfortable.

When you purchase a keyboard, you also need to consider the electrical standards and plug differences of the keyboards. There are two plug types used in today's keyboards: the 5-pin DIN plug and the newer 6-pin miniature DIN plug. The signals carried on the different plugs are the same—this compatibility is a good feature when it comes time to upgrade. To make one compatible with the other, all you need is an adapter to change a 6-pin to a 5-pin or a 5-pin to a 6-pin plug.

Electrical differences can pose a problem. There are two types of keyboards, XT and AT class keyboards. Most of the keyboards built today follow the AT standard. The designations XT and AT refer to the electrical differences in the keyboards, not the types of computers with which they are compatible. For the most part, computers built since 1985, including all those built today, follow the AT standard. The two keyboards are not interchangeable, but this should not pose a problem. Unless you have a computer built before 1984 (which are incapable of running Windows without a major, major upgrade), you will not see this type of keyboard design.

WARNING If you are upgrading an older machine, be warned that on some older computers (such as some models of Dell and Compaq machines) the electrical design of the keyboard is different than keyboards made today. These keyboards use what is known as *proprietary design*. If you plug an industry-standard replacement keyboard into

the connector on these machines, the connector will fit fine, but you won't get the proper keys transmitted as you type. It can be difficult to find replacement keyboards for such machines from anywhere other than the machine's vendor.

Mice

From an operational standpoint, there are two basic kinds of mice: mechanical and optical. Inside the mechanical mouse is a small ball that spins in the different directions of the mouse. Two flywheels, one in a horizontal position, the other in the vertical position, contact the ball and track its movements. The sensors in turn determine how far you have moved the mouse. The software then translates the movements into a position for the mouse pointer on the screen.

The optical mouse uses a different principal to determine the pointer position and distance traveled. The distance is determined by light bouncing off a special mouse pad that is necessary for its operation. Although there are no special parts, and therefore nothing for lint and dirt to get into, you must have the special mouse pad for the mouse to work.

As to the mouse interface used, there are several different types:

- *Serial Mouse:* This mouse is connected to your computer through a serial port. Serial mice are the most common type of mice used today. Their advantages include low cost and adaptability with virtually every PC-compatible made in modern times (because serial ports are standard items on all PCs). The disadvantage of serial mice occurs when you want to use your serial ports for something else. If that will be the case, consider a bus mouse (or a PS/2 mouse if your PC has a connector for it). Figure 16.1 shows a serial mouse. Normally, such a mouse comes with both DB-9 and DB-25 connectors (as shown in the illustration) so you can connect the mouse to either variation of the serial port.

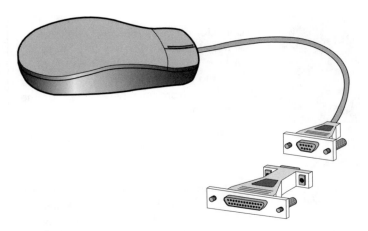

Figure 16.1. *A serial mouse.*

■ *PS/2 Mouse:* Introduced with the IBM PS/2 computer line, this mouse connects to the computer via a 6-pin miniature DIN plug, similar to the kind used by PS/2-style keyboards. An advantage of this type of mouse is that it is easily connected to the computer. The disadvantage is that the computer must have a PS/2-style mouse connector before you can use the mouse. Figure 16.2 shows an example of a PS/2-style mouse.

Figure 16.2. *A PS/2 mouse.*

■ *Bus Mouse:* This mouse is good if you want to save one of your serial ports for some other purpose. It's a bit more expensive because it requires more hardware—you'll need to install a small expansion card. The connector design resembles that of the PS/2 mouse, but the connector is designed to plug into the bus adapter card supplied with the mouse. This type of mouse, as expected, costs more—about $125.

A mouse does use up some of the hardware resources of your computer. However, you can minimize this by using a PS/2 connector if your PC has one. Obviously, if you choose the bus or serial interface, you'll be giving up a serial port or an expansion slot in your computer.

Trackballs

Trackballs (which are built into many laptop computer keyboards) resemble a mouse turned upside down; a trackball is a small ball that you rotate with your palm to cause movement of the pointer on-screen. Many people favor this mutation of the mouse for one good reason: a desk never seems to have enough space. The tracking ball doesn't have to move, which means it doesn't need the square foot or so of space that a mouse needs to move around. The tracking ball requires the same interfaces that the mouse does. As a result, you are again confronted with the question of how to connect it. (Trackballs use the same connection techniques as mice.)

Both mice and trackballs come in two- or three-button models. In the past, the second and third buttons on mice and trackballs served little or no purpose. However, software now makes it possible for those buttons to call up special menus, such as the Properties windows in Windows 95. There are no popular applications that take advantage of mice with a third button, but software often supplied with the mouse may make it possible to assign a special task to the third mouse button. (One example is assigning the mouse button to duplicate the Alt+*key* combination that saves or prints your documents in your favorite word processor.) By reassigning the third mouse button through software, the button does more than sit there and look like a button.

Graphics Tablets

In some cases a mouse is not sufficient for drawing. If you are in a profession that requires you to draw accurate lines, for example, a mouse is not likely to serve your needs. The graphics tablet

II

revolutionized the world of drafting and architecture, and it now enables persons in these professions to draw accurate diagrams and edit them painlessly.

Most graphics tablets use some kind of pointing device—either a light pen or a puck—depending on the type of work being done. The strength of a graphics tablet is its accuracy in translating movements into digitized output. The graphics tablets range in size from a mouse pad to the size of a drafting table. Graphics boards can cost from $150 to $1,500 for a high-end graphics board.

Pens and pucks, the input devices for graphics tablets, both come with or without cords. A cordless pen or puck offers more mobility and enables you to switch between the puck and pen simply by picking up the other. However, you will need to consider whether you are able to keep up with the cordless pen or puck.

Pen technology has advanced to the point where the computer can distinguish between lighter and darker lines according to the pressure applied to the board. High-end graphics programs often incorporate this into the software. Pressure-sensitive graphics programs also go as far as interpreting the pen movements differently based on the pressure applied.

A puck looks similar to a mouse. Sensors keep track of the puck's location based on the light reflected from the tablet. These input devices are great for data transfer from a set of building plans to the computer. Using crosshairs, you can move a puck over the plans for a building to edit the plans. As with a mouse, a puck has several buttons for entering commands to the computer. Because of its capability to be tightly integrated with popular programs, a puck can enable you to do hours of work without the use of the keyboard.

16.1. How do I install a mouse?

If you have a PS/2 port and mouse, and can plug in a toaster, you should have no problems installing your mouse. On the other hand, if you want to install a serial port mouse, you can follow these steps:

1. Connect the mouse connector to the desired serial port on the back of your PC.

2. In Windows, choose Start | Settings | Control Panel.

3. In the Control Panel, choose Add New Hardware.

4. When the Hardware Installation Wizard dialog box appears, choose Next and answer Yes when asked if the device is installed.

5. After choosing Next, choose Mouse from the Hardware Type list.

6. Click Next. Windows will look for the mouse, and you can begin installation.

Installing a bus mouse is the most difficult of all the mouse installations because you must install hardware. Here are the steps you need to follow:

1. After disconnecting all power to your computer, remove the cover from it. Find the slot in which you wish to place the card.

2. You may have to set some of the DIP switches or change some jumper settings; you'll need to consult the mouse's documentation for those answers. This is to prevent IRQ conflicts.

3. Insert the card in the selected slot.

4. Firmly seat the card, and attach the screw to hold it in place.

5. Replace the cover, reconnect the power to your computer, and start it up.

6. Choose Start | Settings | Control Panel. When Control Panel opens, choose New Devices.

7. Choose Next and answer Yes when asked if the device is installed, then choose Next again.

8. Choose Mouse from the Hardware Type list, and choose Next. Windows will find the device and installation can begin.

16.2. I installed a new mouse, but it doesn't work correctly. Now what?

Two points that you may want to consider if you are having trouble with your mouse are as follows:

■ Check to see that the mouse is connected to the proper port on the PC. If the mouse is a serial mouse, it may be connected to the wrong COM port (many recently manufactured PCs have more than one COM port).

■ If the mouse has a switch on its underside that enables you to choose an emulation for the type of mouse, make sure the switch is set in the correct position for the type of mouse driver you chose during installation. Some mice have a switch that lets you choose either Microsoft mouse emulation or Logitech mouse emulation. If the switch is in the wrong position, the pointer either will move erratically on the screen or won't move at all.

Choosing and Upgrading Your Windows Printer

This chapter covers printers that can be used with Windows systems. Although your choice of printers does not necessarily help Windows run any faster on an overall basis, you definitely can gain increased performance when it comes to the overall process of getting your data on paper. Like it or not, as a society we're a long way from the "paperless office." The graphical environment that is Windows seems to encourage the generation of printed documents.

This chapter provides a quick rundown on printer types that are appropriate for use with Windows, and it provides some upgrade tips to help you get the most out of existing printers.

17.1. What types of printers should I consider for use with Windows?

Printer types generally used as Windows printers include dot-matrix, inkjet, laser, LED page printers, and color inkjet or color thermal-transfer printers. The paragraphs that follow explain how these printers work in general, as well as their pros and cons:

- *Laser printers:* These printers use a moving laser to print images on a photosensitive drum. The imaged areas on the drum attract toner, and the toner then is transferred to the paper in the same fashion as in an office copier. Laser printers offer high quality print, quiet printing, and are cost-effective, considering the technology involved. You can purchase a basic model laser for about $500. The per-page cost for a laser printer is significantly higher when compared with a dot-matrix printer, however. A dot-matrix printer costs you about 1 cent per page, and a laser printer costs more in the 3 cents per page range. (This high per-page cost is due to the expense of replacing the one-piece printing cartridge used in most laser printers. Replacing this cartridge routinely costs between $50 and $100.)

- *LED page printers:* An LED page printer works much like a laser, with one exception—the image is written on the drum by a fixed matrix of light-emitting diodes that emit light as opposed to a moving laser. Generally, LED page printers tend to be less expensive than laser printers. This type of printer has basically the same drawback as the laser, which is a relatively high per-page cost.

- *Dot-matrix printers:* These printers use a ribbon to bang images onto a paper much in the way a typewriter does, but at a higher speed. These are by far the most inexpensive printers to operate, and the most durable in text-based environments. These printers also have the capability to handle multipart forms and very wide paper. Dot-matrix printers are very noisy, however. Also, when you print graphics with a dot-matrix printer, the print quality is poor and the image shows banding, and the pounding given the print head tends to shorten its life significantly.

- *Inkjet printers:* These printers work by squirting ink onto paper via tiny nozzles controlled by the computer. Inkjet printers are quiet and compact. They also are cost-effective; prices range from about $150 to $300—less than the cheapest laser printer. On the other hand, inkjets have a higher per-page operating cost: about 4 cents to 8 cents. Also, the ink sometimes has an annoying tendency to smear and streak (this tendency often can be reduced by being careful about the quality of paper you buy for the printer).

■ *Thermal-wax printers:* These printers work by melting wax-based inks onto the page. These printers are inexpensive, and often portable. They also are slow and have a high per-page cost. The quality for photographs is not good either.

■ *Color inkjets and color thermal printers:* These printers use inkjet or thermal technology to print. The colors are achieved by the use of cartridges in multiple colors. Color printers have a high quality output at high resolutions. These printers are perfect for business graphics; in some cases, approximate photo color can be reached. Color printers, however, are very expensive to operate and are extremely slow. They often are bulky and have high per-page operation costs.

By far, the most preferred printers among Windows users are the laser printer and the LED page printer. This preference is due mainly to the relatively inexpensive operating costs and the high-quality copies that can be printed. At one time, laser printers were the selected province of big businesses, but dropping prices have made these printers practical for the average PC user who wants a quiet, cost-effective, high-quality printer.

17.2. What does DPI refer to?

Laser printers (and some other printer types) commonly refer to resolutions as *dots per inch*, or *dpi*. The higher the dpi, the finer the printer's resolution. The standard of 300 dpi for a laser printer remained unchanged until recently. Although a 300 dpi printer produces a pretty good image, a sharp eye can detect the rough edges. The high-end 300-dpi printers manufactured by Hewlett-Packard use RET (Resolution Enhancement Technology), as Hewlett-Packard calls its edge enhancer. IBM also offers a similar technology in the company's laser printers, called Print Quality Enhancement Technology. Regardless of the company that designs edge-enhancement technology into its laser printers, all these printers perform the same function, which is compensating for the jagged edges by filling in dots of different sizes to give the letters a smoother look. Laser printers that print at 600 dpi are common on the market, although they do cost more than the 300-dpi models.

17.3. What features should I look for in a printer?

Speed is definitely something you should keep in mind. Although the page-per-minute ratings are only ballpark figures done under ideal circumstances, they can serve as a general guide to which printer is faster at printing text. When it comes to graphics, however, all those numbers go out the window. Each printer's processor is optimized for different tasks. A printer that may have been rated at eight pages per minute, therefore, may only print one page per minute when printing graphics.

Keep in mind that the fastest printers today are those that have RISC processors. Once again, remember that this is all relative. Any printer that is inundated with many different fonts, graphics, and so on in one massive document will be slowed down by the complexity of the job. Also, if your printer doesn't have sufficient memory, it will be slow regardless of the processor.

Paper handling is another area to look at. Think about the different sizes of paper that you will need to print on in the future. An average printer, for example, will not be able to handle 11-inch-by-17-inch paper (paper that is larger than the standard legal paper). If you need to print on this kind of paper, you need to look for a printer that accepts paper of this size. Also, not all printers will handle envelopes. If you want to print envelopes, you also need to check to see whether the printer you want to buy can print envelopes. Also consider whether you need to print just one envelope once in a while, or a group of envelopes at the same time. Some printers are capable of printing multiple envelopes at one time, but they are in the minority.

Finally, you should consider the paper capabilities of your printer. Some portable printers only handle one sheet of paper at a time. Are you willing to tolerate that for the convenience of portability? Think about these things before you buy your printer so that you can avoid purchasing a printer, only to discover later that you need additional paper-handling capabilities. (You may have to purchase optional paper trays for your laser printer, for example, which can seem incredibly expensive for what amounts to little more than a plastic paper holder.)

A printer's installed memory also is an important consideration when purchasing your printer. Because the print data can move to the printer much quicker than it can be printed, a place to store the information is needed. If your printer has plenty of memory, it can accept the entire document from Windows, leaving you to continue in your other applications without the hassle of waiting or dealing with inferior performance because of printer activity.

Lack of memory can limit what you can print. In order for a laser printer to print a full page of graphic images, you need a minimum of 1M memory. If you plan on printing many graphics pages, you need 3M of memory on your printer. (As with PCs, with printers, you can never have enough memory.) More memory also improves the performance of your printer.

Finally, you need to look at the interface compatibility of your printer. Printers are available with many different compatibility interfaces, serial ports, and parallel ports. Printers also are available with AppleTalk for the Macintosh or Ethernet for network hookups. When you buy your printer, investigate these features after determining which you will be using. If you may be using more than one feature, check to see whether the printer will switch automatically between the interfaces.

17.4. How can I increase the performance of my existing laser printer?

You can add to the performance of most laser printers by adding new memory to the printer, by adding fonts, or by a combination of both of these. The precise methods are different, depending on the model of printer, but most lasers enable you to insert an additional memory expansion card into a slot somewhere in the printer to increase the performance of the printer.

You also can add fonts to your printer. Most printers enable you to vary the fonts you print via the printer. You can use this feature to create better documents, without being confined to the fonts in your word processor. Simply purchase a compatible font cartridge from your vendor, and insert it into a printer's cartridge slot.

The location of these slots varies from printer to printer. On the popular Hewlett-Packard LaserJets, the font cartridge slots are located on the left front panel or on the right side of the printer toward the front edge. (Consult your printer's documentation to determine exactly where these slots are for your particular laser printer.)

17.5. What is PostScript, and can I add it to my existing laser printer?

PostScript is a description language patented by Adobe Systems, Inc., and heavily used by the professional typesetting industry. PostScript offers a wide variety of fonts and a great deal of flexibility in how your pages can be laid out. If you are very involved in desktop publishing or a demanding page layout application, PostScript is worth considering. You can add PostScript to some non-PostScript printers in the following ways:

■ Buy plug-in cartridges that add Adobe PostScript (or a clone of it).

■ For many laser printers, you can purchase an upgrade circuit board with PostScript.

■ Purchase a speed/resolution upgrade kit that includes PostScript.

> **NOTE**   Before you read about the ways to add PostScript to a printer, consider whether you'll need all the benefits of PostScript. If you just want to print the fonts, you only need Adobe Type Manager or some similar software utility—not PostScript. Also, at the time of this writing, most fonts are available in TrueType format.

PostScript built into an upgrade circuit board that you install in your printer gives you the most problem-free and fastest printing. Cartridges, however, perform somewhat slower. One of the less expensive clones of PostScript is offered by Pacific Data Products' PacificPage II. This particular PostScript clone is quite popular and does a decent job for a product that undercuts the true PostScript cartridge by HP. Although it produces the pages rather slowly, it is cost-effective and reliable.

17.6. How do I install a printer?

Installing a printer is not the most difficult of upgrades, but it does require attention. Use the following steps to install a printer:

1. In a safe place, remove the printer from the box and review the documentation. This step helps you to be aware of any special considerations you should have before you proceed. Be sure that all the packing materials are removed. Some printers have packing materials in unusual places, and if you try to operate the printer with the packing intact, you may damage the printer.

2. If there is a ribbon or toner parts to install, you should do this now. The documentation provides exact instructions for your particular printer.

3. Determine whether you are going to use a serial or a parallel port, and connect the appropriate cable to the back of the computer (be sure that the power is off).

4. Connect the other end of the cable to the same type of port on the printer.

5. Connect the power cable to the printer and to the AC power outlet.

6. Now run the self-test on the printer. This helps you determine whether there are any problems early on. If your self-test failed, it may be because it was connected to the port on the computer. If you think this is the case, remove the cord from the back of the monitor and try the self-test again.

7. In Windows, choose Start | Settings | Control Panel.

8. After the Control Panel opens, choose Add New Hardware to launch the Installation Wizard.

9. After the Wizard opens, choose Next. When you are asked whether the device is installed, answer Yes.

10. Choose Next. In the resulting dialog box, choose Printers from the Hardware Type list. After choosing Next again, Windows displays a series of screens that you can use to configure the printer.

II

17.7. Can you offer some suggestions for troubleshooting common installation problems with printers?

Sure. Here are a few quick tips for troubleshooting a printer installation.

- On a dot-matrix printer, be sure that the DIP switches are set correctly. Check the documentation to be sure.

- If the image on your laser printer is too dark or too light, check the density setting and lower or raise it. (You can usually find this setting by opening the printer cover.) Also check the DPI Settings. Gray tones in a low resolution tend to appear too dark or black.

- Be sure that your computer knows to what kind of printer it is connected. Windows doesn't speak the printer language of a Hewlett-Packard LaserJet 4 if you tell Windows that a Panasonic KX-P1180 is the default printer. Having the incorrect printer driver chosen under Windows usually causes unintelligible information to be printed.

- For all printers, be sure that all the cables are connected firmly.

- If your printer isn't getting power at all, a fuse may be blown. Check your documentation to determine where any fuses may be located so you can see whether or not they are blown.

Your documentation can provide you with specialized help for your installation problems. Because many types of printers exist, this chapter cannot cover all the problems you may face. By referring to your printer manual, you can troubleshoot many of the problems you may encounter with your specific printer.

Windows 95 and the Outside World

18   Installing and Using Windows 95 on
     a Network   271
19   Windows Communications   301
20   Windows and Laptop Computing   317
21   Troubleshooting Windows   331

Installing and Using Windows 95 on a Network

This chapter provides the specifics you'll need to fully integrate Windows 95 with an existing Local Area Network (LAN). One of the many advantages to this particular upgrade of Windows is its greatly increased support for local area networks. In the design of its predecessor (Windows 3.1), the operating system underneath was still DOS, and Windows had to reside above DOS. The network shells loaded into memory before Windows, so what you had in the end was DOS in conventional RAM, network shells following DOS (and hopefully loaded into high memory), and Windows in extended memory sitting on top of the first two. With cranky DOS applications, this made for a house of cards all too often; Windows 3.1 on top of Novell NetWare had an annoying tendency to lock up, particularly when dealing with DOS applications and their less-than-stellar manners.

To cure many of these problems, Windows 95 includes the operating system, eliminating the reliance on DOS. It also uses built-in networking components that are designed to work with Novell NetWare, Windows NT, and Microsoft LAN Manager networks. The networking components in Windows 95 are designed into the software as virtual device drivers operating in protected mode, so they don't use any conventional memory.

Those who may be on the verge of implementing a LAN should realize that Windows 95 not only integrates with NetWare and Windows NT as a network client, but that it also has its own peer-to-peer networking built in. Hence, if your network needs are small in scope, it's not necessary to go through the expense of installing a file server running Novell NetWare or Windows NT. You can simply add some relatively inexpensive network adapter cards, the connecting cables, and any hubs needed. (Starter kits for two-, three-, and four-station networks of this type are routinely available through retail computer outlets.) After installing the hardware, you can use the networking options of Windows 95 to allow resource sharing and communications between the PCs connected to the network. With the prior version of Windows, the stand-alone user—someone not connecting to a peer-to-peer network—was content with Windows 3.1. And if you wanted peer-to-peer networking, you switched to Windows for Workgroups 3.11. Windows 95 integrates the stand-alone and peer-to-peer networking capabilities of both of the older products into a single product.

18.1. What kind of network connectivity does Windows 95 provide?

Windows 95 has the capability to support different networks, alone or simultaneously. You can have a workstation connected to Windows 95 servers, to Windows NT servers, and to NetWare servers simultaneously. This multiple-network support is provided by the Network Provider Interface (NPI) that's built into Windows 95. Support for Novell NetWare, Windows NT, and Microsoft LAN Manager is built into Windows 95. Also, this version of Windows supports the following third-party networks:

> Artisoft's LANtastic, versions 5.0 and above
> Banyan VINES, versions 5.5.2 and above
> Beame and Whiteside, BW-NFS 3.0C and above
> DEC Pathworks, versions 4.1 and above (installed as a protocol)
> Novell NetWare, versions 3.11 and above

SunSelect PC-NFS, versions 5.0 and above
TCS 10-Net, versions 4.1 and above

> **NOTE** In all cases, a third-party network should be up and running before you install Windows, so that the installation and setup program run by Windows will detect the network hardware and will install the needed support files for the network.

18.2. How does the user interface for Windows 95 support networking?

The user interface designed into Windows makes navigating a network and using network resources a point-and-click affair. The most significant aspect of network resource use that's different from earlier versions of Windows is that there's no longer any need to hunt for and set up obscure options in Connect dialog boxes for different network devices. This version of Windows places all network objects in one place, the Network Neighborhood. It's accessible by double-clicking the Network Neighborhood icon on the Windows desktop.

Common network tasks like browsing file servers and connecting to a desired network printer are handled in the same way, no matter what type of server you are connected to. Users of Novell NetWare can also choose to run the NetWare utilities through a DOS session. This offers backward compatibility with techniques that users may already be familiar with.

III

> **NOTE** When you open Network Neighborhood, it shows only the network servers you are logged onto, or servers that you most frequently connect to. This "initially restrictive view" makes identifying network resources much less of a hassle from a user's point of view. Additional icons in Network Neighborhood are provided to let users browse among the entire network.

Q 18.3. What are the overall steps involved in setting up peer-to-peer networking for the first time?

The current version of Windows makes going to a small workgroup-type network environment a fairly simple matter. The overall steps involved include the following:

1. Install a network adapter card in each PC you want connected to the network. Generally, you install these as you would install any adapter card (see Appendix B, "PC Assembly," for general tips on working with hardware). Detailed instructions normally accompany the network adapter cards that you purchase. What's important to remember with network adapter cards is that you must carefully follow any configuration steps listed in the installation instructions regarding the setting of jumpers or switches. A common problem that arises with network adapter cards is that you may have the jumpers or switches set to use an interrupt (IRQ) number that is already in use by a modem, sound card, or by some other adapter card. If this happens, neither the network adapter card nor the other adapter card will work properly.

> **NOTE**   With Extended Industry Standard Architecture (EISA) bus computers, and with IBM PS/2s that use Micro Channel architecture, a software program (shipped with the adapter card) is used to set the IRQ settings after you install the card.

2. Connect the cables between each PC in the workgroup. There are many types of cables on the market, and the precise type you use will be more or less governed by which type of network adapter card you are using. With most network adapter designs, you connect the cable to the rear of the adapter either by inserting a plug identical to a telephone cord plug into a jack, or by inserting a round connector into a jack and twisting it firmly into place.

> **TIP** If you are installing a network for the first time, it's a wise idea to purchase one of the network starter kits commonly available at computer retail outlets. These kits come with network adapter cards and matching cables to set up two-, three-, and four-station networks. As the network grows, you can purchase additional adapter cards and cables individually to add more computers to the network.

3. Install Windows 95 on each PC. If you install this version of Windows on a PC that is already running Windows 3.*x*, Windows 95 will add all of your program groups to the menu structure. Also, your configuration settings and printer driver information will be carried over to the new version of Windows.

During the installation process, Windows will sense what type of network adapter cards you have installed, and will automatically activate the proper network drivers needed. If Windows cannot identify your particular network adapter card, it will display a list of network drivers, and ask you to select one from the list.

Once the network is set up and Windows is running, you can use Windows in pretty much the same manner as you did before attaching to a network. What peer-to-peer networking adds to the picture is the capability to designate resources as *shared resources*. An example of a shared resource might be a particular folder located on your PC's hard disk. If you want others in the workgroup to be able to access that folder, you'll have to declare it as shared. (To do this, right-click the folder in Explorer or My Computer, choose Properties to open the window, click the Sharing tab, and fill in the desired options. For more on this, see question 18.20, "How can I set up share-level security on a network?," later in this chapter.)

If you want to selectively provide access to the directory, you assign it a password and tell those users who should have access what the password is. With peer-to-peer networking, the owner of each resource decides whether others can share that resource. If Sue has a massive hard disk drive and John has a laser printer, John controls whether other users can use the laser printer and Sue controls who gets access to what folders on her hard disk.

III

> **NOTE** Any user on a peer-to-peer network can browse among the resources that have been made available by double-clicking the Network Neighborhood icon.

> **TIP** As organizations grow, most peer-to-peer networks reach a point in size where the peer-to-peer model can no longer handle the workload, or doesn't provide the level of security needed by an organization. You'll need to watch for signs that you are approaching this point, and plan your upgrade decisions accordingly. If your four-person network has grown to a couple dozen users and response time slows to a crawl at four in the afternoon every day, it's time to consider a change to the client/server model of networking.
>
> You can add a PC as a fast file server with as much hard disk space as your organization can afford, another PC as a dedicated print server with a high-speed laser (get one with the largest paper tray you can find), and use Novell NetWare or Windows NT as a network operating system. When you do this, you'll need to change your network configuration options to match the type of network software you're now using. See Question 18.11, "How can I set my network configuration options in Windows?" later in this chapter, for specifics on how to do this.

18.4. How can I browse among the shared resources in my workgroup?

To browse the resources within your workgroup, perform the following steps:

1. Double-click the Network Neighborhood icon on the desktop.

2. When Network Neighborhood opens, double-click the computer that has the shared resources you want to view.

> **TIP**
>
> On a peer-to-peer network, it's a wise idea to standardize folder names among users. This can prevent confusion among different users on the network. As an example, if one user stores Word for Windows documents in a folder called MYDOCS inside the WINWORD folder, and another stores them in a folder called MYWORK, and someone else puts them in a folder called DATA, no one intuitively knows how to find Word documents on someone else's hard drive. If everyone has a folder named WORDDOCS established for the purpose of storing documents, one user can easily access another user's work.

18.5. How can I browse among the shared resources in the entire network?

You can browse the shared resources in the entire network to which your computer is connected using the following steps:

1. Double-click the Network Neighborhood icon on the Desktop.

2. When Network Neighborhood opens, double-click the network that has workgroups you want to browse.

3. Double-click the workgroup that has computers you want to browse.

4. Double-click the computer that has shared resources you want to view.

III

18.6. Sharing Windows resources on our peer-to-peer network is slow at times, but we just can't afford a move to a high-performance file server and another network operating system right now. Is there anything else we can do to speed things up?

One step that you can take is to change the Performance Priority setting in the Sharing tab of the shared resource's properties. (Find the shared resource in My Computer or in Explorer, right-click it and choose Properties, then click the Sharing tab in the properties window.) If other users are complaining about how long it takes to access shared resources on your PC, move the Performance slider toward "Resources shared fastest."

18.7. We're already running Microsoft Windows for Workgroups. Will we keep all the peer-to-peer network capabilities that we currently have if we install Windows 95?

Yes. The setup program that's part of Windows will automatically upgrade your networking components of Workgroups for Windows, and Windows 95 will provide you with the peer-to-peer network services that you had previously, as well as the new remote access features built in to this version of Windows. Before installing Windows 95, make sure that your network is already up and running Windows for Workgroups; verify the network's operation by connecting to a shared resource in the network before starting the Windows Setup program.

TIP	Before performing any installation of Windows, it's a wise idea to back up your hard disk drive.

18.8. How can I install Windows on a workstation that's already attached to a local area network?

With existing networks, you have two choices: you can install Windows locally (running the Setup program from the PC's floppy drive or CD-ROM), or you can install Windows from a shared drive on the network. There are advantages to either approach. If you install Windows locally, the Setup program will first copy all needed files into a temporary directory on the hard disk, then it will run itself from the hard disk. If you run the Setup program from a shared drive on a server, the Windows software is downloaded from the server to the workstation, then the Setup program configures the workstation in accordance with the options set by the system administrator. The advantage of installing Windows from the server is that the system administrator is able to exercise tight control over the Setup options.

TIP	Local installation is advantageous to end users because they get more control over all aspects of the setup process.

You'll find more specifics on Windows installation in Appendix A, "Installation." As a quick reference, here are steps you can take to install Windows on a network. Several different circumstances are covered.

If you must install Windows off a shared network drive and you don't have Windows 3.*x* currently installed, perform the following steps:

1. Connect to the shared directory of the network drive.
2. Type SETUP /A and press Enter.
3. Follow the directions that appear on the screen to complete the installation.

If you want to install the administrative installation of Windows off a shared drive, and you are currently running Windows 3.*x* or Windows for Workgroups, perform the following steps:

1. Choose File|Run from the Program Manager menu.
2. Click Browse.
3. In the dialog box, locate the shared network drive and folder that contain the Setup program.

III

4. Click SETUP.EXE to select it, then click OK.

5. In the Command Line text box, click at the end of the command line and type /A, then click OK.

6. Follow the directions that appear on the screen to complete the installation.

If you want to install Windows locally, and you don't have Windows 3.*x* or Workgroups for Windows currently installed, perform the following steps:

1. Insert the Setup disk in the drive.

2. Log onto that drive (for example, enter A: if the Setup disk is in drive A), and enter SETUP.

3. Follow the directions that appear on the screen to complete the installation.

If you want to install Windows locally, and you're already running Windows 3.*x* or Workgroups for Windows, perform the following steps:

1. Insert the Setup disk in the drive.

2. Choose File | Run from the Program Manager menu.

3. Click Browse.

4. In the dialog box, locate the drive and folder that contain the Setup program.

5. Click SETUP.EXE to select it, then click OK.

6. In the next dialog box that appears, click OK again.

7. Follow the directions that appear on the screen to complete the installation.

NOTE When the Setup program detects Novell NetWare, it attempts to install the Microsoft Client for NetWare automatically. Usually, Setup replaces the existing network adapter driver, protocol, and the shell with its own NetWare-compatible protected mode components. (Setup also normally replaces Novell's NETBIOS support program with NWNBLINK, the 32-bit IPX-compatible NetBIOS driver.) If for any reason you don't want this to happen, use the Custom Network dialog box that appears during the Setup process. In this dialog box, delete the Microsoft Client for NetWare setting, and add the desired Novell NetWare client.

18.9. Is there a way to fine-tune the installation options that are used during the install process?

You can create a batch file that controls the installation options when Setup runs. To start Setup—whether from a DOS prompt or from a File Run dialog box within an earlier version of Windows—you can use the command sequence SETUP *filename*, where *filename* is the name of a text file that contains the desired custom settings for Setup to use. Under the control of the text file, you can change the optional components Setup will install, the default installation directory, the network settings, the user name and organization name, and the system settings.

18.10. I've added a new type of network adapter to a new computer that I'm adding to the network. How do I install the software needed by this network adapter?

Perform the following steps to install software for the network adapter:

1. Open the Start menu, and choose Settings | Control Panel.
2. When the Control Panel opens, double-click the Network icon.
3. Click Configuration.
4. Click Change, to the right of the Adapters box.
5. Click Add.
6. From the list that appears, choose the appropriate network adapter, then click OK.

III

18.11. How can I set my network configuration options in Windows?

All of the network options you use to establish different settings can be reached through the Control Panel's Network icon. Open the Start menu and choose Settings | Control Panel. When the Control Panel appears, double-click the Network icon to open its property window (see Figure 18.1). The Property window for Networks has three tabs, labeled Configuration, Identification, and Access Control.

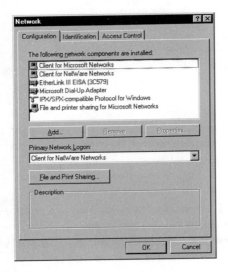

Figure 18.1. *Property window for Networks with Configuration tab displayed.*

The Configuration tab can be used to view and change the information about a user's client software, the network adapter card driver in use, the protocol used by the network, and the shared services available. When you click on Client, the dialog box that appears lets you choose the appropriate client software for the network you are using. (You can use the 32-bit compatible clients supplied with Windows 95, or you can use older "real mode" network clients.)

> **NOTE** When you use the Microsoft Client for NetWare as your choice of client, you don't need to load any Novell drivers in your AUTOEXEC.BAT file. Also, you should be aware that the Microsoft Client for NetWare doesn't read any of the settings in the NET.CFG configuration file. When Windows is first installed in the presence of a Novell NetWare network, all network settings needed by the client are read from the NET.CFG file and stored as information in the Registry. Afterward, NET.CFG is not needed by Windows. If you need to change any of these settings, you can do so through the Control Panel.

Click the Adapter button to display a dialog box that you can use to install drivers for different adapter cards, or to specify hardware settings (such as I/O and IRQ settings) used by the network adapter cards. Clicking the Protocol button displays a dialog box that lets you use other network protocols, and clicking the Service button displays a dialog box used to specify what kind of peer service you want to run, or install and configure additional services.

Clicking the Identification tab reveals the options shown in Figure 18.2.

You can use the options contained in this tab to change the computer name, workgroup name, and description for the workstation. (The information that you enter within the text boxes is used by Windows to identify the workstation on the network.)

Clicking the Access Control tab reveals the options shown in Figure 18.3.

You use the options contained within this tab to control the access that's allowed to shared resources on the network. You can specify share-level security, which conforms to the network security system that uses passwords assigned to each shared resource, or you can specify user-level security, which conforms to the network security system that requires each user on the network to have a valid user name and password.

III

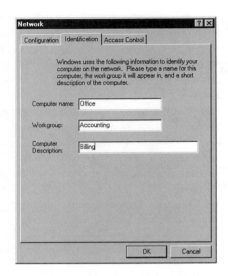

Figure 18.2. *Properties window for Network with Identification tab displayed.*

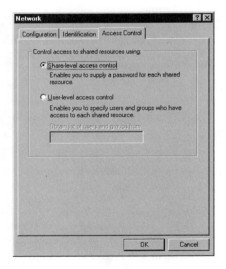

Figure 18.3. *Properties window for Network with Access Control tab displayed.*

18.12. How can I run the NetWare utilities (such as SYSCON, PCONSOLE, and FCONSOLE)?

You can go to a DOS prompt to run all the standard Novell utilities from within Windows. Start a DOS session in the usual manner, log onto the network drive that contains the Novell utilities, and run the desired utility.

18.13. How can I change the settings used for a dial-out network cable connection?

You can do this by performing the following steps:

1. Double-click Network Neighborhood.

2. When Network Neighborhood opens, double-click the Remote Access icon.

3. Right-click the connector icon whose settings you wish to change, and choose Properties from the popup menu.

4. Make the desired changes in the properties window that appears. (The changes will take effect when you access any shared resource that uses this connection, or when you next double-click the connector icon to establish a connection.)

18.14. What is Chat?

Chat is a simple application provided with Windows that lets users of a workgroup converse in real time. To start Chat, open the Start menu, and choose Programs | Accessories | Chat. The Chat window is divided into two halves. What you type appears on one side, and what the other user types appears on the other side. As you type messages to another workgroup member, they appear in that person's Chat window. As such, Chat is closer to the typed equivalent of a phone call than to an e-mail system. Previous users of Windows 3.1 may be new to Chat, but users of Windows for Workgroups will recognize it as a holdover from that version of Windows.

III

18.15. What is Print Server for NetWare, and how can I use it?

Microsoft's "Print Server" (as Novell calls it) for NetWare (MSPRV.EXE) is an interesting little program that lets a local printer behave like one of the network printers. The program lets you de-spool print jobs from a NetWare queue to your local printer. Any local printer that has been granted access to a NetWare server can be configured in this manner.

To use this capability, right-click the local printer, and choose Properties from the popup menu. In the properties window that opens, turn on the "Enable Microsoft Print Server for NetWare" option. When you do this, all NetWare servers that you have been granted access to will appear in a drop-down list box. Choose the desired server, and you'll see a list of available print servers. Select the desired print server, and spooler output for that printer will be redirected to your local printer.

> **NOTE** If the system administrator disables local printer sharing on the network, the Print Server for NetWare program will refuse to load.

18.16. We run a number of NetWare terminate-and-stay-resident utilities (TSRs) that are compatible with the Novell NetWare drivers, but are incompatible with the Microsoft Client for NetWare. How can we install or change Windows to use the Novell NetWare drivers?

Some TSRs, 3270 emulators, and other unusual programs will not cooperate with the Microsoft Client for NetWare. If you are using software like this on your network, you can install a Novell client when you install Windows, or you can replace the use of the Microsoft Client with a Novell NetWare client.

If you've already installed Windows on a network running Novell NetWare and you want to replace the Microsoft Client with the Novell NetWare client software, perform the following steps:

1. Get to a DOS prompt (choose Start | Programs | MS-DOS Prompt).

2. Log onto the network drive containing the NetWare installation software.

3. Run the NetWare installation program, and select the Install NetWare with Windows option.

4. End the DOS session (enter EXIT at the DOS prompt).

5. Get to the Control Panel (from the Start menu, choose Settings | Control Panel), and double-click the Network icon.

6. Click the IPX/SPX-compatible protocol to select it, then click Delete.

7. Click OK to get back to the Configuration property window.

8. Click Microsoft Client for NetWare, then click Delete.

9. Choose Novell NetWare Workstation Shell 3.*x* or Novell NetWare Workstation Shell 4.*x* as desired, then click Add.

10. Click Close to close the property window, then click OK to save the changes.

11. Restart the PC to have the changes take effect.

If you are about to install Windows and you want to keep using your current NetWare client, perform the following steps:

1. When the Setup program asks you whether you want to begin Setup or customize the installation, choose Customize.

2. In the dialog box that appears, click the Network button.

3. In the Custom Network dialog box that appears, click the Client button.

4. In the Change Clients dialog box that appears, click Microsoft Client for NetWare to select it, then click Delete.

5. Click the Add button, then click either the Novell NetWare 3.*x* client or the Novell NetWare 4.*x* client, as desired.

6. Click Close to close the Custom Network dialog box.

7. Click OK.

III

Q 18.17. We don't use NetWare or Microsoft LAN Manager. Can we install Windows 95 to support another existing third-party network?

Yes. Windows includes support for a number of third-party networks. The ones for which Microsoft provides specific details are listed in Question 18.1. Also, any other networks that are 100 percent NetBIOS-compatible should operate with Windows 95.

Use the following instructions to install Windows on a network other than one using Novell NetWare, Microsoft Networks, or Microsoft LAN Manager. These first six steps should be performed regardless of the network you plan to install. Additional steps are required if the network is Banyan VINES, DEC Pathworks, or SunSelect PC-NFS; follow the steps specific to the network you are using.

1. Make sure that the network software is already installed and running under DOS. If you currently use Windows 3.*x*, it should also be loaded.

2. Start the Windows 95 Setup program (see Question 18.3, "What are the overall steps involved in setting up peer-to-peer networking for the first time?" for specifics), and choose Custom Setup from the dialog box that appears.

3. Click Network Options. Setup should display the type of network you are running, and display it in the Clients section of the dialog box. If the type of network chosen by Setup is correct, click OK to exit the dialog box and continue with the setup process.

4. If the network client shown is incorrect, click Client, then click Add to display the Network Options dialog box. Choose the network vendor in the left pane, and the name of the network client in the right pane. Click OK, then click Close.

5. Click OK to exit the Network Configuration dialog box.

6. If you are using Banyan VINES, DEC Pathworks, or SunSelect PC-NFS, follow the additional steps required for that network.

Banyan VINES

To install Windows 95 to support Banyan VINES, perform the preceding steps 1 through 6, and then perform these additional steps:

1. Restart the computer, and immediately hold down the Shift+F5 key combination (doing so prevents Windows from loading).

2. Use a text editor to edit the AUTOEXEC.BAT file stored in the root directory of the startup disk. Make sure that the following lines have been included in the AUTOEXEC.BAT file by the Setup program:

```
\winboot\net init /dynamic
cd banyandirectory
```

   (Usually, the Setup program will add these lines to the end of the existing AUTOEXEC.BAT file.)

3. Make sure that the net start line includes a full path to the C:\WINBOOT directory, and that this line is between the redirall and arswait lines.

If you install Windows after installing the Banyan VINES client, a Banyan dialog box appears when the VINES.DRV driver loads. Perform these additional steps when you see the dialog box:

1. Turn on the option for keeping files on the network.

2. Click Install. Windows will exit and restart.

3. When the Banyan dialog box appears again, turn on the option for keeping files on the network.

4. Click Cancel.

DEC Pathworks

To install Windows 95 to support DEC Pathworks, begin the Windows installation by performing the following steps:

1. Start the Windows Setup installation program, and choose Custom Setup from the dialog box.

2. Click Network Options.

3. Click Client, then click Add.

III

4. Click Microsoft in the left pane to select it, then click Microsoft Network Client in the right pane. Click OK, then click Close.

5. Click Protocols, then click Add.

6. Click DEC in the left pane to select it, then click Pathworks 4.*x* or Pathworks 5.*x*, as is appropriate, in the right pane.

7. Click OK, then click Close.

8. Click OK to exit this dialog box and to continue with Setup.

SunSelect PC-NFS

To install Windows 95 to support SunSelect PC-NFS, perform these additional steps:

1. Make sure that the files SOCKDRV.SYS, PCNFS.SYS, and NFSDIS.SYS are copied to the C:\WINBOOT directory.

2. Copy PCNFS.386 to the WINDOWS\SYSTEM directory.

3. Remove the PC-NFS netbind command from the AUTOEXEC.BAT file.

18.18. What levels of security are provided by Windows 95?

Windows 95 includes both local security and network security. *Local security* applies to users that access a PC in a stand-alone fashion. Windows provides this type of security on a user-by-user basis, using the user names and passwords to establish the desired level of security. Local security is useful in a situation where a number of different users share the same PC; each user can be assigned a user name and password that determines what local resources that particular user is able to work with.

By comparison, *network security* refers to the ability of users to access the shared resources that are available on a local area network. Two overall methods of security are built into Windows 95: share-level security and user-level security. With share-level security, passwords are associated with the different shared files and other resources that are on the network. With user-level security, access to a network's shared resources is granted or denied based on the rights of the user who is trying to access the resources. (Networks running Novell NetWare are based on the share-level security model.)

> **NOTE** If you are using Windows' own peer-to-peer networking, or if you are running Microsoft Network File and Print Sharing, you can use either security method. If you are running Windows along with Novell NetWare, you cannot use share-level security on NetWare drives. Also, if you are running Microsoft Network File and Print Sharing, the user list and authentication of passwords must be provided by a Windows NT Advanced Server, or a Windows NT domain. If you are running Microsoft File and Print Sharing for NetWare, the user list and authentication of passwords must be provided by a Novell NetWare 3.*x* server, or by a Novell NetWare 4.*x* server running Bindery emulation. Refer to your Windows NT or NetWare documentation for specifics on enabling user names and passwords on the server.

III

18.19. How do I access the security options built into Windows?

1. Open the Start menu and click Settings | Control Panel.

2. When the Control Panel opens, double-click the Passwords icon. In a moment, the Properties for Security window opens, as shown in Figure 18.4.

Under the Change Passwords tab, you can use the Change the Windows password for the current Windows session. Another dialog box, shown in Figure 18.5, prompts you for password changes in other network environments so that you can synchronize passwords, making it much easier to log into multiple networks. (See Figure 18.5.)

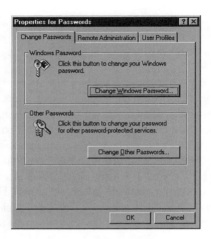

Figure 18.4. *The Properties for Security window.*

Figure 18.5. *The dialog box for new passwords in other networks.*

After selecting the other network or networks, click the OK button. Now you are prompted for your old password, as a check for who you are, and the new password. The new password must be entered twice as a check against a mistyped password. If you don't enter the same new password twice, the password will not be changed. This protects you from having the password become something other than what you thought you changed it to. Use the Tab key to move between the fields in this dialog box. Only after you have correctly entered the old and new password, click the OK button or press Enter. (See Figure 18.6.)

Figure 18.6. *The dialog box for changing the password.*

Under the User Profiles tab (see Figure 18.7), you can choose whether all users get the same desktop settings, or whether different Windows users using the same PC are able to customize their desktop settings.

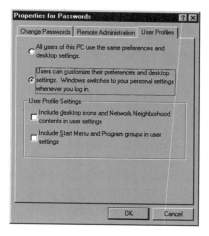

Figure 18.7. *The Profiles tab.*

Under the Remote Administration tab (see Figure 18.8), you can turn on or off an option that tells Windows to allow a remote user to administer files and settings on this local system.

If you are running Windows on a network, the Properties for Security window will also contain a Remote Administration tab. You can use the options shown on this tab to allow (or deny) administration of security on your PC from a remote site.

III

294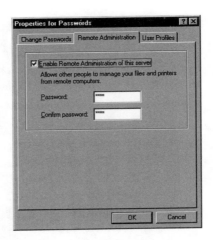

Figure 18.8. *The Remote Administration dialog box.*

18.20. How can I set up share-level security on a network?

As long as you are not running Microsoft File and Print Sharing for NetWare, share-level security is established by default. Each shared directory (or folder) and shared printer can be assigned a read-only password, and/or a full access password. To establish the password for a shared directory or printer, use the following steps:

1. Find the desired directory or printer in My Computer or in Explorer.

2. Right-click the desired directory, and choose Properties from the popup menu.

3. Click the Sharing tab to open the Sharing property window.

4. In the property window, specify that you want to share the directory.

5. Specify whether users should be allowed read-only access or full access.

6. In the Password text box, enter the password that will be required to access the resource.

7. Click OK to close the window.

To establish a password for remote administration on a shared computer, perform the following steps:

1. Open the Start menu, and choose Settings | Control Panel.
2. In the Control Panel, double-click the Passwords icon.
3. In the Properties for Security window that opens, click the Remote Administration tab.
4. Turn on the Enable Remote Administration option.
5. In the Password text box, enter the desired password.
6. Click OK.

18.21. How do I establish user-level security?

Assuming you are running Windows within a server-based environment that supports user-level security, you can set up security by performing the following steps:

1. Open the Start menu, and choose Settings | Control Panel.
2. Double-click the Network icon.
3. Click the Access Control tab.
4. Turn on the option for User-level Security in the window that opens.
5. In the text box, enter the name of the NetWare server or the Windows NT domain that will provide the user list and authentication of passwords.

III

> **NOTE** For every resource or service controlled by user-level security, Windows maintains groups (also known as *trustees*) who are given rights to that resource. What kinds of rights you can assign will depend on what kind of resource you are controlling.

For shared directories, you can let users have read-only access, full access, or custom access. (Custom access lets you grant different read, write, create, list, delete, change file attribute, and change file permissions rights for different users.)

For shared printers, you can grant the user the right to access the printer, or you can deny access.

For network DDE objects, you can grant a user read-only or full access.

For remote access, you can grant or deny the right to dial into your PC from a remote location.

For remote administration, you can grant or deny the right for a user to perform administration from a remote site.

18.22. How do I grant permissions to shared directories and printers?

To establish permissions for shared directories or shared printers, perform the following steps:

1. Find the desired directory or printer in My Computer or in Explorer.

2. Right-click the desired directory, and choose Properties from the popup menu.

3. Click the Sharing tab to open the Sharing property window.

4. Select the allowed access to the directory or the printer, and enter a password to be used to gain access.

To establish permissions for remote administration, use the following steps:

1. Open the Start menu, and choose Settings | Control Panel.

2. In the Control Panel, double-click the Passwords icon.

3. In the Properties for Passwords window that opens, click the Remote Administration tab.

4. Put a check mark in the box by clicking next to the enable remote administration.

5. Enter the Remote Password.

18.23. How can I monitor resource usage on a peer-to-peer network?

As your network grows in size, a way to monitor network traffic can become an important aid in keeping things running smoothly.

Windows includes a tool called NetWatcher. NetWatcher monitors network activity, showing you which resources are being used, who they are being used by, and how the resources are being used (as read-only or as read-write operations). You can also use NetWatcher to disconnect users who have connected to your computer's resources and have perhaps forgotten to disconnect.

To start NetWatcher, open the Start menu and choose Programs | Accessories | System Tools | NetWatcher. In the left side of the NetWatcher window that appears, you see the names of all users connected to your PC. Click any user in the list, and you'll see all folders, printers, and other resources in use by the selected user. The toolbar buttons perform the same tasks as the corresponding four options of the Connection menu, as explained in Table 18.1.

Table 18.1. Menu options and toolbar buttons in NetWatcher.

Menu Option/Toolbar Button	Function
Properties	Displays a dialog box containing additional information for the selected user
Disconnect	Disconnects selected user from your PC (see the Warning at the end of this topic)
Close File	Closes selected file that another user has opened (see the Warning at the end of this topic)
View Event Log	Displays the Event Log for your PC

III

The options menu contains choices for displaying or hiding the toolbar, for displaying or hiding the Status Bar, and (using the Split Window option) for changing the size of either window with the arrow keys on the keyboard.

You can use NetWatcher to disconnect a user who is connected to your computer, or to close a file on your PC that has been opened by another user, by performing the following steps (also see the Warning that follows):

1. Select the desired user (or file) by clicking the user name in the left side of the NetWatcher window, or by clicking the file name in the right side of the NetWatcher window.

2. Open the Connection menu and choose Disconnect, or click the Disconnect button in the toolbar to disconnect a user. Or, choose Close File or click the Close File button in the toolbar to close a file that a user has open.

3. When the confirmation dialog box appears, click Yes to disconnect the user or close the file.

WARNING	If you disconnect a user or close a file from your PC, the other user can lose data he was working on at the time. On a peer-to-peer network, you should always contact other users and give them the opportunity to save files before kicking them off your computer.

NetWatcher also offers the use of an *event log*. You can enable the event log, and then view events (which are a record of all network activity) on your PC. This can help in planning to meet the demands of network traffic, which has a tendency to grow in most organizations. To enable the event log, perform the following steps:

1. Open the Start menu, and choose Programs | Accessories | System Tools | NetWatcher.

2. Select the type of resource you wish to monitor.

Once you've enabled the event log with these steps, you can use the lists shown in the dialog box to specify what events should be logged. (Click any event in the right side of the dialog box, then click the Add button to add it to the list of events to be logged, shown at the left side of the dialog box.)

When you are finished setting the desired options in the Event Log Settings dialog box, click OK. From then on, you can view the event log by choosing the View Event Log option from the Connection menu in NetWatcher.

18.24. How can I monitor network activity on a peer-to-peer network?

Windows provides a management tool called the System Monitor. System Monitor is a utility that tracks the percentage of CPU time spent on running your applications, versus the CPU time spent providing shared resources for others. To start System Monitor, open the Start menu, and choose Programs | Accessories | System Tools | System Monitor. The System Monitor appears, as shown in Figure 18.9.

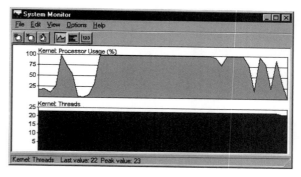

Figure 18.9. *The System Monitor.*

You can use the statistics shown by System Monitor to monitor performance trends on your network; its indications can be useful in determining the optimal value for the Performance Priority settings. (You'll find this setting in the Sharing tab of the property window for any shared resource on the network.)

III

CHAPTER 19

Windows Communications

This chapter covers a number of topics specific to communications and Windows, and includes details on the online services and the Internet, which are among the prime reasons for adding communications to many Windows machines.

19.1. How do I install an external modem?

Follow these steps to install an external modem:

1. Decide to which serial port you want to attach your modem.

2. Connect the modem cable to the back of the modem.

3. Connect the opposite end of the modem cable to the correct serial port on the back of your system. Don't forget to write down which port you connected the cable to (COM1 or COM2). You will need to remember this port when you choose your configuration settings.

4. Restart Windows. Choose Start|Shut Down from the toolbar. After you exit Windows, press Ctrl+Alt+Del to reboot Windows.

5. After Windows comes up again, choose Settings | Control Panel from the Start menu.

6. Double-click the Modems icon.

7. Follow the instructions that appear on-screen to configure Windows to recognize the modem.

19.2. How can I install an internal modem?

To install an internal modem, first set the appropriate jumpers on the modem (as directed by the modem's documentation) to choose the COM port setting for the modem. Then, follow these steps:

1. Remove your computer's cover (see Appendix B, "PC Assembly," for steps regarding cover removal).

2. Remove the expansion slot cover of a slot that is not in use. You will use the screws from the cover to attach the modem to the chassis.

3. Firmly insert the modem into the empty slot. Be sure that the edge connector—the end with the gold markings—is lined up by the edges with the slot on the motherboard. You may need to rock the modem horizontally to insert it completely.

4. Now that the card is inserted, fasten the screw to the slot connector at the top right. Then, replace the computer's cover, reconnect all cables, and power up the machine. Then return to Windows.

5. The New Device Found dialog box appears. Click Use Default driver in the dialog box and follow the instructions that appear.

6. From the Start menu, choose Settings | Control Panel.

7. Double-click the Modems icon.

8. Follow the instructions that appear on-screen to configure Windows to recognize the modem.

19.3. I just installed an external modem, but it isn't functioning. How can I fix it?

Ask yourself the following questions; answering them may help you to get your modem to function:

■ *Is the serial cable installed correctly?*

Typically a serial modem has a 25-pin male connector on one end and a 9-pin female connector at the other end. The 25-pin male connector can be attached to the back of the modem only. The 9-pin connector, however, can be attached to the wrong area because many PCs contain multiple 9-pin connectors. Be sure that the 9-pin connector is in the correct port on the back of your computer. If the 9-pin connector seems to fit, you can use a 9- to 25-pin adapter and try to connect the cable to the other port to see whether the problem is resolved.

■ *Was the configuration of the external modem performed correctly?*

If the settings for your external modem are not correct from the setup process, your modem may not function properly, or it may not function at all.

■ *Is the modem receiving power?*

Most external modems need an AC power pack to function. You should find the AC power pack in the package in which the modem was shipped. Also check to see whether the modem is plugged into a working AC power outlet.

■ *Is there a phone wire plugged into the modem?*

This may seem obvious, but not having a phone line plugged into your modem does not enable you to get very far in terms of communications. Check to make sure that the other end of the phone line is connected firmly in its jack.

■ *Was the communications software installed to use the proper COM port and I/O address for the modem?*

Your mouse and external modem should not use the same port. If they do, you need to change one of the two. Your computer also may not find your modem because it was configured for a port other than the one the software is told to use. Also, the particular port being used for the modem may be assigned to another device that you are not aware of.

19.4. I just installed an internal modem, but it isn't functioning. How can I fix it?

Ask yourself the following questions; answering them may help you to get your modem to function:

■ *Are the jumpers set correctly to avoid conflicts with other serial devices?*

Refer to the documentation that came with your modem, compare the diagrams of the jumpers and or DIP switches, and set them accordingly.

Also, if your computer already is using COM1 or COM2 for a serial port, don't attempt to set an internal modem to either of them. (Attempting to do so creates a device conflict.) If your mouse is connected to one of the COM ports, you shouldn't attempt to assign the modem to the same port that the mouse is connected to either. Again, this can create a potential device conflict.

■ *Is there a phone wire plugged into the modem?*

■ *Was the installation and configuration of the communications software done correctly, using the proper COM port and I/O address for the modem?*

Your computer may not find your modem because it was configured for a port other than the one the software is told to use.

Also, the particular port being used for the modem may be assigned to another device that you are not aware of.

This section does not cover all the possible problems you may have installing your modem, but it does address some of the more common problems. If you still have a problem after reading these tips, you should look at the documentation for your modem to get specific help. The manufacturer often has some tips for that specific kind of modem.

19.5. Should I buy an external or an internal modem?

External modems are probably your best choice if you are short on expansion slots, or if you want to use the same modem with a desktop PC and with a laptop. If your computer already has two serial ports installed, an external modem also may be less troublesome to install because you easily can connect it to one of the two serial ports.

> **NOTE** Internal modems often are troublesome to install in machines that have two existing serial ports, because most internal modems are set up by default to use the same COM port and interrupt setting as one of the existing serial ports in the PC; you'll have to change them in order to work correctly.

External modems tend to cost more because the manufacturing cost must include a case and a power supply.

Internal modems are the preferred choice if you are looking to minimize cost, if you don't need to move the modem between machines, or if you just don't want to surrender real estate on your desk to yet another piece of electronics. Before deciding on an internal modem, be sure that you have enough expansion slots to cover your future upgrade possibilities. If you later start adding things like a CD-ROM drive, tape backup, sound card, and network adapter, you easily can run out of slots.

19.6. What are surge suppressors, and should I buy one?

A *surge suppressor* is a relatively inexpensive electronic device that plugs into a wall outlet, grounding the phone line. If there is any electrical surge on the phone line (such as one caused by a lighting strike), a surge suppressor can deflect the surge from entering your modem through the phone cable. Surge suppressors are well worth the cost, given that they routinely retail for about $20, and replacements for fried modems or baked Pentium-based motherboards cost much more.

19.7. How can I use HyperTerm to connect to another computer?

HyperTerm is a communications program included with this version of Windows; it replaces Windows Terminal, which shipped with prior versions of Windows. To access HyperTerm, open the Start

III

menu and choose Programs | Accessories | HyperTerminal Connections. In the window that opens, double-click the HyperTerm icon to start the program. When you are inside HyperTerm, you need to set up the program's dialog box options to dial the phone numbers of other computers or online services to which you want to connect. You can use the HyperTerm Help screens for specifics on the use of the program.

19.8. How can I dial phone calls from my PC?

Assuming that you already have installed and configured your modem as described earlier in this chapter, you can use the Phone Dialer feature of Windows to dial the phone. Open the Start menu and choose Programs | Accessories | Phone Dialer. After the Phone Dialer appears, enter the number in the Number to Dial text box and click the Dial button.

19.9. Which of the online services should I consider?

Online services have fast become an extremely popular way to find and share information. These services have grown beyond that now, giving you the capabilities to shop, make airline reservations, receive technical help for computer and automotive problems, and send e-mail messages and faxes.

Currently, five major online services are available: America Online (AOL), CompuServe Information Service (CIS), Dow Jones News/ Retrieval with MCI Mail (DJN/R), GEnie, and Prodigy Interactive Personal Service. Also, there is the Internet, which cannot be thought of as an individual service, but is definitely an online resource for millions of people. Each one of the different online services has its good and bad points, and some have more to offer than others. This section considers which are the good and bad points for each of the systems and, based on your current online needs, it offers some guidance on which service you should subscribe to.

All the services offer a few common elements, such as communications services and information. The forums on CompuServe are an outstanding source of information for having questions answered fairly quickly. Many computer companies have forums to answer software questions and post software fixes and updates.

> **TIP** These forums can be invaluable for information systems professionals who don't have the time to stay on hold when calling a support line.

Each of the services gives users the opportunity to meet other professionals—potential business partners or collaborators, business resources, or people who simply have a common interest. All the services covered in this chapter at the very minimum offer an e-mail gateway to the Internet.

The Internet by far offers the most depth in information—so in-depth, that it often surprises those who are able to get at the information. Because Internet is not a service, you may find it difficult to locate all that you are looking for. Now there are software packages, however, that make searching the Internet easier than in the past.

19.10. How can I select the right online service?

When you go shopping for an online system, you should consider the cost of each of the services. Also, consider how easy each one of the services is to use. This ease of use can have a direct effect on the cost of the system. If you choose a system that is difficult to get around in, you will need to spend more time looking for what you want, with a corresponding increase in your online bill.

Ease of use should be a very important part of your consideration. If you want to use the services and information found on the online system, you need to be able to find them. America Online and Prodigy are examples of the newer graphical services. Subscriptions to these services come with software for your computer to help you in your navigation. The more business-oriented services such as the Dow Jones News/Retrieval with MCI Mail usually tend to be more text-based systems directed at the business user who, more often than not, knows where to look for what.

If you prefer to use the more text-oriented systems, you can make use of communications front ends. These communications packages are designed specifically to aid in your navigation through the online systems. They also do some work for you, such as enabling you to compose and read e-mail on the local computer, which enables you to be offline and not incur charges for the reading of your mail. CompuServe offers about 20 front ends, and eight front ends are available for MCI Mail. Also, there are enhancements for the standard Prodigy, including the soon-due Prodigy for Windows front end (which should be out by the time this book is printed). GEnie users can use an interface called Aladdin, while waiting for the upcoming GEnie for Windows, which is due to be released this year.

Also, when you are shopping for an online system, consider the information available for each system. Do you want a business-oriented online system, or do you want a system that offers generalities with an easy interface? What you find on each system varies. However, most systems have a general mix of news, along with financial information. You find more specific databases for business, hobbies, and entertainment in some online systems than others; if you are more interested in the business end of online systems, you will want to find an online system that carries a more business-oriented selection of topics.

All these services except Dow Jones offer software for downloading. Many free and shareware titles are available on the online systems. (These programs can be downloaded and used for a specified time without having to pay for the software; many programs ask for a voluntary donation.) Of the systems available, CompuServe has the most software available for downloading. America Online has the nicest search capability for finding some of these titles, however. America Online enables you to find files by searching titles and keywords from a single screen, making it easy to find a shareware program on a topic of your interest.

Cost also comes into play when you choose an online system. The next section considers the cost of each of the online systems considered here, as well as what is offered by each to help you choose your online systems.

19.11. What is America Online? (AOL)

America Online has a well-designed graphical interface; in fact, it is the most outstanding in the group. Although the services from AOL are not as deep as those of its principal competitor (Prodigy), it is positioned to attract the more personal user, as you can see from its graphical interface alone.

AOL's graphical user interface and flexible account structure make it an excellent choice if you are just entering the world of online services. AOL enables up to six people to share an account with different user names. All the billing is done via the master account. (This is excellent for families with one PC and more than one user of the system.) AOL enables each person to keep track of the time spent on the system and to pay only for his or her time. Many college students find this beneficial also; students with several roommates can keep account of the time each person spends looking for that information for the college paper due at the end of the week.

At the time of this writing, users of America Online pay $9.95 a month for access. This fee includes five hours of online time, which again is ideal for the family or college student that may not use the system every day. Additional hours are $3.50. (You must pay extra for fax transmissions and online classes.)

Omni, Time, and *USA Today* are carried by AOL. However, although AOL claims that it carries full text and runs forums in which readers can discuss issues with the editors of the magazines, the publications aren't found in full text and the editors don't appear in the forums very often. This is a definite disadvantage for those who would enjoy entering a forum of this kind or who want to read an updated publication.

In spite of this disadvantage, AOL does have an advantage over some of the other services offered; it offers message-sending to an Internet address as easily as to a local address. Also, both Internet and local addresses can be included in the online book or mailing list.

Searching for software in AOL is easy. You look through a single main library. From here, you search for a title by using radio

III

buttons, check boxes, and keywords, which enable you to find a match quickly.

You also find about 28 bulletin boards on AOL. At each bulletin board, there are subtopics. According to the volume of messages, a chain system is used, or, in the more active boards, a limited-thread system is used that supports one level of replies in addition to the main thread.

Aside from the fact that AOL is somewhat light on services, it is easy to use and informative for the beginning user, or someone who is not an incredibly frequent user of the system. (AOL is an excellent way to begin your trek onto the information highway without a major collision.)

19.12. What is CompuServe (CIS)?

With the exclusion of the Internet, CompuServe can be considered the mother of all online systems. On CIS, you find a host of forums, databases files, and other services. CIS also has an excellent e-mail facility—one of the best. The only thing that could be considered a drawback is the price, which is $8.95 per month for access. However, this price provides you with unlimited access to many of the services available on CIS. Here are some of the more commonly used services:

News, Sports, and Weather

Accu-Weather Maps and Reports
Associated Press Online (Summarized hourly)
Deutsche Presse-Agentur
Kurznachrichtendienst (German language news summary)
National Weather Service Reports
Press Association Online (UK)
Syndicated Columnists (20 popular journalists in America)
U.S. News and World Report

Electronic Mail

CompuServe Mail (send about 60 free messages per month)

Reference Library

American Heritage Dictionary of the English Language
Consumer Reports Complete Drug Reference
Grolier's Academic Encyclopedia
Handicapped Users Database
HealthNet

Financial Information

Basic Service Current Stock Quotes
Loan Analyser

Travel & Leisure

EAASY SABRE and WORLDSPAN Travelshopper (airline, hotel, and rental car information)
U.S. Department of State Advisories

Entertainment & Games

Biorhythms, BlackDragon, Hollywood Hotline, Science Trivia Quiz, Soap Opera Summaries, and Hangman Membership Support. (This section provides help with navigation for new members. It also contains a software support forum and a practice forum that helps you learn the fundamentals of real-time, online communication.)

These are some of the services available through CompuServe. This list helps you appreciate the size of CIS, and why it is considered the mother of online systems.

CompuServe has a few front ends available to help you navigate through the vast field of information. The two most popular are CIM (CompuServe Information Manager for DOS) and WinCIM (CompuServe Information Manager for Windows). These two front ends are provided by CIS for about $10, but a $10 usage credit is given, so it is virtually free.

The mail service on CIS also is outstanding. CIS mail handles local Internet, fax, Telex, and postal addresses via a single interface. This enables the easy creation of mail with a variety of addresses.

Some users are overwhelmed by the size of CIS. Sometimes asking for an answer can prompt many, many responses. This fact, however, also is CIS's strength; more than 600 forums are offered that can provide answers to a variety of computer problems or other needs.

CompuServe also has a good share of news feeds and business information. CIS is a solid choice for the general home or business user. However, if you need more than just the business services available on CIS, you should consider Dow Jones News/Retrieval with MCI Mail.

19.13. What is Dow Jones News/Retrieval with MCI Mail (DJN/R)?

For business users, Dow Jones News/Retrieval with MCI Mail is the preferred choice. The DJN/R service offers a wealth of business news, detailed financial data, and general information. The service is coupled with MCI Mail, the largest e-mail service in the United States. The per-month cost for a corporate account may seem a bit steep at $75. This fee does include 10 hours of free connect time, however, and after that, a $1.30 per minute and $78 per hour fee is assessed to search the majority of the databases. Also, there is a charge of 76 cents for each 1,000 characters retrieved. (This is about 10 times what you pay on CIS or GEnie.) MCI Mail charges 50 cents for the first 500 characters of a message.

In spite of its high prices, DJN/R offers high-quality financial information. The prices show that this service is not aimed at the personal user, but at the corporate market instead.

This service is built on information provided daily by Dow Jones Co., *The Wall Street Journal*, and the Dow Jones News Service (a financial wire service). This quality and detail in financial information, for the most part, cannot be found in other places. From these two sources, you can receive a large amount of current and historical stock and commodity prices, corporate financial reports, and so on. Important news of the day, derived from DJN/R's many sources, is available through a list of top stories for the day.

Two Windows-based front ends have been created in order for this service to keep down online costs. News/Retrieval link changes the cryptic commands into buttons and windows, which enables the average user to have access to this online service.

TextSearch Plus is the other Windows-based front end that is available. This front end enables you to search any of the many newspapers, journals, and magazines for words, phrases, or topics. You can search publications individually by categories. The TextSearch Plus front end enables easy access to the DJN/R sea of publications.

Currently, there is no other online service that provides so much day-to-day business information. If you run a business with the need for this type of information, this is the online service for you.

19.14. What is GEnie?

GEnie is geared to the professional who needs occasional access to vast databases of information. GEnie excels in its array of information databases, news, and financial information.

GEnie gives you a rather inexpensive way to access these databases. You pay $30 or more for the searches. Because GEnie costs only $8.95 per month for access and $3 an hour for the first four hours, it may be a more cost-effective choice than Dow Jones News/ Retrieval for some users.

The strength of GEnie lies in its third-party database access. Charles Schwab Investing, for example, has more than 400 databases, including business wire, Paterson College database, and TRW credit profiles. A broad selection of forums covering many subjects also is available on GEnie. You can find forums related to hobbies, Borland, and Microsoft.

Another strength of GEnie is its capability to excel in research tasks. Also, you can access DJN/R dialog, Bradstreet corporate profiles, The Thomas Register, and the world-wide Patent Center, among others. Also available on GEnie is the Newsstand, a searchable database of full text from about 900 publications. Don't forget that most of these are considered premium services—you must pay extra for their use. Newsstand costs from $2.50 to $29 per search, for example.

E-mail service is not very easy in GEnie. Choices for reading are unclear, and creating a new message is slow and somewhat difficult. This can prove to be a problem for novice users.

GEnie has an interesting place in the group of commercial online services. If you need detailed research and like to discuss your ideas with 300,000 to 400,000 other users—and you don't want to pay Dow Jones News Retrieval kind of prices—this may be the online service for you.

19.15. What is Prodigy?

This joint venture between IBM and Sears excels in hobby and entertainment information, and informational databases. Prodigy is a personal online service. It does not offer you the depth of information that CIS, DJN/R, or AOL does.

On Prodigy, you find subjects from movie reviews to sport scores, and so on. The information you find is more data-browser oriented, rather than serious business-user or research oriented.

Prodigy also is the only service to display advertisements on-screen. You will notice this as you move around in Prodigy. Prodigy's interface tends to slow it down, and it puts a lot of demands on your system in terms of resources.

Prodigy's monthly fee is $14.95. This gives you unlimited access to the basic features with two hours of service time for non-basic features. Then you are charged $3.60 per hour for non-basic features, and if more than 30 e-mail messages are sent, a 25-cent fee is assessed for each message.

Although Prodigy lacks in some areas in terms of depth, it does have excellent home-user research tools, such as Grolier's Academic American Encyclopedia and Consumer Reports.

Prodigy does not offer much depth; however, it provides an excellent way to familiarize yourself with the world of online services. Prodigy can be a good choice for families who want to use an online service.

19.16. What is the Internet?

The Internet is the world's largest network. The word *Internet* often leaves many people in the dark as to what it actually is. The Internet is a collection of computers, cables, and people. Some have called it a *Global Village*.

The Internet offers many features; it would be impossible to list all of them in this book. A few of these features range from e-mail service to virtual sex, to sending faxes, to downloading Mortal Kombat II secrets. All of this can be done on the Internet.

Service to the Internet is not free (as some users have been falsely led to believe). This is due in part to the fact that some businesses and colleges make the use of the Internet available to students and employees at no charge. However, Internet service providers may charge $1 an hour for access, but this will give you access to everything that the Internet has to offer; the trick is finding your way around.

19.17. How can I access the Internet?

An easy way to get started in your quest for Internet access is to use a communication online service that gives you access to the Internet. These online service providers are slowly beginning to offer access to the Internet as part of the services they offer. The depth of the access varies from service to service. Most of the major online services offer at least e-mail service to and from the Internet. AOL, however offers a more extensive door to the Internet.

Unlike public-access providers, the commercial services enable you to use your own modem (which cannot be done directly on the Internet because you would need a high-speed digital modem). The disadvantage to commercial service access is the obvious, limited access. Some commercial services (like CIS at the time of this writing) offer e-mail only. If that is all you need, you are set.

III

19.18. Which of the online services offers true Internet access?

As stated, CIS, MCI Mail, and GEnie enable you to send and receive e-mail to and from the Internet. If you want more access, however, AOL is the service that will provide it to you.

AOL offers the same services as the other online services, as well as Usenet Newsgroups access. Usenet is the largest, most active, most varied forum available. As of this writing, there are an estimated 120,000 forums on Usenet with about 4.2 million participants. AOL also has Gopher Access in the works. Gopher is designed to enable you to search and browse for information on the Internet.

Q 19.19. What's the Microsoft Network?

At the time of this writing, Microsoft was in the process of developing the company's own variation of an online service to provide the types of features that Windows users find popular on other commercial services such as CompuServe and America Online. The Microsoft Network can be optionally installed as part of the Windows 95 installation process, or you can add it later (see your Windows documentation for further details). Because the product was still in development as this book went to press, we weren't able to provide a full breakdown of its services as we did with the other commercial services. However, according to Microsoft, the service will let you exchange messages with people around the world; read the latest news, sports, weather, and financial information; find answers to your technical questions; download from a collection of thousands of useful programs; and connect to the Internet.

To log on to the Microsoft Network, open the Start menu, and choose Programs|Microsoft Network. If you have never used the service before, an introductory screen for the Microsoft Network will appear. Click OK, and another screen will ask you to supply an area code (and possibly a country name and city name). Provide the requested information, and click OK. In the next dialog box that appears, click the Connect button to proceed. Once you have logged on to the network, it will provide you with additional instructions on its use.

Windows and Laptop Computing

This chapter discusses important issues behind the use of Windows on a laptop or other "portable" (read: fewer-resources-than-on-your-desk) computer. Laptops are truly phenomenal tools to have around, but the design limitations involved in shoehorning a PC into that limited space means that you give up some things. Many laptop users put up with a more cramped keyboard; they also settle for monochrome screens. And laptops typically have less memory and smaller hard disks than their desktop cousins. To get around these kinds of limitations, there are steps you can take to adapt your laptop software and your hardware to better deal with the demands of Windows. Windows 95 adds a feature called the Briefcase that makes it easier to synchronize files between laptops and desktop PCs.

> **NOTE** Throughout this chapter, the term *laptop* is used as a generic reference to any portable computer capable of running Windows 95. This includes machines that actually fall into the "notebook" and "subnotebook" classes of computers.

20.1. Can I install Windows so that it doesn't take up as much disk space?

Because there are so many 386 laptops with 60–80M hard drives out there, this is a common desire. Windows 95 weighs in at around 25M fully loaded. (That easily can represent one-third the size of your hard drive for the operating system alone, which doesn't leave a lot of room for your applications.) You can cut this size down to around 15M by performing a custom installation.

Start Windows Setup in the usual manner (see Appendix A, "Installation," for details). After the Setup program loads, you'll see the Customize Options dialog box asking whether you want to install an Express Setup or a Custom Setup. Choose Custom Setup, and Windows displays the Custom Setup dialog box, shown in Figure 20.1.

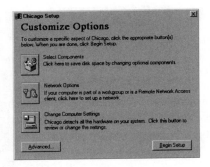

Figure 20.1. *The Customize Options dialog box.*

In the dialog box, you can click any of the check boxes to deselect the items shown. Or, if you want to deselect some of the items in a category (for example, to let Windows install Solitaire but leave all other games off the system), you can leave the check box for that particular category turned on, and click the Files button to the right of the category. Another dialog box appears, and you can delete the desired item by clicking it in the list box and clicking the Remove button. When you're done, click OK.

Q **20.2. I've already installed Windows on my laptop. Is there any way I can remove parts of it without running Setup to reinstall the program all over again?**

Open the Start menu and choose Programs | Main | Windows Setup. The same dialog box that was shown earlier in Figure 20.1 appears, and you can deselect any of the selected items to remove these options, as described in Question 20.1.

Q **20.3. Are there any files installed by Windows that I can delete to free up disk space?**

Any time you delete files that were installed with an operating system, there's always a danger of deleting something that you need. However, if you're careful about what you delete, this can be an acceptable way to free up disk space. You can use Table 20.1 as a guide to some of the Windows files you can delete, *if you're sure that you don't need the program or feature in the "Used for" column.*

Table 20.1. Optional Windows files.

File	Location	Used for
CALC.EXE	WINDOWS	Calculator.
CALENDAR.EXE	WINDOWS	Calendar.
CLOCK.EXE	WINDOWS	Clock.
MSPAINT.EXE	WINDOWS	Windows Paint.
PBRUSH.EXE	WINDOWS	Windows Paintbrush (exists if you installed Windows 95 over an older version of Windows).
WRITE.EXE	WINDOWS	Windows Write (exists if you installed Windows 95 over an older version of Windows).

continues

Table 20.1. continued

File	Location	Used for
WRITE.HLP	WINDOWS	Windows Write help files (exists if you installed Windows 95 over an older version of Windows).
WORDPAD.EXE	WINDOWS	WordPad.
Files with .BMP	WINDOWS	Various Paint files extensions (you'll have to decide if you don't need them).
Files with .TTF extensions	FONTS	TrueType fonts. Make sure you delete only those fonts that you don't need. For example, if you never use the Arial font on-screen or when printing, you can delete ARIAL.TTF.
Files with .HLP extensions	Various folders	Help files. Make sure you delete only those help files associated with applications that you'll never need help on. You can usually tell which application the file is associated with by its name. For example, MSHEARTS.HLP is used with

File	Location	Used for
		the Hearts game, and WINCHAT.HLP is used with Chat.
.WAV, .MID, and .AVI files	MEDIA	.WAV files are sound files in WAVE format; .MID files are sound files in MIDI format; .AVI files are video files used with Video for Windows. You can delete any file you're sure you won't need. If you never play sound or video, delete all of them.
MSD.EXE	WINDOWS/ COMMAND	Microsoft Diagnostics program.
MSD.INI	WINDOWS/ COMMAND	Microsoft Diagnostics program.
APPEND.EXE	WINDOWS/ COMMAND	DOS program; delete it if you don't need it.
ASSIGN.COM	WINDOWS/ COMMAND	DOS program; delete it if you don't need it.
COUNTRY.COM	WINDOWS/ COMMAND	DOS program; delete it if you don't need it.
DISKCOMP.COM	WINDOWS/ COMMAND	DOS program; delete it if you don't need it.

III

continues

Table 20.1. continued

File	Location	Used for
DISKCOPY.COM	WINDOWS/ COMMAND	Useless if you use Windows to copy files.
EDIT.COM	WINDOWS/ COMMAND	DOS Editor; delete it if you don't use the Editor.
EDIT.HLP	WINDOWS/ COMMAND	DOS Editor; delete it if you don't use the Editor.
FASTOPEN.EXE	WINDOWS/ COMMAND	DOS program; delete it if you don't need it.
PRINT.EXE	WINDOWS/ COMMAND	Useless if you always print in Windows.
QBASIC.EXE	WINDOWS/ COMMAND	Useless unless you create DOS programs using QBASIC.
QBASIC.HLP		Help files for QBASIC; delete it if you don't need it.
README.DOC READ.ME	Can be found in various folders	You can delete any "read-me" files that contain reference notes about your software packages as long as you read them first and feel you don't need them as a reference.

TIP

Another step that you can take to reduce space is to compress data files that you don't need to use on a daily basis but want to keep on your laptop for occasional use. You can use popular compression software such as PKZIP to compress files individually or in groups, often saving 50 to 90 percent in space over the original files. You also can compress programs if you know you're not going to use them for some time. You'll need to uncompress any files before you can use them. PKZIP (and its uncompression partner, PKUNZIP) are available on most computer bulletin boards, on CompuServe in the IBM Systems/Utilities forum, or from the programs' vendor, PKWARE (listed in Appendix C, "Resources").

In addition to deleting files for which Windows was responsible, you also should consider whether you can get by with less in terms of your applications. You'll need to refer to the documentation that came with your application to determine whether you can easily remove components. Many applications let you run a setup program for that application after the installation to remove parts of the installation. (All the Microsoft programs that are part of Microsoft Office let you do this.) You may be able to live without many of the extras that typically come with today's Windows applications. Spell checkers, grammar checkers, and thesauruses in word processors, equation solvers and analyzers in spreadsheets, and import/export routines or SQL database drivers in database programs often can be omitted from applications to save space.

III

TIP

If you have Windows programs that you are no longer using, you should uninstall them. Removing a program from the Start menu or deleting an icon from the Desktop does not remove the software from your hard disk. Newer Windows programs often have an option (usually reached from some kind of setup utility) for removing the

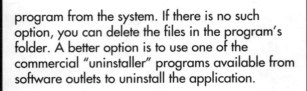

program from the system. If there is no such
option, you can delete the files in the program's
folder. A better option is to use one of the
commercial "uninstaller" programs available from
software outlets to uninstall the application.

20.4. How can I make the display on my laptop's LCD screen easier to read?

Right-click on any blank area of the screen, and choose Properties
from the popup menu that appears. When the Properties for
Display window opens, click the Appearance tab. This window,
shown in Figure 20.2, can be used to modify the color schemes and
colors of the individual items.

Figure 20.2. *The Appearance tab in the Properties for Display window.*

Often, changing the colors used by Windows will provide a more
readable screen, even on a monochrome laptop, because of the
resulting changes in contrast. When you finish making changes to
the color settings, click OK to apply the new color settings.

20.5. How can I make the mouse pointer easier to see?

Click Start, and choose Settings | Control Panel. When the Control Panel opens, double-click the Mouse icon to open the Properties window for the mouse. Click the Motion tab, and turn on the Show option under Pointer Trail, then slide the Short/Long slider toward Long to increase the visible trail of the mouse pointer. When you finish making changes, click OK to put them into effect.

20.6. What is the Briefcase, and how do I use it?

The Briefcase is a feature of Windows that enables users of portable PCs to keep files in sync with those on a desktop PC, meaning you can automatically keep the latest files on both machines. The Briefcase helps you keep the most recent files on both PCs by keeping track of the relationship between files on the laptop and files on the desktop PC. The Briefcase uses the analogy of an actual briefcase in which you carry the latest documents from one work location to another to keep the files synchronized between the laptop and the desktop PC.

After you create a Briefcase on one of the PCs, you can specify which files and folders you want to keep updated between the PCs by dragging and dropping the desired folders into the Briefcase. When you reconnect the portable to the desktop PC, open the Briefcase and choose Update from the Briefcase menu. Doing so automatically replaces the unchanged files with the changed files.

III

To create a new briefcase, open the Start menu and choose Programs | Accessories | Create a Briefcase.

| **TIP** | Microsoft recommends that you have just one Briefcase, and that you keep it on the PC that you use the least often. |

After you create a briefcase, follow these steps to synchronize files on PCs that are connected to each other:

1. Copy all the files or folders that you want to work on from the other computer to the briefcase.
2. Make the desired changes to your files, either in the original location or in the briefcase.
3. With the PCs connected, double-click the Briefcase icon.
4. From the Briefcase menu, click Update All, or select the files you wish to update, then click Update Selection.

20.7. I don't have a cable I can use to connect my laptop to my desktop PC. Is there some way I can keep the files synchronized using a disk?

You can use the Briefcase features of Windows with the disk drives in your PCs by performing the following steps:

1. Open the Briefcase and copy to the Briefcase any files or folders on which you want to work.
2. Insert a formatted disk into the drive.
3. Find the drive in Explorer or in My Computer, and drag the Briefcase to the disk.
4. When the copying process is done, you can take the disk to another computer, open it under Windows 95, and edit the files that are stored in the Briefcase.
5. After your editing is done, insert the disk that contains the Briefcase into the PC that contains the original files.
6. Double-click the Briefcase icon to open the Briefcase.
7. From the Briefcase menu, click Update All, or select the files you wish to update, then click Update Selection.

> **TIP** Instead of editing the files in the Briefcase on the disk (which can be a slow operation), you can drag the Briefcase from the disk to your hard disk. Then select the files, choose Update from the

Briefcase menus, move your briefcase to the original computer, select the files, and choose Update again.

20.8. Can I upgrade my laptop's memory?

In most cases, yes. A memory expansion is a needed process for most laptops, because so many laptops are often shipped with only 4M of RAM. But due to their compact design, laptops have advantages and disadvantages when it comes to adding memory, so the steps outlined for memory expansion in Chapter 12, "Upgrading Your Memory," don't apply to laptops.

An advantage of laptops is that their design usually makes memory addition a much simpler task than with desktop PCs. Generally, the most you need to remove is some sort of small cover or door to gain access to the memory expansion slots. Some laptops accept memory by means of PCMCIA cards; with these, all you need to do is insert a PCMCIA card containing additional memory into one of the PCMCIA slots. These are usually accessed behind a door in the side or the rear of the laptop.

The disadvantage of many laptops is that they often require DRAM memory chips or SIMMs (Single In-line Memory Modules) of a proprietary design, rather than accepting off-the-shelf SIMMs or DRAM chips. As a result, you often pay considerably more per megabyte for a laptop's memory expansion than you would for the same memory on a desktop PC. Also, on many laptops, the 4M that came standard with the machine must be completely replaced to upgrade the memory. For example, to go to 8M you often have to remove all the memory chips and replace them with larger-capacity chips, leaving you with 4M of useless memory.

III

Because the expansion designs of laptops vary so widely, you'll need to consult the documentation for your laptop to determine the precise steps to take for adding memory. Except for the laptops that accept off-the-shelf memory chips or PCMCIA memory cards, the best source of memory will probably be the retail outlet that sold you the laptop in the first place. If your laptop is made by one of the big names in PCs (such as Compaq, IBM, or Toshiba), you may be able to find memory expansion kits specifically designed for your laptop from mail-order suppliers or other third-party vendors.

> **TIP** If memory must be added to your laptop in the form of a PCMCIA card, you may have to remove any installed fax/modem PCMCIA card to get to the slot for the memory card. You may also need to run some sort of setup utility on the laptop to get it to address the existing memory. Consult your laptop's documentation for details.

20.9. Can I upgrade my laptop's processor?

Rarely, and even when you can, it's generally not wise to attempt it (unless the laptop was designed for an easy processor upgrade). The compact design of the laptop makes it a nightmare to disassemble down to the motherboard. Because laptop motherboards use a proprietary design to cram all that stuff into that little case, you can't just swap motherboards as you can with desktop PCs. This leaves replacement of the CPU chip as the only viable option, but even that presents a potential problem. Larger, faster CPU chips often generate more heat. Although a desktop PC usually has plenty of ventilation, your laptop may not stand for much more heat than what's already generated by its design components. If you really need a faster processor, do something nice for a friend, family member, or high school student: give them your old laptop and buy another that offers what you really want.

20.10. What are some features I need to look for if I'm buying a laptop to run Windows?

If it's time for that "ultimate upgrade" that means a new machine, some points to consider as part of your purchase include the following:

- *Pentium processor, if possible:* At the time of this writing, Intel was preparing to ship low-power versions of its Pentium chip for use in laptops. As such chips become available, they'll be well worth the investment for any laptop that you plan to keep for a long time.

■ *486SL or other similar low-power CPU:* Look for a laptop with a processor that uses one of the more energy-efficient CPU chips specially designed for laptop use, such as the 486SL chip. Battery life is one of the major shortcomings of laptops, and one with a low-power CPU will give you better performance between recharges.

■ *Nickel-hydride battery:* To achieve a longer battery life, more laptop manufacturers are going to this new battery design, which produces laptops that run considerably longer between recharges than ones that rely on the more conventional rechargeable nickel-cadmium batteries.

■ *Memory expansion capabilities of 16M or more:* Don't get locked into a laptop that doesn't leave plenty of room for memory expansion. Any laptop you purchase should be able to expand to at least twice what you think you'll need as a maximum during the time you'll have the machine.

■ *Color:* Even though the feature still adds around a thousand or more U.S. dollars to the cost of a laptop, color is gradually coming down in cost. And for a lot of Windows applications, it's a significant feature to have. You'll pay considerably more for active-matrix color than you will for passive-matrix color, but active-matrix color provides a richer, sharper screen display.

III

■ *PCMCIA slots:* Laptops that adhere to the PCMCIA standard as a means for expansion make it easier for you to add peripherals such as modems and network adapter cards by inserting a PCMCIA-compatible card into an easily accessible slot.

■ *Easy connection to a desk-based expansion system:* The laptop should have some way to connect to a type of docking adapter that lets you add the kind of conventional accessories that you would add to a desktop PC. A good example is a CD-ROM drive; you could add one that uses a parallel port adapter, but such a solution provides much slower access time than a drive added through an expansion bus system docked to the laptop.

- *Large hard-disk drives:* Like memory, hard-disk space is something you can't get enough of. If putting off the purchase for a month or two means you'll be able to buy a much larger hard disk, wait for the larger disk. You'll be glad you did.

Troubleshooting Windows

This chapter provides suggestions and techniques that you can use to solve common problems throughout Windows. You will learn solutions for common problems with Windows installation, general Windows use, program crashes, printing, and communications.

Installation Problems

Installing new software doesn't always proceed as expected. The following questions and answers address problems that may arise during the installation of Windows 95.

21.1. Windows fails during the installation process, displaying an error message. What can I do?

In most cases, Windows runs through its installation process from start to finish, performing a thorough technical evaluation of your hardware setup and then installing all necessary files. If your hardware lacks an important resource that Windows needs, or if software currently occupying the system's memory is incompatible

with Windows, the installation process grinds to a halt, and
Windows displays some sort of dialog box. Usually, the message in
the dialog box indicates the source of the problem. If the message
doesn't provide a clue as to what is wrong, quit the installation and
try these solutions:

- If you were running any memory-resident applications along
  with DOS, remove these applications from memory (or
  reboot the machine and don't allow these applications to
  load). If the memory-resident applications are loaded
  automatically due to the contents of an AUTOEXEC.BAT
  file, you can edit the file using an editor such as DOS EDIT
  and comment out or remove the line in the file that loads the
  memory-resident software.

- If you were running a memory manager like 386MAX or
  QEMM386, remove it from your CONFIG.SYS file or delete
  any lines that refer to the memory manager in your
  AUTOEXEC.BAT file.

- Try booting your system with a DOS disk that doesn't
  contain any memory-resident programs or device drivers.
  Then try running SETUP again.

- Rerun the Windows Setup program. This time, when
  Windows displays the dialog box asking whether you want a
  Custom Setup or an Express Setup, choose Custom Setup.
  When Windows finishes analyzing your hardware and
  displays the list of installed hardware, make sure that this list
  is correct. (If it isn't, see the next question.)

21.2. The list of installed equipment shown by Windows doesn't match the actual hardware. What's wrong?

If Windows' installation routine cannot find or properly identify
existing hardware installed on a system, the problem usually is due
to an incompatibility between existing device drivers and Windows.
Note the device that's missing or shown incorrectly in Windows' list
of installed devices, call Product Support Services at Microsoft, and
ask whether an updated Windows driver for the device in question
is available. (You also may want to contact the manufacturer of the
hardware device to obtain the latest needed driver.)

21.3. The mouse pointer appears, but it is frozen on-screen or jumps wildly around the screen. Why is this happening?

In addition to being caused by a defective mouse, this problem commonly is caused by three other possibilities: an interrupt conflict between the serial port you have attached the mouse to and another serial device, a wrongly set switch on the underside of the mouse, or the wrong mouse driver selected within Windows.

> **NOTE** If the mouse pointer is not jumping wildly, but is just somewhat erratic, this probably is due to a dirty mouse; check the underside of the mouse for instructions on cleaning the ball.

First, check the underside of the mouse for a switch setting. Some mice contain a switch that enables the mice to work in a Microsoft-compatible mode or in a Logitech-compatible mode. Try changing the setting and restarting Windows; if this does not solve the problem, be sure to put the switch back in its original position.

Next, check to see that the mouse driver chosen in the Windows Control Panel matches the kind of mouse you have installed. Because your mouse isn't working, you will have to get to the Control Panel from the keyboard. Press Ctrl+Esc to open the Start menu, and choose Settings | Control Panel. When the Control Panel opens, use the arrow keys to highlight the Mouse icon, and then press Enter. When the Properties window for the mouse opens, press the Tab key until the Buttons tab at the top of the dialog box is highlighted, then use the right arrow key to highlight the General tab of the dialog box. Next, press Alt+C for Change. Use the arrow keys to highlight the correct mouse driver, press Alt+D if you have a driver disk for the mouse, and press the Tab key until the OK button is highlighted; then press Enter. If any additional dialog boxes appear, you can make selections from the keyboard by pressing Alt plus the underlined key of any option to select it, and by using the arrow keys to move among the folder tabs and the available options of each tab.

III

If these approaches are not successful, the likely cause of the problem is a defective mouse or a conflict in the interrupt request (IRQ) settings. You probably have an IRQ problem if your mouse stopped working immediately after you installed another adapter card. Using the appropriate hardware documentation, you need to check the jumper or switch settings on the card to which your mouse is attached, and compare its IRQ settings to those of any cards you just installed. An aid in determining what installed equipment is using what interrupts is the free Microsoft Diagnostics program (MSD.EXE) supplied with Windows. To run it, choose Programs|MS-DOS Prompt from the Start menu to go directly to DOS. At the DOS prompt, enter MSD to start the program. From the program's main menu, press Q to display the IRQ status of your system.

21.4. The installation or setup program for my Windows application halts abruptly, and I have leftover files on my hard disk. How do I fix this?

The presence of the files in itself is not a problem, if you plan to install the application. Shut down all other applications that may be running within Windows, make sure you have enough disk space for the application, and rerun the application's installation program. The installation overwrites any files that originally were copied to your hard disk the first time you ran the installation. If you no longer want to install the software, the only way to get rid of the files that the partial installation added to your hard disk is to delete them. You need to be extremely careful, deleting any files that were added by the attempted software installation.

> **NOTE** The problem with getting rid of Windows software is that most Windows applications not only create their own folders, but they usually add some files to the contents of the WINDOWS folder.

> **TIP** The safest rule of thumb is *If in doubt about a particular file, don't delete it.*

Windows Problems

The following questions and answers address problems that may arise after Windows 95 is installed and running on your system.

21.5. Windows is running very slowly and behaving erratically. How do I fix it?

Once Windows is operational, slow performance generally is due to one of three causes: insufficient memory, too many applications running at once, or a badly fragmented and nearly full hard disk drive. If Windows seems to be just plain slow (but not so slow as to be excruciating), you probably are looking at an available resource problem that can be cured only with the addition of memory. If your machine has just 4M of RAM, the addition of another 4M can make a significant difference in terms of speed; you see far more improvement in going from 4M to 8M than you do in going from 8M to 16M. Having multiple applications open also causes major performance problems, especially in machines with limited memory installed. The only inexpensive solution is to shut down some of the applications that are running. Also, if you are performing operations that involve Object Linking and Embedding (OLE), you can throw Microsoft's claim of 4M being a minimum memory standard right out the window. OLE operations demand 8M of RAM to behave reliably and run with any semblance of speed.

If Windows is running far below the level of just plain slow, to the point where individual windows and dialog boxes take an agonizing amount of time just to paint themselves on-screen, you may be running very low on hard disk space. Windows needs at least 2M of free disk space to operate in a normal fashion.

Erratic behavior of Windows often is due to the same problem (a lack of disk space). As free space drops below 2M on the drive that Windows is installed on, you start to experience bizarre occurrences, such as screens that paint themselves partially and freeze, and system

III

crashes within applications for no apparent reason. You also are
likely to experience lockups when trying to print documents,
because Windows must build temporary files on the hard disk
during a print operation. The obvious solution is to free up disk
space (or install a larger hard disk; see Chapter 13, "Upgrading Your
Hard Drive," for more information on this). One other possible
cause of bizarre operation is any accidental erasure of critical files
needed by Windows. If Windows was running at one point, and
someone does some housekeeping in the Windows folder of the
default drive, files that Windows needs to operate properly may
have been erased. The only solution here is to reinstall Windows.

21.6. Windows displays an *Out of memory* error when my application starts, even though my PC has plenty of installed RAM. Why does this happen?

The error message you are seeing in this instance actually refers to
the portion of memory used by Windows to manage system
resources (such as window sizes and where you put all your icons on
the desktop). You therefore can have 16M of memory installed, and
under the right combination of circumstances, still see this error
message. A few suggestions for reducing the chances of seeing this
error follow:

- Ensure that the drive used to store the WINDOWS folder is
  not very low on disk space; clear off disk space as needed.

- Close any extra applications you aren't using.

- If you are using wallpaper on your desktop, consider turning
  it off. (Wallpaper can use a significant amount of system
  resources.)

21.7. Windows hangs every time I run a certain Windows application. How can I prevent this from happening?

This problem usually is due to a corrupted program file belonging
to the application, and not to Windows itself. Because some
Windows applications hang when used with certain video drivers,

try changing the Windows display mode back to standard VGA, and try running the application again. If the application runs, contact the technical support line at the application's supplier, and ask whether there is an updated video driver for the application that supports the mode of video you are using. If an unusual video mode is not the source of the problem, you probably will have to reinstall the application to get this problem to cease.

21.8. I get an error message indicating that my hard disk is full in the middle of a Windows operation. What should I do?

Don't panic. You can interrupt whatever you are doing and delete files to free up disk space. Bring up My Computer or Explorer, and delete unneeded files. After you have freed sufficient disk space, you can click on the appropriate icon in the taskbar to get back to what you were doing.

21.9. I can't save a file to a floppy disk. How can I fix this problem?

Discounting the possibility of a defective disk drive (which is rare), the usual reasons for this problem are that the drive is unformatted, the write-protect tab on the disk is in the open position, or the disk is full. If the disk is full, you can use Explorer or My Computer to delete the files on the disk. If the write-protect tab is in the open position (you can see through the hole on the disk), slide it into the closed position and try again.

III

> **NOTE** On some older machines with the right combination of ROM BIOS, an erratic inability to write to a floppy disk can be caused by ill-behaved DOS applications. When this is the case, restarting the PC cures the problem. If you routinely have trouble writing to floppy disks after running a particular DOS application, the only cure is to avoid that particular DOS application, or to restart the PC after its use when you want to write to a floppy disk.

Q 21.10. When I try to play a particular WAV sound file, I get the error message *Unable to play sound*, or no sound plays. How can I fix this problem?

If this problem occurs with some sound files that you obtain, the *sampling frequency* of the sound file probably is incompatible with Windows' Sound Recorder. Sound Recorder is limited to playing sound files recorded using a 22.05 KHz sampling rate. You may need to obtain a shareware or commercial replacement for Sound Recorder that offers more in terms of flexibility.

Q 21.11. My printer isn't working. How can I fix it?

Printers are surprisingly complex electromechanical devices, and problems getting printers to print are often as likely to be due to a mechanical difficulty with the printer as to a software problem. Look for the obvious, such as whether the printer is turned on, on-line, not out of paper, and not in a paper-jam condition. Beyond the obvious possible solutions, here are other common causes of printing problems:

- Ensure that the printer cable is connected firmly both at the printer and the computer ends.

- If you are using a switch box to allow more than one computer to use the printer (or more than one printer to be connected to the computer), make sure that the switch box is set in the proper position. Then try connecting the computer directly to the printer. If the printer prints, you probably have a defective switch box.

- Most printers have some type of self-test to confirm that the printer is fully operational independent of the computer. On many printers, you can perform the self-test by pressing a button (usually the on-line or test button) while turning on the printer's power. If your printer prints normally when you run its self-test, chances are that the problem is *not* with the printer.

■ Ensure that the correct printer is chosen, and that its ports and other options are set correctly from within Windows. Open the Start menu and choose Settings | Printers. After the Printers Folder opens, right-click the icon for the printer you're trying to use, and choose Properties from the popup menu. After the Properties window opens, make sure that the printer is set for use as the default printer, and that any port settings (in the case of serial printers) are correct.

21.12. My printer works, but some text is missing from the printout. How can I fix this?

This problem usually is the result of one of three possibilities: a defective printer cable, a poor connection between the cable and printer or computer, or a defective printer port. (It also could be caused by a defective subsystem in the printer itself, but this is pretty rare.) Try swapping cables with a cable from another system. If your PC has more than one printer port, you also can try connecting the printer to the other port (and be sure to make the corresponding change in the Printers Folder). This solution is based on the assumption that by "some text is missing," you mean that a few characters here and there are gone—not an entire half-page or more at a time. If you are printing a complex document on a laser printer (particularly a document loaded with graphics) and you get a printed page that's missing a substantial part of the printed image, the cause most likely is insufficient memory installed in the laser printer itself to handle the page you are trying to print.

21.13. My HP laser printer displays an *Error 20* message in its LCD panel in the midst of a document I've sent from within Windows. What does this mean?

This message means that you have exceeded the maximum number of downloadable soft fonts for the printer. Press the Continue button on the printer's LCD panel, and the printing continues (but the printer substitutes some basic fonts for the fancy ones used in your document). To avoid this problem, use fewer soft fonts in your documents.

21.14. My communications software produces a *Cannot Access Serial Port* error message. What does this mean?

If the PC has been running just fine until now, the error probably is caused by an attempt by a Windows program to use a COM port that another Windows program already is using. A COM port can be used by only one Windows program at a time (Windows may be multitasking, but the UART chip on the serial interface card is not). You must shut down one program until you are done with the other one. If you have just performed any hardware upgrades, the problem probably is due to an incorrect COM port setting for the device you are trying to use, or a conflict among your interrupt request (IRQ) settings. You can use Microsoft Diagnostics (type MSD at a DOS prompt) to check the COM and interrupt settings of the serial ports installed in your computer.

21.15. My communications software produces errors when it runs at 9600 bps or more, but it works fine at 2400 bps or less. What should I do?

This indicates a hardware problem of sorts, but it is one that is solvable at a minimum expense (if you can deal with changing IC chips, and if the communications chip on your serial card or your motherboard is socketed). The Universal Asynchronous Receiver-Transmitter (UART) chip used by the serial port is of an older design that cannot reliably handle communications at and above speeds of 9600 bps. These chips carry a designation of 8250A or 16450, and they were almost universally used in PCs. (Microsoft Diagnostics, which you can run by entering MSD at the DOS prompt, can tell you which UART chip is used by the serial ports in your PC.) A pin-compatible replacement for the 8250A and 16450 UART chips, called the 16550A, is readily available. If your system uses the commonly used 8250 or 16450 chip as a UART chip, communications data can be lost as Windows switches the CPU to different tasks. The more modern 16550A chip includes a buffer in its design that solves the data-loss problem when running at high speeds in multitasking environments such as Windows.

You can remove a chip bearing the 8250A or 16450 designation from its socket and replace it with an updated version carrying the designation 16550. (The 16550 directly replaces the 8250A or the 16450.) Computer retail outlets that cater to do-it-yourselfers and many mail-order forms can supply this chip; before ordering one, make sure that your existing UART chip is an 8250A or a 16450, and that it is socketed. When you replace the chip, use a chip-puller tool (available from outlets such as Radio Shack) to avoid damage to the pins or damage by static. Also, make sure that you insert the new chip with pin 1 (usually marked by a notch or a dot on one end of the chip) facing in the same direction as pin 1 for the old chip you removed.

III

IV

Appendixes

A   Installation   345

B   PC Assembly   353

C   Resources   357

Installation

Before you install Windows 95, you should determine which version of Windows currently is installed on your machine, if any. If you currently are using Windows 3.*x* or Windows for Workgroups, you have two options. You can upgrade to Windows 95, or you can install Windows 95 in a new directory.

The two types of installation have positive and negative points. If you upgrade, all applications from your earlier version of Windows migrate over to Windows 95. If you install Windows 95 in a new directory, you need to reinstall all Windows applications before they will appear as part of your Windows 95 menu structure. If you install Windows 95 in a different directory, you can create a dual-boot system that enables you to access earlier installed versions of Windows. If you install Windows 95 over an existing version of Windows, you cannot run the earlier version of Windows.

Setting Up Windows

You can install Windows from one of two sources: from floppy disks, or from a CD-ROM drive. With either type of media, you can start the SETUP program by inserting the Setup disk into the correct drive. Change to that drive, and enter the following at the DOS prompt:

setup

Alternatively, from the Windows 3.*x* Program Manager menus, choose File | Run, type x:setup (where *x* represents the drive identifier), and choose OK. Next, follow the instructions that appear on-screen (for installation from disks, insert disks as the program prompts you).

Although you can simply use the default method for starting Windows Setup by entering the setup command from within Windows 3.*x* or at the DOS Prompt, you should be aware of some advanced options for running setup. You add these options directly after the setup command. The command line's syntax follows, and Table A.1 describes these options.

```
setup [/d] [/i] [/id] [/nostart] [batch file]
```

Table A.1. *SETUP* advanced options.

Option	Function
batch file	Specifies the name of the batch file that contains Setup options. This option enables administrators to customize an installation of Windows 95 to ensure uniformity between the different workstations.
/d	Does not check for disk space. Windows 95 uses approximately 20M of hard disk space. Usually, the Setup program verifies the amount of hard disk space before installing, but not if you use this option.
/i	Ignores the automatic hardware detection so that the user must check settings and make corrections on the System Information screen during setup.
/id	Causes the existing version of Windows not to be used for setup. Use this option to set up Windows 95 in a directory other than the directory used for your early version of Windows.
/nostart	Copies the minimal installation of Windows 3.1. Don't forget that you must reinstall the different applications if you install Windows 95 in a different directory to add the programs to the menu structure of Windows 95.

Upgrading from Windows 3.x to Windows 95

Follow these steps to upgrade your system from Windows 3.*x* or Windows for Workgroups to Windows 95:

1. Back up your hard drive to protect your data against unforeseen occurrences.

2. Start Windows or Windows for Workgroups on your computer.

3. Insert the CD-ROM or the first Setup floppy disk into the correct disk drive.

4. Double-click Windows SETUP.EXE to begin the setup.

Windows 95 runs entirely in graphics mode. It does so from the existing Windows or Windows for Workgroups installation and upgrades it to Windows 95. All the current system settings, such as program groups, carry over to the Windows 95 Desktop. Setup also causes previous supported network configurations to be used.

You also can run setup from the MS-DOS prompt by entering the following, where *x* is the letter of the disk drive containing the startup disk.

```
x:setup
```

Uninstalling Windows 95

If you want to remove Windows 95 from your machine, follow these steps:

1. Reboot your computer via a bootable MS-DOS 5.0 or 6.*x* disk.

2. At the C:\ prompt, enter the **SYS** command. (This may need to be run from a boot disk in some cases.)

3. Next, restore the pre-Windows 95 CONFIG.SYS and AUTOEXEC.BAT files from your emergency boot disk or from your hard disk.

4. Delete the following files from your hard drive where Windows was installed:

   SULOGO.SYS
   SETUPLOG.TXT

IV

DETLOG.TXT
BOOTLOG.TXT
WINBOOT.SYS
SYSTEM.*xxx*
USER.*xxx*

WARNING The DELTREE command removes the entire Windows directory structure. All information stored by applications in these folders is lost. Also, if you uninstall Windows 95, your Windows 3.*x* and MS-DOS configuration must be restored.

5. To remove the directory tree (or root folder and all folders within it), use the DELTREE command where Windows 95 was installed on the hard disk. (The command DELTREE c:\WINDOWS, for example, removes the WINDOWS folder and all folders within it.)

6. Restore your original MS-DOS and Windows 3.*x* configuration.

Learning How Setup Works

You can start the Setup program for Windows 95 in two ways. The first (and recommended) way is to run Setup from within the previous version of Windows. This is possible because Windows 95's SETUP.EXE is a Windows 3.*x* application.

The second way you can start Setup is by installing Windows 95 from MS-DOS. This method causes Setup to run a *stub*, or short application. This application is limited to activating the essential Windows portion of the installation. It originates in real mode, but begins the installation process in protected mode. This stub starts a miniversion of Windows 3.1 in order to run the Windows 95 Setup program.

The real-mode stub does the following:

1. It searches the hard disk for earlier versions of Windows. If it finds a prior version of Windows, the Setup program asks the user whether this is the version of Windows it should use.

After approval from the user, the already installed version is started by the real-mode stub. Then, the Windows version of Windows 95 Setup is started.

2. A minimum systems check is performed to be sure that Windows 95 can be run on the machine. (It checks the available memory, disk space, CPU, and MS-DOS version to see whether they can be used successfully by this version of Windows.)

3. Setup checks for an XMS (extended memory) provider; if an XMS is not located, one is installed.

4. Problematic terminate-and-stay-resident programs are detected, along with device drivers. (If any are detected, Windows displays an error message asking you to remove them from memory and start the installation over again.)

5. Mini-Windows 3.1 components are installed, and the miniversion of Windows 3.1 is launched to run the Windows 95 Setup program using the SHELL=SETUP.EXE option.

Copies of all files needed by the installation are copied into a temporary folder early in the process. From that point on, Setup runs the installation totally from the temporary folder on the local hard drive.

Ultimately, Setup modifies the boot records along with the boot track to point to WINBOOT.SYS. This file replaces the old MS-DOS files IO.SYS and MSDOS.SYS.

Taking Advantage of Setup's Failure Detection and Recovery

Some safeguards are created by Setup that can be used in case of trouble during and after system setup:

- The Event Log
- The Detection Crash Recovery Log
- The emergency boot disk

Descriptions of these safeguards follow.

The Event Log

If something occurs during setup that causes it to fail, the best choice is to restart the Setup program without deleting files or making any other changes.

An Event Log is created in the root folder by Setup called SETUPLOG.TXT. If Setup fails and has to be rerun, the Event Log is used. This shows Setup which parts were installed, and the failures that occurred (if any). Setup can use this information to avoid having the same problem occur twice.

The Detection Crash Recovery Log

Another recovery file is created by Setup called the Detection Crash Recovery Log: DETLOG.TXT. Setup uses this to track the detection process. As with the SETUPLOG.TXT file, the information recorded here before a crash is stored and used in order to avoid a second crash. The module that caused the crash is identified and then is skipped.

Windows 95's new design continues Setup after almost any interruption. Setup keeps the base files for the original version of MS-DOS, Windows, and any networking software intact until after they are installed on the user's system. If Setup is interrupted, it still can boot the user's original MS-DOS, Windows, and networking configurations. Next, the Setup Log and Detection Crash Recovery Log are read and the setup process continues. The user is prompted to run Setup again.

After all the Windows 95 files are copied by Setup, any changes required are made so that the real-mode components can access the hard disk and then reboot. If Windows 95 does not reboot into real mode, simple default CONFIG.SYS and AUTOEXEC.BAT files are installed and the setup is restarted.

After the real-mode components are loaded, WIN.COM runs to start the entire Windows 95 environment.

Deciding Whether to Use Custom Setup

During the installation process, Windows Setup provides you with the option of using Express Setup or Custom Setup. Although Express Setup will work for most users, Custom Setup offers the power user much more control over how Windows is installed on the system. With Custom Setup, you can change the default folders (subdirectories) in which Windows is installed. Also, if you have a Super VGA or better video adapter and monitor combination and you want to run Windows at a higher resolution, you should choose Custom Setup to use Standard VGA (640×480) settings (of course, you always can let Express Setup do the install, and later change your video resolution from within Windows). Custom Setup is a good idea if you know that you need special printer options included with the installation. Also, if you're installing Windows on a laptop, you may want to use Custom Setup to deselect certain Windows components from the list of installed ones in order to save space on your hard drive.

Looking At Hardware Requirements

Table A.2 lists the hardware requirements for Windows 95.

Table A.2. Hardware requirements for Windows 95.

Item	Requirements
Computer	386SX processor (or higher) with high-density floppy-disk drive and hard-disk drive.
Memory	At least 4M of RAM; more is recommended.

continues

IV

Table A.2. continued

Item	*Requirements*
Disk Space	30M of free hard-disk space is recommended. 14M of hard disk space is required for a minimal installation. The full installation requires 19M of hard-disk space. You also need at least 5M free for the swapfile that is created by Windows.
Video Display	Video graphics adapter (VGA) or Super VGA monitor recommended.
Modem	Needed in order to use remote access.

PC Assembly

This appendix provides basic instructions and techniques that supplement Chapters 12–16 of this book. The appendix is designed as a helpful guide for those who are unfamiliar with the mechanics of working on a PC.

The Basics of a System

Virtually all desktop PCs are made up of three basic components: the system unit, monitor, and keyboard. Because any monitor or keyboard upgrades involve replacements of the entire unit, the system unit is the only part of the trio that upgraders need to become familiar with. As the heart of any PC setup, the system unit contains the components illustrated in Figures B.1 and B.2.

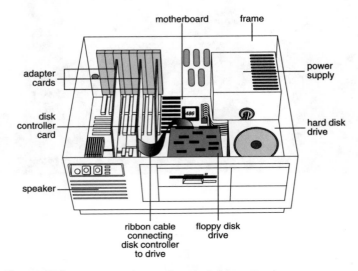

Figure B.1. *Component layout of a typical system unit.*

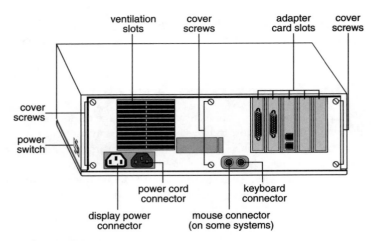

Figure B.2. *Typical rear view of a system unit.*

Common Tools Needed

If you plan to perform hardware upgrades on your PC, you should possess the following basic tools:

3/16-inch nut driver
1/4-inch nut driver
Small Phillips screwdriver
Medium Phillips screwdriver
Small flat-blade screwdriver
Medium flat-blade screwdriver
Chip puller/inserter
Tweezers
Needlenose pliers

> **TIP** Sets of tools like these, packaged in a carrying case, are sold by many computer retail outlets.

System Unit Cover Removal

The following steps can be used as a general guide to removing the cover. You should consult your PC's documentation for more precise specifics.

1. Turn off the PC's power and unplug the power cord from the system unit.

2. Remove all cables attached to the rear of the system unit.

3. Using the 1/4-inch nut driver, remove the screws attaching the cover to the frame.

4. To remove the cover on typical desktop PCs, slide the cover toward the front of the system and lift upward as you slide the cover forward. On most tower or mini-tower designs, tilt the rear of the cover upward slightly at the back of the machine, and pull the cover toward the rear of the frame.

IV

Adapter Card Removal

> **TIP** Before handling any adapter cards or other circuitry within your PC, you should make sure that your body is not carrying any static charges that could damage the circuitry. You can discharge your body of static by touching any metal that is attached to an earth ground source.

Use the following steps as an overall guide to removing adapter cards:

1. Remove the cover of the system unit by following Steps 1–4 in the previous section.
2. Using a 3/16-inch nut driver, remove the screw holding the adapter in place.
3. If any cables are connected to the adapter, make a note of how the ends of the cables are connected, then remove the cables from the adapter card.
4. Lift the adapter card using an even force at both ends of the card to remove it.

> **TIP** Always make a note of the existing positions of any jumpers or switches on an adapter card immediately after its removal. That way, if any jumper or switch setting is accidentally disturbed, you can restore it without having to hunt for the card's documentation.

You can reverse the basic order of these four steps to install an adapter card.

For specific procedures on installing motherboards, hard drives, video controllers, and memory expansion, refer to Chapters 12–16. For specifics on installing internal modems, see Chapter 19.

Resources

This appendix lists hardware and software vendors, with names, addresses, and phone numbers for each vendor. Many of the vendors are mentioned at various places throughout this book.

Adobe Systems
1585 Charleston Road
P.O. Box 7900
Mountain View, CA
(800) 833-6687
Adobe Type Manager, Fonts & Utilities

America Online
8619 Westwood Canter Drive
Vienna, VA 22182-9806
(800) 827-6364
Online service

ATI Technologies
3761 Victoria Park Avenue
Scarborough, Canada M1W 3S2
(416) 756-0718
Windows accelerator cards

Bitstream
215 First Street
Cambridge, MA 02142
(671) 497-6222
Fonts and utilities

Buffalo Products
2805 19th Street SE
Salem, OR 97302
(800) 345-2356
CPU upgrades

Compaq Computer Corp.
P.O. Box 692000
Houston, TX 77269-2000
(800) 345-1518
PCs, notebook PCs, Windows accelerators, printers

CompuServe
5000 Arlington Center Blvd.
Columbus, OH 43220
(800) 848-8199
Online service

Corel Systems
1600 Carling Avenue
Ottawa, Ontario K1Z 8R7
(800) 836-SCSI
Graphics software, SCSI management software

Creative Labs
1901 McCarthy Blvd.
Milpitas, CA 95035
(800) 998-5227
Sound boards, multimedia kits

Dell Computer
9505 Arboretum Blvd.
Austin TX 78759
(800) 289-3355
PC hardware

Delrina Technology
895 Don Mills Road
500-2 Park Centre
Toronto, Ontario M3C 1W3
(800) 268-6082
Fax software

Edge Technology
915 E. Harcher Road
Nampa, ID 83687
(800) 438-3343
Windows accelerator cards

Genoa Systems
75 E. Trimble Road
San Jose, CA 95131
(408) 432-9123
Windows accelerator cards

Hayes Microcomputer Products
P.O. Box 105203
Atlanta, GA 30348
(800) 93-HAYES
Modems, Windows communication software

Hewlett-Packard Company
Ms 5111-SJ
P.O. Box 58059
Santa Clara, CA 95051
(800) 752-0900
Printers, Windows utility software

Intel Corp.
2200 Mission College
P.O. Box 58119
Santa Clara, CA 95052
(800) 538-3373
Processor upgrades, fax/modems

IV

Kensington Microware
2855 Campus Drive
San Mateo, CA 94403
(800) 535-4242
Pointing devices

LaserMaster Corp.
6900 Shady Oak Road
Eden Prairie, MN 55344-9959
(800) 365-1144
Laser printers, printer enhancements

Lexmark International
740 New Circle Road
Lexington, KY 40511
(800) 258-8575
IBM printers

Logitech
6505 Kaiser Drive
Fremont, CA 94555
(800) 231-7717
Pointing devices, scanners

Lotus Development Corp.
55 Cambridge Parkway
Cambridge, MA 02142
(800) 343-5414
Business software on CD-ROM with multimedia

Media Vision
3185 Laurelview Court
Fremont, CA 95438
(800) 348-7116
Sound boards, multimedia kits

Metheus
1600 N.W. Compton Drive
Beaverton, OR 97006-6905
(503) 690-1550
Windows accelerator cards

Microsoft Corp.
One Microsoft Way
Redmond, WA 98052
(800) 426-9400
Windows software, application software, mouse, sound system, printing system, keyboards

Microsoft Download Service
Modem: 206-936-67-35

Mouse Systems
47505 Seabridge Drive
Fremont, CA 94538
(510) 656-1117
Pointing devices

National Semiconductor Corp.
2900 Semiconductor Drive
Santa Clara, CA 95052
(800) 838-8510
Combination fax/modem/voice mail board

NEC Technologies
1255 Michael Drive
Wooddale, IL 60191
(800) 366-0476
CD-ROM drives, notebook PCs, monitors

NEC Technologies
1414 Massachusetts Avenue
Boxborough, MA 01719
(800) 300-8888
Printers

Okidata
532 Fellowship Road
Mopunt Laurel, NJ 08054
(800) OKI-DATA
LED-page printers, combination printer/scanner/copier/fax

Orchid Technology
45365 Northport Loop
West Fremont, CA 94538
(800) 767-2443
Windows accelerator cards

Pacific Data Products
9125 Rehco Road
San Diego, CA 92121
(619) 625-3638
Printer enhancements

IV

PKWARE
9025 N. Deerwood Drive
Brown Deer, WI 53223
(414) 354-8699
File compression/decompression software

Prodigy
P.O. Box 791
White Plains, NY 10601
(800) 284-5933
Online information service

Samtron
14251 E. Firestone Blvd.
Suite 101
La Mirada, CA 90638
(310) 802-8425
Monitors

Seiko Instruments
111 MacArthur Blvd.
Mahwah, NJ 07430
(800) 553-5312
Printers

Tektronix
P.O. Box 1000
M/S 63-583
Wilsonville, OR 97070
(800) 835-6100
Printers

Toshiba America Information Systems
9740 Irvine Blvd.
Irvine, CA 92718
(714) 583-3111
CD-ROM drives, notebook PCs, printers

Turtle Beach Systems
1600 Pennsylvania Avenue
Suite 33
York, PA 17404
(717) 843-6916
Sound boards

ZEOS International Ltd.
1301 Industrial Blvd.
Minneapolis, MN 55413
(800) 554-7161
PC hardware

IV

I N D E X

Symbols

characters, numeric data in cells, 119

* characters, numeric fields in reports (Microsoft FoxPro for Windows), 141

- (hyphen), displaying as text (Microsoft Excel), 122-123

/ (slash), displaying as text (Microsoft Excel), 122-123

1-2-3 for Windows (Lotus), 125-127

486DRX/2 processors (Cyrix Corporation), 242

84-key keyboard, 253

8088 processors (Intel), 240

80286 processors (Intel), 240

80386DX processors (Intel), 241
upgrades, 246

80386SX processors (Intel), 241
upgrades, 246

80486DX processors (Intel), 241-242

80486DX2 processors (Intel), 242

80486SX processors (Intel), 241

A

Access (Microsoft), 130-137

Access Control tab (Properties for Networks window), 283, 295-296

Accessories command (Programs submenu)
Chat, 285
Create a Briefcase, 325
HyperTerminal Connections, 306
Media Player, 180
Multimedia | Sound Recorder, 177
Phone Dialer, 306
System Tools
NetWatcher, 297
System Monitor, 299

adapter cards, removing, 356

Add Fonts dialog box, 61-62

Add New Hardware icon (Control Panel), 174, 267

Add Printer dialog box, 47

Add Printer Wizard dialog box, 47

Adobe Systems, 357

Advanced tab (Properties for Multimedia window), 176-177

aligning
  labels across columns (Lotus
    1-2-3), 126
  snap to grid, disabling
    (Microsoft FoxPro for
    Windows), 140
America Online (AOL) online
  service, 309-310, 357
Appearance tab (Properties for
  Display window), 19-22, 41-42,
  324-325
applications, *see* programs
Arrange Icons command (View
  menu), 37, 53
ASCII
  text, lining up columns
    (Microsoft Word), 111
  text files, exporting
    (Novell Quattro Pro
    for Windows), 129
associating files with programs, 42
asterisk (*), numeric fields in
  reports (Microsoft FoxPro for
  Windows), 141
AT class keyboards, 254
ATI Technologies, 357
attributes (files), changing, 38
AutoExec macro, disabling
  (Microsoft Access), 135
AUTOEXEC.BAT file, 11, 185
automatic
  cell width adjustment
    Microsoft Excel, 125
    Novell Quattro Pro for
      Windows, 129
  decimal points, disabling
    (Microsoft Excel), 122
  opening at startup
    folders (Borland dBASE for
      Windows), 142
    speadsheets (Lotus
      1-2-3), 126
    workbooks (Microsoft
      Excel), 123
autosaving documents (Windows
  word processors), 103-104

B

Background tab (Properties for
  Display window), 22-23
backgrounds
  colors, changing in graphics, 95
  creating, 23
  patterns, changing, 22-23
backup programs (third-party),
  from prior Windows versions, 44
backups, Autosaving documents
  (Windows word processors),
  103-104
banner pages, disabling, 56
Banyan VINES, Windows 95
  installation, 289
batch files
  running before DOS
    applications, 149-150
  Windows 95 installation
    customized settings, 281
Bitstream, 358
blank pages in reports (Microsoft
  Access), 134
Borland
  dBASE for Windows, 141-143
  Paradox for Windows, 143-144
breaking links with linked
  objects, 80
Briefcase, 325-327
Brightness control, 234
Browse window, changing field
  headings (Borland dBASE for
  Windows), 142-143
browsing shared resources, 276-277
Buffalo Products, 358
built-in printer fonts, 58-59
  versus TrueType fonts, 62
bullets
  inserting, 87-88
  instead of field codes (Microsoft
    Word), 114
bus mouse, 256-257
  installation, 259
buses, 227
  Enhanced IDE drives, 212
  hard drive performance, 209

buttons
Start, customizing, 18
Toolbar, assigning macros to
(Microsoft Word), 114
Buttons tab (Properties for Mouse
window), 24-25

C

cables for dial-out connections,
changing settings, 285
caching, drive caching, 210-211
calculated fields (Microsoft
Access), 133
call waiting, disabling, 99
Cannot Access Serial Port message
(communications software), 340
capitalization, reversing (Windows
word processors), 107
capturing screens, 73, 155
CDs, playing, 179-180
cells
combining contents (Microsoft
Excel), 121
date and time, entering
(Novell Quattro Pro for
Windows), 128
formats
copying (Lotus 1-2-3), 126
formatting, 119
formulas
converting to values (Lotus
1-2-3), 126
entry errors, 120
printing (Microsoft
Excel), 122
numeric data, as series of #
characters, 119
protecting most (Microsoft
Excel), 123-124
widths, automatically adjusting
Microsoft Excel, 125
Novell Quattro Pro for
Windows, 129
Central Processing Units (CPUs),
see processors

CGA standard, 226
Change Passwords tab (Properties
for Security window), 291-293
Chat, 285
chips, 193-194
CPU types, 240-242
installation, 201-202
circles, drawing, 94
CIS online service, *see* CompuServe
Clipboard, 72-74
Close command (File menu), 52
Close Program dialog box, 154
closing
crashed DOS applications
safely, 154
folders, 33
Color Difference control, 235
color inkjet printers, 263
color schemes
changing, 19-20
custom, 20-21
color thermal printers, 263
colors
background, changing in
graphics, 95
custom, creating, 21-22
screen text, changing, 89
columns
aligning labels across (Lotus
1-2-3), 126
ASCII text, lining up (Microsoft
Word), 111
commands
DOS
DIR, 37
not runnable under
Windows 95, 155-156
Edit menu, 53
Copy, 34
Cut, 34
Delete, 40
Insert Object, 77
Links, 80
Paste, 34
Paste Link, 76-77
Paste Link versus Paste, 79
Paste Special, 76-78

File menu, 52
  Empty Recycle Bin, 39
  New, 39
  Print, 39
  Quick View, 42-43
  Restore, 39
Insert menu, Object, 77
Printer menu
  Pause Printing, 54
  Printer Properties, 55
Start menu, 13-15
  Programs | Accessories | Chat,
    285
  Programs | Accessories | Create
    a Briefcase, 325
  Programs | Accessories |
    HyperTerminal Connec-
    tions, 306
  Programs | Accessories | Media
    Player, 180
  Programs | Accessories | Multi-
    media, 177
  Programs | Accessories | Phone
    Dialer, 306
  Programs | Accessories | System
    Tools, 297, 299
  Programs | Main | Windows
    Setup, 319
  Programs | Microsoft
    Network, 316
  Programs | MS-DOS
    Prompt, 17, 148
  Programs | Windows
    Explorer, 33
  Settings | Control Panel, *see*
    Control Panel command
  Settings | Printers, 46,
    48-51, 55
  Settings | Taskbar, 15-16, 18
Tools menu, Find, 35-36
View menu, 37-38, 53
  Details, 37, 38
  Options | File Types tab, 42
  Options | View tab, 37, 43
communications software,
  troubleshooting, 340-341
Compaq Computer Corp., 358

compatibility interfaces, printer
  considerations, 265
compound documents, moving, 79
CompuServe (CIS) online service,
  310-312, 358
  software libraries for Microsoft
    Excel, 124
computers
  dialing, 305-306
  PC components, 353-354
  see also laptops
CONFIG.SYS file, 11, 185
Configuration tab (Properties for
  Networks window), 281-283
configurations
  NetWare servers, to support
    drag-and-drop printing, 57-58
  networks, setting options in
    Windows, 282-283
connecting to network printers, 57
connectivity, networks, 272-273
Contrast control, 234
Control Panel command (Settings
  submenu), 19
  Add New Hardware icon,
    174, 267
  Display icon, 19
  Fonts icon, 59
  Keyboard icon, 26-27
  Modems icon, 302
  Mouse icon, 24, 325
  Multimedia icon, 176
  Network icon, 58, 281-282
  Passwords icon, 291
  Printers icon, 54
  Regional Settings icon, 27-28
  Sounds icon, 28-29, 179
  System icon, 67
controls for monitors, 234-235
conventional memory, 190
Convergence control, 235
conversing in real time, 285
Copy command (Edit menu), 34
copying
  cell formats (Lotus 1-2-3), 126
  files, 34-35

folders, 34
graphics to other applications, 96
records (Microsoft Access),
131-132
text between documents, 87
windows to Clipboard, 73
copyright symbol, inserting
(Microsoft Word), 116
Corel Systems, 358
cost, memory, 199
covers of system units,
removing, 355
CPU chips, 240-242
CPUs (Central Processing Units),
see processors
crashed DOS applications, safely
terminating, 154
Create Shortcut command (File
menu), 52
Creative Labs, 358
currency symbols, foreign
(Microsoft Excel), 125
Currency tab (Properties for
Regional Settings window), 28
curved lines, drawing, 94
custom color schemes, 20-21
custom colors, creating, 21-22
Custom Setup, 351
Customize Options dialog box,
318-319
Cut command (Edit menu), 34
cutting data in DOS applications,
153
Cyrix Corporation 486DRX/2 CPU
chips, 242

D

data files, 31
Database Documentor (Microsoft
Access), 131
databases
Borland
dBASE for Windows,
141-143

Paradox for Windows,
143-144
Microsoft
Access, 130-137
FoxPro for Windows,
137-141
Date tab (Properties for Regional
Settings window), 28
dates
adding to documents, 86
Windows word processors,
108-109
entering in cells (Novell Quattro
Pro for Windows), 128
on printed pages (Novell
Quattro Pro for Windows),
128-129
dBASE for Windows (Borland),
141-143
DDE (Dynamic Data Exchange),
74-75
DEC Pathworks, Windows 95
installation, 289-290
decimal points (automatic),
disabling (Microsoft Excel), 122
defaults
DOS applications, changing to
full-screen, 148
folders, for Windows word
processor files, 102-103
fonts
changing for Windows word
processors, 101-102
designating (Microsoft
Excel), 123
for all new spreadsheets
(Lotus 1-2-3), 127
icons for DOS applications,
changing, 149
MS-DOS Application Toolbar
presence/absence, setting, 153
Delete command (Edit menu), 40
Delete Printer command (File
menu), 52
deleting
files, 40

freeing laptop disk space, 319-324
from print queues, 54
Lotus 1-2-3, 126
Microsoft Word, 113
folders, 40
hard returns (Windows word processors), 106
links between linked objects, 80
multimedia drivers, 176-177
shortcuts, 40-41
tab stops, 90
text from documents, 85
Dell Computer, 358
Delrina Technology, 359
Desktop, 5-6
displaying icons, 10-11
screen display
fonts, changing, 63
saving layout, 41-42
Detail View command (View menu), 53
Details command (View menu), 37-38
Details tab (Properties for Printer window), 49-50
Detection Crash Recovery Log (Setup program), 350
DETLOG.TXT file, 350
device drivers
multimedia, 173-177
Novell NetWare, 286-287
printer, Windows versus WordPerfect, 118
virtual, 66-67
Device Options tab (Properties for Printer window), 51, 55-56, 63
devices, 32
dial-out network cable connections, changing settings, 285
dialing
computers/online services, 305-306
modems (Microsoft Access), 135
phone calls, 306
dialog boxes
Add Fonts, 61-62

Add Printer, 47
Add Printer Wizard, 47
Close Program, 154
Customize Options, 318-319
Find: All Files, 35-36
Form Expert, disabling (Borland dBASE for Windows), 142
Low Memory, avoiding, 69-70
Virtual Memory, 68-69
DIR command, 37
Direct Random Access Memory (DRAM), 193-194
installation, 201-202
directories, 31
default, for Windows word processor files, 102-103
listing contents, 37
shared
establishing passwords, 294
granting permissions to, 296
see also folders
discharging static, 356
disk space, freeing
customizing Windows 95 for laptops, 318-319
deleting files, 319-324
disks
formatting, 40
hard, *see* hard drives
properties, viewing, 40
Windows installation, keeping, 99-100
Display icon (Control Panel), 19
DJN/R (Dow Jones News/Retrieval with MCI Mail) online service, 312-313
documents, 32
adding date and time, 86
Windows word processors, 108-109
appearance, screen display versus printouts (Windows word processors), 110
Autosaving (Windows word processors), 103-104
compound, moving, 79
copying text between, 87

creating, 84
deleting text, 85
finding text, 85
inserting graphics (Windows
    word processors), 109
logos/decorative titles,
    adding, 81
moving information
    between, 87
opening, 85
password-protection (Windows
    word processors), 106-107
printing, 91
    most-often used,
        shortcuts, 46
replacing text, 86
saving, 85
selecting entire document (Win-
    dows word processors), 105
Documents command (Taskbar
Start menu), 14
DOS
    DIR command, 37
    running alone, 149
    switching between Microsoft
        Word and, 114-115
DOS applications
    crashed, safely terminating, 154
    customizable properties,
        156-162
    cutting and pasting data, 153
    default icons, changing, 149
    fonts, changing sizes, 153-154
    loading multiple, 150
    MS-DOS Application Toolbar,
        152-153
    optimizing performance,
        162-163
    running, 17
        not to run under Windows
            95, 155-156
        running batch files before
            running DOS application,
            149-150
        under Windows 95,
            145-146

running within windows
    default, changing to
        full-screen, 148
    switching between running
        full-screen and, 147
    shortcuts, 148
    Single MS-DOS Application
        Mode, 151-152
    starting, 146
    using Clipboard, 73-74
DOS prompt in Windows 95, 148
dot pitch, 233
dot-matrix printers, 262
Dow Jones News/Retrieval with
    MCI Mail (DJN/R) online
    service, 312-313
dpi (dots per inch), 263
draft copies, printing (Microsoft
    Word), 112
drag-and-drop
    moving files/folders, 34
    printing, configuring NetWare
        servers to support, 57-58
    printing files, 39
dragging Taskbar, 15
DRAM (Direct Random Access
    Memory), 193-194
    installation, 201-202
drawing
    lines, 93-94
    shapes, 94
drive caching, 210-211
drive letters, mapping, 101
drives, changing, 33
DX2 CPU designation, 245
Dynamic Data Exchange (DDE),
    74-75

E

Edge Technology, 359
Edit menu commands, 53
    Copy, 34
    Cut, 34
    Delete, 40
    Insert Object, 77

Links, 80
Paste, 34
Paste Link, 76-77
   versus Paste, 79
Paste Special, 76-78
editing
   application self-assigned
      names, 18
   graphics, 95
   linked objects, 79-80
   sound files, 178
editors
   PIF Editor, 156
   Registry Editor, 183-185
EGA standard, 226
electrical standards for keyboards,
   254-255
embedding objects, 75-78
   logos/decorative titles, 81
   WordPad word processor, 91-93
Empty Recycle Bin command (File
   menu), 39
Enhanced IDE standard, 209-210
   expansion buses, 212
envelopes, printing (Microsoft
   Word), 113-114
ergonomically designed keyboards, 254
Error 20 message (laser printer LCD
   panel), 339
error messages, *see* messages
errors, entering formulas in
   cells, 120
Event Log (Setup program), 350
Excel (Microsoft), 120-125
expanded memory, 191
expansion buses
   Enhanced IDE drives, 212
   hard drive performance, 209
Explorer, 7-9
   running DOS applications, 17
   screen display, customizing,
      37-38
   starting, 33
   versus File Manager, 32
Explorer window, 53

exporting files
   ASCII text (Novell Quattro Pro
      for Windows), 129
   Microsoft Excel, 120-121
Extended Graphics Array (XGA)
   standard, 227
extended memory, 191
extensions (files), displaying, 43
external modems, 301-305

F

field codes, bullets instead of
   (Microsoft Word), 114
fields
   adding to reports (Microsoft
      FoxPro for Windows), 139
   calculated (Microsoft
      Access), 133
   changing headings in Browse
      window (Borland dBASE
      for Windows), 142-143
   general, displaying contents
      (Microsoft FoxPro for
      Windows), 138
   memo
      formatting text (Microsoft
         Access), 132
      printing multiple lines
         (Microsoft FoxPro for
         Windows), 140
   numeric, * characters (Microsoft
      FoxPro for Windows), 141
   tab order, changing (Microsoft
      FoxPro for Windows), 138
File is in use message (Microsoft
   FoxPro for Windows), 137
File Manager, 7-8
   versus Explorer, 32
File menu commands, 52
   Empty Recycle Bin, 39
   New, 39
   Print, 39
   Quick View, 42-43
   Restore, 39

File Types tab (View | Options command), 42
file viewers, 42-43
files
    accessing on other computers, 101
    associating with programs, 42
    attributes, changing, 38
    AUTOEXEC.BAT, 11, 185
    batch, Windows 95 installation customized settings, 281
    changing order in print queues, 54
    CONFIG.SYS, 11, 185
    copying, 34-35
    data, 31
    deleting, 40
        freeing laptop disk space, 319-324
        from print queues, 54
        Lotus 1-2-3, 126
        Microsoft Word, 113
    DETLOG.TXT, 350
    examining, 42-43
    exporting, ASCII text (Novell Quattro Pro for Windows), 129
    extensions, displaying, 43
    hidden, viewing, 43
    importing/exporting (Microsoft Excel), 120-121
    .INI, 185
    listing, 37
    moving, 34-35
    names, preserving when copying files to disks, 43
    printing, 39
        multiple (Microsoft Excel), 124-125
        multiple (Windows word processors), 108
    redirecting printing output to, 55
    renaming, 39
    saving to floppy disks, troubleshooting, 337
    searching for, 35-36
    SETUPLOG.TXT, 350
    sorting, 38
    sound, 177-180
    synchronizing between laptops and desktop PCs, 325-327
    undeleting, 39
    video, playing, 179-180
filling shapes, 94
Find command
    Start menu, 14
    Tools menu, 35-36
Find: All Files dialog box, 35-36
finding
    files/folders, 35-36
    text in documents, 85
fixed frequency monitors, 233
flat memory models, 66
flicker, 225
Folder tab (Explorer window), 53
folders, 32
    closing, 33
    copying, 34
    creating, 39
    default, changing for Windows word processor files, 102-103
    deleting, 40
    moving, 34
    names
        renaming, 39
        standardizing, 277
    opening, 33-34
        automatically at startup (Borland dBASE for Windows), 142
    Printers, 47, 52-53
    searching for, 35-36
    see also directories
font cartridges, fonts not displaying, 58
Font tab (Properties for *DOS application* window), 158-159
fonts
    built-in printer, 58-59
        versus TrueType fonts, 62

default
  changing (Windows word
    processors), 101-102
  designating (Microsoft
    Excel), 123
  for all new spreadsheets
    (Lotus 1-2-3), 127
  Desktop display, changing, 63
  selecting, 88
  sizes, changing (DOS applica-
    tions), 153-154
  soft, 59-62
  TrueType, sources for
    obtaining, 62
Fonts icon (Control Panel), 59
Fonts tab (Properties for Printer
  window), 51, 58-59
Fonts window, 59-61
footers, dates/page numbers
  (Novell Quattro Pro for
  Windows), 128-129
foreign currency symbols (Microsoft
  Excel), 125
Form Expert dialog box,
  disabling (Borland dBASE
  for Windows), 142
Format bar, hiding/displaying, 84
formatting
  cells, 119
    copying (Lotus 1-2-3), 126
  disks, 40
  text
    in memo fields (Microsoft
      Access), 132
    WordPad, 87-90
forms, creating
  Borland dBASE for
    Windows, 142
  Microsoft Access, 132
  Microsoft FoxPro for
    Windows, 138
formulas
  converting to values (Lotus
    1-2-3), 126
  entering in cells, errors, 120
  printing (Microsoft Excel), 122

FoxPro for Windows (Microsoft),
  137-141
free-form lines, drawing, 93
freeing disk space
  customizing Windows 95 for
    laptops, 318-319
  deleting files, 319-324
full hard drives,
  troubleshooting, 337

G

games, running, 150-152
general fields, displaying
  contents (Microsoft FoxPro
  for Windows), 138
General Protection Fault message
  Microsoft Access, 130
  Microsoft FoxPro for
    Windows, 141
General tab
  Properties for *DOS application*
    window, 157
  Properties for *drive* window, 40
  Properties for Keyboard
    window, 26
  Properties for Mouse
    window, 26
  Properties for Printer window,
    48-49, 56-57
GEnie online service, 313-314
Genoa Systems, 359
graphics
  adding text, 95
  background colors, 95
  copying to other applica-
    tions, 96
  drawing, 93-94
  editing, 95
  filling, 94
  inserting into documents (Win-
    dows word processors), 109
  printing, 63
  viewing, 95-96
graphics accelerator cards, 229

Graphics tab (Properties for Printer
window), 50-51
graphics tablets, 257-258
grids, disabling snap to grid
(Microsoft FoxPro for
Windows), 140
grounding phone lines, 305

H

hanging Windows 95, troubleshooting, 336-337
hard drives
adding second drive, 213-214
Enhanced IDE, expansion
buses, 212
full, troubleshooting, 337
installation, 214-222
MPC-2 standard, 168
performance consideration
factors, 206-207
planning for enough space, 214
types, 207-209
upgrading
economic considerations,
211-212
reasons for, 205-206
hard page breaks, viewing
(WordPerfect), 117
hard returns, deleting (Windows
word processors), 106
HardCard drives (Quantum
Corporation), 219-220
hardware
multimedia requirements, 166
not matching list of installed
equipment, 332
upgrades, necessary tools, 355
vendors, addresses, 357-363
Windows 95 requirements,
351-352
Hardware Installation Wizard,
174-176
Hayes Microcomputer
Products, 359

headers, dates/page numbers
(Novell Quattro Pro for
Windows), 128-129
headings for fields, changing in
Browse window (Borland dBASE
for Windows), 142-143
heat generated by processors, 243
Help Topics command (Taskbar
Start menu), 15
Hertz, 225
Hewlett-Packard Company, 359
DeskJet printers, printing
multiple copies (Novell
Quattro Pro for Windows),
127-128
hidden files, viewing, 43
hiding
Format bar, 84
Ruler, 84
Status bar, 84
system tables (Microsoft
Access), 131
Taskbar, 15-16, 100
Toolbar, 84
Horizontal Position control, 235
Horizontal Size control, 235
HyperTerm, 305-306
hyphen (-), displaying as text
(Microsoft Excel), 122-123

I-J

I/O Channel Ready, 210
icons
Control Panel
Add New Hardware,
174, 267
Display, 19
Fonts, 59
Keyboard, 26-27
Modems, 302
Mouse, 24, 325
Multimedia, 176
Network, 58, 281-282
Passwords, 291

Printers, 54
Regional Settings, 27-28
Sounds, 28-29, 179
System, 67
displaying on Desktop, 10-11
DOS applications, changing
default, 149
Remote Access (Network
Neighborhood), 285
IDE (Integrated Drive Electronics)
standard, 207-208
drive installation, 214-219
Identification tab (Properties for
Networks window), 283
importing files (Microsoft Excel),
120-121
Industry Standard Architecture
(ISA) bus, 244
.INI files, 185
inkjet printers, 262-263
Insert menu, Object command, 77
Insert Object command (Edit
menu), 77
installation
hard drives, 214-222
memory, 199-204
memory expansion cards,
202-203
modems, 301-304
monitors, 235-237
motherboards, 247-250
network adapters on
networks, 281
OverDrive processors (Intel),
250-251
printers, 46-48, 267-268
sound cards, 172-173
video cards, 231-232
troubleshooting, 236-237
Windows 95
batch files for customized
settings, 281
customizing for laptops, 318
on third-party networks,
288-290
on workstations attached to
LANs, 278-281

Setup program, 345-346
troubleshooting, 331-335
Windows applications under
Windows 95, 100
WordPerfect 6.0 and
WordPerfect 5.2, 117
installation disks for Windows,
keeping, 99-100
Installation Wizard, 267
installed equipment list, hardware
not matching, 332
Insufficient memory message
(Novell Quattro Pro for
Windows), 127
Integrated Drive Electronics
standard, *see* IDE
Intel Corp., 359
CPU chips, 240-242
OverDrive processors, 245-246
installation, 250-251
interface compatibility, printer
considerations, 265
interlaced monitors versus
noninterlaced monitors, 226
internal modems, 302-305
international
currency symbols (Microsoft
Excel), 125
languages, changing keyboard
character layouts, 27
settings, customizing, 27-28
Internet, 314-316
ISA (Industry Standard Architecture) bus, 244

K

Kensington Microware, 359
Keyboard icon (Control Panel),
26-27
keyboard shortcuts
common to Windows
applications, 98-99
Next application (Alt+Tab), 17
Screen Capture (Alt+PtrSc), 73

keyboards
    character layouts for other
        languages, 27
    repeat speeds, changing, 26
    types, changing, 26
    upgrades, 253-255
keys, PrtSc, 155

L

labels, aligning across columns
    (Lotus 1-2-3), 126
Language tab (Properties for
    Keyboard window), 27
LANs (Local Area Networks),
    see networks
laptops
    Briefcase, 325-327
    consideration factors, 329-330
    freeing disk space, 318-324
    memory upgrades, 327-328
    mouse pointer, making more
        visible, 325
    processor upgrades, 328
    screen displays, making more
        readable, 324-325
Large Icons command (View
    menu), 37, 53
laser printers, 262
    Error 20 message (LCD
        panel), 339
    performance, increasing,
        265-266
LaserMaster Corp., 360
LED page printers, 262
Lexmark International, 360
light pens, 258
lines, drawing, 93-94
linked objects
    breaking links, 80
    creating links, 75-77
        WordPad word processor,
            91-93
    documents with multiple
        links, 80

editing, 79-80
    moving compound
        documents, 79
    optimizing performance, 78-79
Links command (Edit menu), 80
List View command (View
    menu), 53
Lists command (View menu), 37
loading multiple DOS
    applications, 150
local bus, 244-245
    video, 227-229
local printers as network
    printers, 286
local security, 290
Locked Record message (Borland
    Paradox for Windows), 144
Logical Block Addressing, 209-210
Logitech, 360
logos, adding to documents/
    spreadsheets, 81
Lotus Development Corp., 360
    1-2-3 for Windows, 125-127
Low Memory dialog box, avoiding,
    69-70

M

macros
    assigning to Toolbar buttons
        (Microsoft Word), 114
    AutoExec, disabling (Microsoft
        Access), 135
    for switching between Microsoft
        Word and DOS, 114-115
Main command (Programs
    submenu), 319
manual page breaks (Microsoft
    Excel), 124
mapping drive letters, 101
margins
    changing, 89-90
    outside printable area (Microsoft
        Word), 112
    setting for printing, 91

Margins outside printable area
of page message (Microsoft
Word), 112
math coprocessors, 247
mechanical mouse, 255
Media Player, 179-180
Media Vision, 360
megahertz (MHz), 242
memo fields
formatting text (Microsoft
Access), 132
printing multiple lines
(Microsoft FoxPro for
Windows), 140
memory
address spaces, 190-191
conserving, 69-70
cost, 199
faster than processors, 198
flat memory models, 66
installation, 199-204
insufficient (Novell Quattro
Pro for Windows), 127
printers
considerations, 265
usage, changing, 55-56
RAM
minimum Windows 95
requirements, 69
MPC-2 standard, 168
requirements, 191-192
sources, 199
types, 192-198
upgrades
laptops, 327-328
reasons for, 189-190
video, amounts and types,
224-225
virtual, 67-69
memory boards, 198
memory expansion cards, installation, 202-203
memory management, reasons
for, 65
memory managers, third-party from
prior versions, 66

Memory tab (Properties for *DOS
application* window), 159-160
messages
Cannot Access Serial
Port (communications
software), 340
Error 20 (laser printer LCD
panel), 339
File is in use (Microsoft FoxPro
for Windows), 137
General Protection Fault
Microsoft Access, 130
Microsoft FoxPro for
Windows, 141
Insufficient memory
(Novell Quattro Pro for
Windows), 127
Locked Record (Borland
Paradox for Windows), 144
Margins outside printable area
of page (Microsoft Word), 112
#NAME? (Microsoft Access),
132-133
Not enough disk space
(Microsoft FoxPro for
Windows), 137
Out of memory
Microsoft Access, 134
Windows 95, 336
Unable to play sound (Windows
95), 338
Word has caused a General
Protection Fault in module
WINWORD.EXE, 111
Metheus, 360
MHz (megahertz), 242
microprocessors, *see* processors
Microsoft Corp., 360
Access, 130-137
Download Service, 360
Excel, 120-125
FoxPro for Windows, 137-141
Microsoft Network, 316
Word for Windows, 101-116
Misc tab (Properties for *DOS
application* window), 161-162

missing text in printouts, troubleshooting, 339
modems
dialing (Microsoft Access), 135
disabling call waiting, 99
external versus internal, 304-305
installation, 301-304
Modems icon (Control Panel), 302
monitors
controls, 234-235
dot pitch, 233
installation, 235-237
interlaced versus noninterlaced, 226
matching with video cards,
230-231
multiscanning, 230
resolution, 224
consideration factors, 232
types, 233-234
video standards, 226-227
see also screen displays; video
motherboards
installation, 247-250
local bus, 244-245
memory types, 192-198
sizes, 243
Motion tab (Properties for Mouse
window), 25, 325
mouse
installation, 258-260
settings, changing, 24-26
types, 255-257
Mouse icon (Control Panel),
24, 325
mouse pointer
making more visible, 325
troubleshooting, 333-334
Mouse Systems, 361
moving
compound documents, 79
files, 34-35
folders, 34
paragraphs (Microsoft
Word), 112
rows (Microsoft Word), 112

tables (Borland Paradox for
Windows), 144
Taskbar, 15
MPC-2 standard, 166-168
MS-DOS Application Toolbar,
152-153
MS-DOS Prompt command
(Programs submenu), 17, 148
multicolumn reports (Microsoft
FoxPro for Windows), 140
multifrequency monitors, 233-234
multimedia, 165-166
assigning sounds to system
events, 178-179
component requirements, 166
Media Player, 179-180
MPC-2 standard, 166-168
sound cards, installing, 172-173
Sound Recorder, 177-178
multimedia drivers, 173-177
Multimedia icon (Control
Panel), 176
multiscanning monitors, 230, 234
Multiword Direct Memory
Access, 209
My Computer, 8-9
running DOS programs, 17
screen display, single
window, 38

N

#NAME? message (Microsoft
Access), 132-133
names
applications, editing self-
assigned, 18
files
preserving when copying
files to disks, 43
renaming, 39
folders
renaming, 39
standardizing, 277
National Semiconductor Corp., 361
NEC Technologies, 361

NetWare (Novell)
  drivers, 286-287
  servers, configuring to support
    drag-and-drop printing, 57-58
  utilities, running, 285
NetWatcher, 297-298
network adapters, installation on
  networks, 281
Network icon (Control Panel), 58,
  281-282
Network Neighborhood, 9, 273
  Remote Access icon, 285
Network Provider Interface
  (NPI), 272
network security, 290-291
  share-level, 294-295
  user-level, 295-296
networks
  banner pages, disabling
    printing, 56
  configuration options, setting
    in Windows, 282-283
  connectivity, 272-273
  dial-out cable connections,
    changing settings, 285
  network adapter installa-
    tion, 281
  peer-to-peer
    monitoring network
      activity, 299
    monitoring resource usage,
      296-298
    optimizing perfor-
      mance, 278
    setting up, 274-276
    with Workgroups for
      Windows, 278
  printers, connecting to, 57
  shared resources, browsing,
    276-277
  third-party, installing Windows
    95, 288-290
  user interface, 273
  Windows 95 advantages,
    271-272
  workstations, installing
    Windows 95, 278-281

New command (File menu), 39
noninterlaced monitors versus
  interlaced monitors, 226
Not enough disk space message
  (Microsoft FoxPro for
  Windows), 137
notebook computers, *see* laptops
Novell
  NetWare
    drivers, 286-287
    servers, configuring to
      support drag-and-drop
      printing, 57-58
    utilities, running, 285
  Quattro Pro for Windows,
    127-129
  WordPerfect for Windows,
    101-110, 117-118
NPI (Network Provider
  Interface), 272
Number tab (Properties for
  Regional Settings window), 28
numeric coprocessors, 247
numeric data in cells as series of #
  characters, 119
numeric fields, * characters (Micro-
  soft FoxPro for Windows), 141

O

Object command (Insert menu), 77
objects, 31-32
  database, listing (Microsoft
    Access), 131
  see also devices; documents;
    folders; programs
Okidata, 361
OLE (Object Linking and
  Embedding), 75-76
  embedding objects, 77-78
    logos/decorative titles, 81
  linked objects
    breaking links, 80
    creating links, 76-77
    documents with multiple
      links, 80

editing, 79-80
moving compound
documents, 79
optimizing performance,
78-79
WordPad word processor, 91-93
one-to-many relationships (Microsoft FoxPro for Windows), 140
online services, 306-307
accessing Internet, 315-316
America Online (AOL),
309-310
CompuServe (CIS), 310-312
dialing, 305-306
Dow Jones News/Retrieval with
MCI Mail (DJN/R), 312-313
GEnie, 313-314
Microsoft Network, 316
Prodigy, 314
selecting, 307-308
Open command (File menu), 52
opening
documents, 85
folders, 33
automatically at startup
(Borland dBASE for
Windows), 142
multiple, 34
sound files, 177
speadsheets, automatically at
startup (Lotus 1-2-3), 126
workbooks, automatically at
startup (Microsoft Excel), 123
optical mouse, 255
optimizing performance
DOS applications, 162-163
linked objects, 78-79
Microsoft Access, 130
startup speed, 136
Microsoft Word, 115-116
peer-to-peer networks, 278
WordPerfect, 118
Option Compare Database
(Microsoft Access), 136
Options command (View menu),
37-38, 42-43, 53

Orchid Technology, 361
Out of memory message
Microsoft Access, 134
Windows 95, 336
ovals, drawing, 94
OverDrive processors (Intel),
245-246
installation, 250-251

P

Pacific Data Products, 361
page breaks
manual (Microsoft Excel), 124
viewing (WordPerfect), 117
page numbers on printed pages
(Novell Quattro Pro for
Windows), 128-129
pages
blank in reports (Microsoft
Access), 134
printing
disabling banner pages, 56
selected pages (Microsoft
Word), 113
with graphics, 63
Paint program, 93-96
paper
printer handling considerations, 264
sizes, changing (Windows word
processors), 105
Paper tab (Properties for Printer
window), 50
Paradox for Windows (Borland),
143-144
paragraph marks, deleting
(Windows word processors), 106
paragraphs
moving (Microsoft Word), 112
selecting (Windows word
processors), 106
passwords
establishing for share-level
security, 294

shared-resource access, 275
Windows word processors,
106-107
Passwords icon (Control
Panel), 291
Paste command (Edit menu), 34
Paste Link command (Edit menu),
76-77
versus Paste command, 79
Paste Special command (Edit
menu), 76-78
pasting data in DOS applications, 153
Pathworks (DEC), Windows 95
installation, 289-290
patterns (background), changing,
22-23
Pause Printing command
File menu, 52
Printer menu, 54
PC-NFS (SunSelect), Windows 95
installation, 290
PCI (Peripheral Component
Interconnect) bus standard,
228-229, 244
PCs (personal computers),
components, 353-354
peer-to-peer networks
monitoring
network activity, 299
resource usage, 296-298
optimizing performance, 278
setting up, 274-276
with Workgroups for
Windows, 278
Pentium CPU chips, 242
performance
hard drives, consideration
factors, 206-207
optimizing
DOS applications, 162-163
laser printers, 265-266
linking objects, 78-79
Microsoft Access, 130
Microsoft Access startup
speed, 136

Microsoft Word, 115-116
peer-to-peer networks, 278
WordPerfect, 118
slow, troubleshooting, 335-336
Peripheral Component Interconnect
(PCI) bus standard, 228-229, 244
permissions, granting, 296
Phone Dialer, 306
phone lines, grounding, 305
PIF Editor, 156
pixels, 224
PKWARE, 362
playing
CDs/video files, 179-180
sound files, 177, 179-180
plugs in keyboards, 254
Pointers tab (Properties for Mouse
window), 25
pointing devices (Microsoft FoxPro
for Windows), 138
portable computers, *see* laptops
ports, assigning printers to, 56-57
PostScript description language
(Adobe Systems, Inc.), 266
previewing
documents, 91
WYSIWYG (WordPerfect), 117
Print command (File menu), 39
Print Manager, 11
print queues
changing order of files, 54
deleting files, 54
viewing, 53
Print Server for NetWare, 286
printer drivers, Windows versus
WordPerfect, 118
printer fonts, built-in, 58-59
versus TrueType fonts, 62
Printer menu commands
Pause Printing, 54
Printer Properties, 55
printers
assigning to ports, 56-57
changing options, 91
consideration factors, 264-265
dpi (dots per inch), 263

font cartridges, fonts not
displaying, 58
HP DeskJet, printing multiple
copies (Novell Quattro Pro
for Windows), 127-128
installation, 46-48, 267-268
laser
    Error 20 message (LCD
    panel), 339
    increasing performance,
    265-266
memory usage, changing, 55-56
missing text, troubleshooting, 339
network
    connecting to, 57
    local printers as, 286
PostScript description language
(Adobe Systems, Inc.), 266
settings, changing, 48-51
shared
    establishing passwords, 294
    granting permissions to, 296
troubleshooting, 338-339
types, 261-263
Printers command (Settings
submenu), 46, 48-51
    Details tab, 55
Printers Folder, 11, 47, 52-53
Printers icon (Control Panel), 54
printing
banner pages, disabling, 56
documents, 91
    document appearance, versus
    screen display appearance
    (Windows word proces-
    sors), 110
    most-often used documents,
    shortcuts, 46
draft copies (Microsoft
Word), 112
drag-and-drop, configuring
NetWare servers to support,
57-58
envelopes (Microsoft Word),
113-114

files, 39
formulas (Microsoft Excel), 122
in Microsoft FoxPro for
Windows, 141
in Windows applications, 99
multiple copies (Novell Quattro
Pro for Windows), 127-128
multiple files
    Microsoft Excel, 124-125
    Windows word processors,
    108
new Windows 95 features,
45-46
pages with graphics, 63
pausing, 54
redirecting output to files, 55
reports to files (Microsoft
Access), 133
resuming, 54
reverse order (Microsoft
Word), 113
selected pages (Microsoft
Word), 113
specific areas of spread-
sheets, 121
processors
Intel OverDrive, 245-246
upgrades
    80386, 246
    consideration factors,
    240-243
    laptops, 328
    types, 239
Prodigy online service, 314, 362
program groups, 36
Program tab (Properties for
DOS application window),
149-152, 158
programs, 32
associating files with, 42
backup (third-party), from prior
Windows versions, 44
Chat, 285
communications software,
troubleshooting, 340-341

CompuServe software libraries
for Microsoft Excel, 124
DOS, *see* DOS applications
HyperTerm, 305-306
NetWatcher, 297-298
Novell NetWare utilities,
running, 285
Paint, 93-96
Phone Dialer, 306
Print Server for NetWare, 286
running, 17-18
self-assigned names, editing, 18
Setup, 345-346
storing in multiple databases
(Microsoft Access), 136-137
System Monitor, 299
uninstalling, freeing laptop disk
space, 323-324
vendor addresses, 357-363
Windows, *see* Windows
applications
WordPad word processor, 84-93
Programs command (Start
menu), 14
Accessories
Chat, 285
Create a Briefcase, 325
HyperTerminal Connec-
tions, 306
Media Player, 180
Multimedia | Sound
Recorder, 177
Phone Dialer, 306
System Tools | Net-
Watcher, 297
System Tools | System
Monitor, 299
Main | Windows Setup, 319
Microsoft Network, 316
MS-DOS Prompt, 17, 148
Windows Explorer, 33
properties, 9-10
Properties command (File
menu), 52
Properties for Display window
Appearance tab, 19-22, 41-42,
324-325

Background tab, 22-23
Screen Saver tab, 23-24
Settings tab, 63
Properties for *DOS application*
window, 157-162
Program tab, 149-152
Screen tab, 153
Properties for *drive* window, 40
Properties for *filename* window, 38
Properties for Keyboard window
General tab, 26
Language tab, 27
Speed tab, 26
Properties for Mouse window,
24-26
Motion tab, 325
Properties for Multimedia window
Advanced tab, 176-177
Properties for Networks window,
282-283
Access Control tab, 295-296
Configuration tab, 281
Properties for Printer window,
48-51
Device Options tab, 55-56, 63
Fonts tab, 58-59
General tab, 56-57
Properties for Regional Settings
window, 27-28
Properties for Security window,
291-293
Remote Administration tab,
295, 296
Properties for Shared Resources
window, Sharing tab, 278
Properties for Sounds window,
28-29, 179
Properties for Taskbar window,
15-17
proprietary memory, 194
protecting
documents, password-
protection, 106-107
most worksheet cells (Microsoft
Excel), 123-124
PrtSc key, 155

PS/2 mouse, 256
    installation, 258
pucks, 258
Purge Printer command (File
    menu), 52

Q

Quantum Corporation HardCard
    drives, 219-220
queries
    calculated fields (Microsoft
        Access), 133
    creating forms for
        Borland dBASE for
            Windows, 142
        Microsoft Access, 132
        Microsoft FoxPro for
            Windows, 138
    creating reports for
        Borland dBASE for
            Windows, 143
        Borland Paradox for
            Windows, 144
        Microsoft Access, 133
        Microsoft FoxPro for
            Windows, 139
queues
    changing order of files, 54
    deleting files, 54
    viewing, 53
Quick View command (File menu),
    42-43

R

RAM
    DRAM (Direct Random Access
        Memory), 193-194
    minimum Windows 95
        requirements, 69
    MPC-2 standard, 168
    VRAM (Video Random Access
        Memory), 225

records
    copying (Microsoft Access),
        131-132
    sorting (Borland Paradox for
        Windows), 143-144
recovery safeguards (Setup
    program), 349-350
rectangles, drawing, 94
Recycle Bin, 39
Refresh command (View menu),
    37, 53
refresh rate, 225-226
Regional Settings icon (Control
    Panel), 27-28
Regional Settings tab (Properties for
    Regional Settings window), 28
Registry, 181-183
Registry Editor, 183-185
Remote Access icon (Network
    Neighborhood), 285
remote administration
    establishing passwords, 295
    granting permissions to, 296
Remote Administration tab
    (Properties for Security window),
    293, 295-296
Rename Printer command (File
    menu), 52
renaming files/folders, 39
repeat speeds (keyboard), 26
replacing text in documents, 86
reports
    * characters in numeric fields
        (Microsoft FoxPro for
        Windows), 141
    adding fields (Microsoft FoxPro
        for Windows), 139
    blank pages (Microsoft
        Access), 134
    creating
        Borland dBASE for
            Windows, 143
        Borland Paradox for
            Windows, 144
        Microsoft Access, 133
        Microsoft FoxPro for
            Windows, 139

FoxPro for DOS, in Microsoft
  FoxPro for Windows, 139
multicolumn (Microsoft FoxPro
  for Windows), 140
printing multiple lines in memo
  fields (Microsoft FoxPro for
  Windows), 140
printing to files (Microsoft
  Access), 133
resolution, 224
  consideration factors, 232
resources
  conserving, 69-70
  shared, 275-277
Restore command (File menu), 39
restoring
  autosaved documents (Windows
    word processors), 103-104
  files, 39
resuming printing, 54
returns (hard), deleting, 106
reverse order, printing (Microsoft
  Word), 113
rotational speeds, hard drive
  performance factors, 207
rows, moving (Microsoft
  Word), 112
Ruler, hiding/displaying, 84
Run command (Taskbar Start
  menu), 15

S

Samtron, 362
saving
  custom color schemes, 21
  Desktop screen display layout,
    41-42
  documents, 85
  files to floppy disks, trouble-
    shooting, 337
  reports to files (Microsoft
    Access), 133
Screen Builder pointing devices
  (Microsoft FoxPro for
  Windows), 138

screen captures, 73, 155
screen text colors, changing, 89
screen displays
  Desktop, saving layout, 41-42
  document appearance, versus
    printout appearance (Win-
    dows word processors), 110
  Explorer, customizing, 37-38
  laptops, making more readable,
    324-325
  My Computer, single
    window, 38
  refresh rate, 225-226
  sorting data (Microsoft
    Access), 133
  WordPad word processors,
    customizing, 84
  see also monitors
Screen Saver tab (Properties for
  Display window), 23-24
Screen tab (Properties for *DOS
  application* window), 153,
  160-161
SCSI (Small Computer Systems
  Interface) standard, 208
  drive installation, 220-222
security
  accessing options, 291-293
  granting permissions, 296
  levels, 290-291
  monitoring
    network activity on peer-to-
      peer networks, 299
    resource usage on peer-to-
      peer networks, 296-298
  network
    share-level, 294-295
    user-level, 295-296
Seiko Instruments, 362
selecting (Windows word processors)
  entire documents, 105
  words/sentences/para-
    graphs, 106
serial mouse, 255-256
  installation, 258-259

Settings command (Start menu), 14
  Control Panel, *see* Control Panel
    command
  Printers, 46, 48-51
    Details tab, 55
    Taskbar, 15-16, 18
Settings tab (Properties for Display
  window), 63
Setup program
  Custom Setup, 351
  failure detection and recovery
    safeguards, 349-350
  stub (short), 348-349
  upgrades from Windows 3.*x* or
    Windows for Workgroups to
    Windows 95, 347
  Windows 95 installation,
    345-346
SETUPLOG.TXT file, 350
shapes, drawing/filling, 94
share-level network security,
  290-291, 294-295
shared
  directories or printers
    establishing passwords, 294
    granting permissions to, 296
  resources, 275-277
Sharing tab (Properties of Shared
  Resources window), 278
shells, 32
shortcuts
  deleting, 40-41
  DOS applications, 148
  printing most-often used
    documents, 46
Shutdown command (Taskbar Start
  menu), 15
SIMMs (Single In-Line Memory
  Modules), 193-201
Single MS-DOS Application Mode,
  151-152
SIPs (Single In-line Packages),
  193-201
sizes
  fonts, changing (DOS
    applications), 153-154

motherboards, 243
paper, changing (Windows word
  processors), 105
slash (/), displaying as text
  (Microsoft Excel), 122-123
slow performance, troubleshooting,
  335-336
Small Computer Systems Interface
  (SCSI) standard, 208
  drive installation, 220-222
Small Icons command (View
  menu), 37, 53
Snap Grid command (View
  menu), 53
snap to grid, disabling (Microsoft
  FoxPro for Windows), 140
soft fonts, 59-62
soft page breaks, viewing
  (WordPerfect), 117
sorting
  displayed data (Microsoft
    Access), 133
  files, 38
  records (Borland Paradox for
    Windows), 143-144
sound cards, installing, 172-173
sound files
  editing, 178
  opening and playing, 177
  playing, 179-180
Sound Recorder, 177-178
sounds
  assigning to system events,
    28-29, 178-179
  creating, 178
  troubleshooting, 338
Sounds icon (Control Panel),
  28-29, 179
speakers, 168
special characters, inserting
  (Windows word processors), 104
speed
  communications software,
    high speed troubleshooting,
    340-341
  CPU chips, 242-243

hard drive rotation, performance factors, 207

hard drives, performance factors, 206-207

memory, faster than processors, 198

printer considerations, 264

SIMMs, 197-198

slow performance, troubleshooting, 335-336

Speed tab (Properties for Keyboard window), 26

spreadsheets
logos/decorative titles, adding, 81
Lotus 1-2-3 for Windows, 125-127
Microsoft Excel, 120-125
Novell Quattro Pro for Windows, 127-129
Windows applications, 119-120

SQL tables, write privileges (Microsoft Access), 135

squares, drawing, 94

standards
Enhanced IDE, 209-210
IDE (Integrated Drive Electronics), 207-208
local bus, 244-245
MPC-2, 166-168
SCSI (Small Computer Systems Interface), 208
video
local bus, 227-229
monitors, 226-227

Start button, customizing, 18

Start menu commands, 13-15
Programs
Accessories | Chat, 285
Accessories | Create a Briefcase, 325
Accessories | HyperTerminal Connections, 306
Accessories | Media Player, 180
Accessories | Multimedia | Sound Recorder, 177

Accessories | Phone Dialer, 306
Accessories | System Tools | NetWatcher, 297
Accessories | System Tools | System Monitor, 299
Main | Windows Setup, 319
Microsoft Network, 316
MS-DOS Prompt, 17, 148
Windows Explorer, 33

Settings
Control Panel, *see* Control Panel command
Printers, 46, 48-51
Printers | Details tab, 55
Taskbar, 15-16, 18

startup
DOS applications, 146
Explorer, 33
General Protection Fault message
Microsoft Access, 130
Microsoft FoxPro for Windows, 141
insufficient memory (Novell Quattro Pro for Windows), 127
opening automatically
folders (Borland dBASE for Windows), 142
spreadsheets (Lotus 1-2-3), 126
workbooks (Microsoft Excel), 123
optimizing performance (Microsoft Access), 136
Word 6.0, troubleshooting, 111

static, discharging, 356

Status bar, hiding/displaying, 84

Status Bar command (View menu), 37, 53

storing programs in multiple databases (Microsoft Access), 136-137

straight lines, drawing, 93

stub (short) Setup program, 348-349

SunSelect PC-NFS, Windows 95 installation, 290

Super VGA (Super Video Graphics Array) standard, 227

surge suppressors, 305

swapfiles, 67-69

switching between running programs, 17

synchronizing files between laptops and desktop PCs, 325-327

system events, assigning sounds to, 28-29

System icon (Control Panel), 67

System Monitor, 299

system tables (Microsoft Access), 131

system units, removing covers, 355

T

tab order of fields, changing (Microsoft FoxPro for Windows), 138

tab stops, 90

tables
creating in word processing documents, 109-110
creating forms for
Borland dBASE for Windows, 142
Microsoft Access, 132
Microsoft FoxPro for Windows, 138
creating reports for
Borland dBASE for Windows, 143
Borland Paradox for Windows, 144
Microsoft Access, 133
Microsoft FoxPro for Windows, 139
moving (Borland Paradox for Windows), 144
SQL tables, write privileges (Microsoft Access), 135

system tables (Microsoft Access), 131

task switching, 7

Taskbar, 6-7
customizing, 16-17
hiding/displaying, 15-16, 100
moving, 15
Start menu, 13-15

Taskbar command (Settings submenu), 15-16, 18

Tektronix, 362

telephone calls, dialing, 306

text
adding to graphics, 95
aligning labels across columns (Lotus 1-2-3), 126
ASCII, lining up columns (Microsoft Word), 111
capitalization, reversing, 107
copying between documents, 87
deleting from documents, 85
finding in documents, 85
formatting, 87-90
in memo fields (Microsoft Access), 132
hard returns, deleting, 106
missing in printouts, troubleshooting, 339
moving
between documents, 87
rows/paragraphs (Microsoft Word), 112
replacing in documents, 86
selecting
all, 105
words/sentences/paragraphs, 106
slash (/) or hyphen (-), displaying as text (Microsoft Excel), 122-123
special characters
copyright/trademark symbols, inserting (Microsoft Word), 116
inserting (Windows word processors), 104

thermal-wax printers, 263
third-party backup programs from
  prior Windows versions, 44
three-finger salute
  (Ctrl+Alt+Del), 154
time
  adding to documents, 86
    (Windows word processors),
    108-109
  entering in cells (Novell Quattro
    Pro for Windows), 128
Time tab (Properties for Regional
  Settings window), 28
titles (decorative), adding to
  documents/spreadsheets, 81
Toolbar command (View menu),
  37, 53
Toolbars
  assigning macros to buttons
    (Microsoft Word), 114
  hiding/displaying, 84
  MS-DOS Application Toolbar,
    152-153
Tools menu, Find command, 35-36
Tools tab (Properties for *drive*
  window), 40
Toshiba America Information
  Systems, 362
trackballs, 257
trademark symbol, inserting
  (Microsoft Word), 116
transfer rates, hard drive performance factors, 207
transferring data
  between WordPad docu-
    ments, 87
  Clipboard, 72-74
  embedding objects, 77-78
    logos/decorative titles, 81
  linking objects, 76-79
troubleshooting
  communications software,
    340-341
  hard drives
    full, 337
    installation, 222

memory installation, 203-204
modem installation, 302-304
monitor installation, 236-237
mouse installation, 259-260
printers, 338-339
  installation, 268
  missing text, 339
saving files to floppy disks, 337
Setup program, failure detection
  and recovery safeguards,
  349-350
slow performance, 335-336
sound, 338
video card installation, 236-237
Windows 95
  hanging, 336-337
  installation, 331-335
  see also messages
TrueType fonts
  sources for obtaining, 62
  versus built-in printer fonts, 62
trustees, 295
Turtle Beach Systems, 362
type colors, changing, 89
type size, changing, 89

U

Unable to play sound message
  (Windows 95), 338
undeleting files, 39
uninstalling
  programs, freeing laptop disk
    space, 323-324
  Windows 95, 347-348
upgrades
  80386 processors, 246
  from Windows 3.*x* or Windows
    for Workgroups to Windows
    95, 347
  hard drives
    economic considerations,
      211-212
    installation, 214-222
    reasons for, 205-206

hardware, necessary tools, 355
keyboards, 253-255
laptops, consideration factors,
    329-330
memory
    installation, 199-204
    laptops, 327-328
    reasons for, 189-190
monitor installation, 235-236
motherboard installation,
    247-250
mouse
    installation, 258-260
    types, 255-257
printer installation, 267
processors
    consideration factors,
        240-243
    Intel OverDrive installation,
        250-251
    laptops, 328
    types, 239
video card installation, 231-232
upper memory, 190
user interface, 4-5
    networks, 273
User Profiles tab (Properties for
    Security window), 293
user-level network security,
    290-291, 295-296

V

values, converting formulas to
    (Lotus 1-2-3), 126
vendors
    addresses, 357-363
    memory sources, 199
Vertical Position control, 235
Vertical Size control, 235
VGA (Video Graphics Array)
    standard, 226-227
video
    graphics accelerator cards, 229
    local bus video, 227-229

memory, amounts and types,
    224-225
MPC-2 standard, 168
standards, 226-227
see also monitors
video cards
    alternatives to, 230
    consideration factors, 229
    installation, 231-232
        troubleshooting, 236-237
    matching with monitors,
        230-231
Video Electronics Standards
    Association (VESA), 244
video files, playing, 179-180
Video Graphics Array (VGA)
    standard, 226-227
Video Random Access Memory
    (VRAM), 225
View menu commands, 37-38, 53
    Details, 37-38
    Options
        File Types tab, 42
        View tab, 37, 43
View tab (Explorer window), 53
VINES (Banyan), Windows 95
    installation, 289
virtual device drivers, 66-67
virtual memory, 67-69
Virtual Memory dialog box, 68-69
VL (VESA local) bus standard,
    228-229, 244
VRAM (Video Random Access
    Memory), 225

W

wallpaper, 22-23
warranties, hard drives, 207
windows
    Browse, changing field headings
        in, (Borland dBASE for
        Windows), 142-143
    copying to Clipboard, 73

DOS applications, switching
between running within
windows and running full-
screen, 147
Explorer, 53
Fonts, 59-61
My Computer screen display,
single window, 38
Properties for Display
Appearance tab, 19-22,
41-42, 324-325
Background tab, 22-23
Screen Saver tab, 23-24
Settings tab, 63
Properties for *DOS application*,
157-162
Program tab, 149-152
Screen tab, 153
Properties for *drive*, 40
Properties for *filename*, 38
Properties for Keyboard
General tab, 26
Language tab, 27
Speed tab, 26
Properties for Mouse, 24-26
Motion tab, 325
Properties for Multimedia,
Advanced tab, 176-177
Properties for Networks,
282-283
Access Control tab, 295-296
Configuration tab, 281
Properties for Printer, 48-51
Device Options tab,
55-56, 63
Fonts tab, 58-59
General tab, 56-57
Properties for Regional Settings,
27-28
Properties for Security, 291-293
Remote Administration tab,
295-296
Properties for Shared Resources,
Sharing tab, 278
Properties for Sounds,
28-29, 179

Properties for Taskbar, 16-17
Taskbar Options, 15-16
Windows 95, 3-4
comparing to earlier Windows
versions, 4
hanging, troubleshooting,
336-337
hardware requirements, 351-352
installation
batch files for customized
settings, 281
customizing for laptops, 318
on third-party networks,
288-290
on workstations attached to
LANs, 278-281
Setup program, 345-346
troubleshooting, 331-335
uninstalling, 347-348
upgrades from Windows 3.*x*
or Windows for Workgroups
to, 347
Windows applications
accessing files on other
computers, 101
Borland
dBASE for Windows,
141-143
Paradox for Windows,
143-144
common keyboard shortcuts,
98-99
installation under Windows 95,
100
Lotus 1-2-3 for Windows,
125-127
Microsoft
Access, 130-137
Excel, 120-125
FoxPro for Windows,
137-141
Word for Windows,
101-116
Novell
Quattro Pro for Windows,
127-129

WordPerfect for Windows, 101-110, 117-118
printing in, 99
spreadsheets, 119-120
Windows Explorer command (Programs submenu), 33
Windows installation disks, keeping, 99-100
Windows Terminal, 305
Wizards
Hardware Installation Wizard, 174-176
Installation, 267
Word 2.0, using Word 6.0 files in, 116
Word for Windows (Microsoft), 101-116
Word has caused a General Protection Fault in module WINWORD.EXE message, 111
word processors
Microsoft Word for Windows, 101-116
Novell WordPerfect for Windows, 101-110, 117-118
WordPad, 84-93
word wrap, turning on/off, 87
WordPad word processor, 84
documents, 84-87
printing, 91
embedding and linking objects, 91-93
formatting text, 87-90
screen display, customizing, 84
WordPerfect for Windows (Novell), 101-110, 117-118
words, selecting (Windows word processors), 106
workbooks, opening automatically at startup (Microsoft Excel), 123
Workgroups for Windows with peer-to-peer networks, 278
worksheets, protecting most cells (Microsoft Excel), 123-124
workstations attached to LANs, installing Windows 95, 278-281

write privileges, SQL tables (Microsoft Access), 135
WYSIWYG (what-you-see-is-what-you-get) (WordPerfect), 117

X–Z

XGA (Extended Graphics Array) standard, 227
XT class keyboards, 254

ZEOS International Ltd., 363

Add to Your Sams Library Today with the Best Books for Programming, Operating Systems, and New Technologies

The easiest way to order is to pick up the phone and call

1-800-428-5331

between 9:00 a.m. and 5:00 p.m. EST.

For faster service please have your credit card available.

ISBN	Quantity	Description of Item	Unit Cost	Total Cost
0-672-30520-8		Your Internet Consultant	$25.00	
0-672-30562-3		Teach Yourself Game Programming in 21 Days (Book/CD-ROM)	$39.99	
0-672-30466-x		Internet Unleashed (Book/Disk)	$44.95	
0-672-30617-4		The World Wide Web Unleashed	$39.99	
0-672-30570-4		PC Graphics Unleashed (Book/CD-ROM)	$49.99	
0-672-30595-x		Education on the Internet	$25.00	
0-672-30413-9		Multimedia Madness! Deluxe Edition (Book/Disk/CD-ROM)	$55.00	
0-672-30638-7		CD-ROM Madness (Book/CD-ROM)	$39.99	
0-672-30590-9		The Magic of Interactive Entertainment, 2nd Edition (Book/CD-ROM)	$44.95	
❏ 3 ½" Disk		Shipping and Handling: See information below.		
❏ 5 ¼" Disk		TOTAL		

Shipping and Handling: $4.00 for the first book, and $1.75 for each additional book. Floppy disk: add $1.75 for shipping and handling. If you need to have it NOW, we can ship product to you in 24 hours for an additional charge of approximately $18.00, and you will receive your item overnight or in two days. Overseas shipping and handling adds $2.00 per book and $8.00 for up to three disks. Prices subject to change. Call for availability and pricing information on latest editions.

201 W. 103rd Street, Indianapolis, Indiana 46290

1-800-428-5331 — Orders   1-800-835-3202 — FAX
1-800-858-7674 — Customer Service

Book ISBN 0-672-30611-5